OUTSOURCING AND MANAGEMENT

OUTSOURCING AND MANAGEMENT

WHY THE MARKET BENCHMARK WILL TOPPLE OLD SCHOOL MANAGEMENT STYLES

Thomas Nelson Tunstall

OUTSOURCING AND MANAGEMENT
© Thomas Nelson Tunstall, 2007.

First published in 2007 by
PALGRAVE MACMILLAN™
175 Fifth Avenue, New York, N.Y. 10010 and
Houndmills, Basingstoke, Hampshire, England RG21 6XS
Companies and representatives throughout the world.

PALGRAVE MACMILLAN is the global academic imprint of the Palgrave Macmillan division of St. Martin's Press, LLC and of Palgrave Macmillan Ltd. Macmillan® is a registered trademark in the United States, United Kingdom and other countries. Palgrave is a registered trademark in the European Union and other countries.

ISBN-13: 978–1–4039–7967–4
ISBN-10: 1–4039–7967–7

Library of Congress Cataloging-in-Publication Data

Tunstall, Thomas Nelson.
    Outsourcing and management : why the market benchmark will topple old school management styles / by Thomas Nelson Tunstall.
        p. cm.
    Includes index.
    ISBN 1–4039–7967–7 (alk. paper)
        1. Management. 2. Industrial organization. I. Title.

HD31.T83 2007
658.4'058—dc22   2006051389

A catalogue record for this book is available from the British Library.

Design by Newgen Imaging Systems (P) Ltd., Chennai, India.

First edition: March 2007

10 9 8 7 6 5 4 3 2 1

Printed in the United States of America.

Transferred to digital printing in 2007.

For Renee

CONTENTS

LIST OF FIGURES

ACKNOWLEDGMENTS

Something is happening to modern organization that will have a big impact on management. A fundamental change unlike anything we have seen for a hundred years is now underway. What drives this change? Why now? We will be stuck in a management paradigm rooted in the manufacturing era until we can answer these questions. Unless we just want to guess how to build good organization, we need to dig deep.

The answer as to why organizational management will change will be found in the characteristics of service and information. In the new economy these will be the issues with which we must come to terms. This book attempts to do that. In a way, just as Thomas A. Anderson (a.k.a. Neo) says at the end of the first installment of "The Matrix," I am not going to tell you how the story will end. I can only tell you how it begins.

I adhere to the "Why" theory of management. Who, What, When, Where, and How make great questions too, but Why cuts to the chase. It is the questions that drive us. Questions of all sorts irritate more people in my journeys than anything else I can think of. Questions often produce discomfort but they also keep us out of a lot of trouble down the road. It is important to recognize that questions are good. What other tool can annoy so many people up line on the organizational hierarchy? At the same time questions motivate people in the trenches to do better. Not all governance structures or management styles find themselves receptive to the Why school of thought, as you will see on the pages that follow. They pay a price for that.

I believe the story of sorts that unfolds below imparts useful perspective that will entertain as well as enlighten. This book answers many questions that nag about why managers struggle in the new economy.

You may find this book different because it offers no pat answers. Good management in a world full of challenges does not come from a cookbook. Other management guides often make that claim. They serve up solutions in the form of three, five, seven, or ten easy steps to enlightenment. They may peddle one-size-fits all packages. This is not one of those books.

My approach places management theory at the foundation of the argument, supported by economic fundamentals. Areas of specific emphasis include operations, outsourcing, and transaction costs. Theory is one thing. To be of any use to us, it must also be guided by practical experience. It has to come to terms with the real world.

In the course of my consulting work in the real world, it has become clear to me that organizations will soon undertake fundamental changes that will change the nature of management in the process. New governance options will require new forms of organization. New managerial mindsets will become necessary also. The information economy or new economy or knowledge economy (whichever you prefer) will be morphing for some time to come.

The concept of the market benchmark as a means to dissect the inner works of organization started as a doctoral dissertation on outsourcing. It ended up as a much more comprehensive look at governance.

My firsthand experience in the service industry, the consulting world, and academia have all been instrumental in this process of discovery. I have consulted in both, the public and private sectors, and served as an economic development advisor to the Afghanistan Ministry of Finance and later to the Central Bank of Afghanistan for nearly three years in the post-9/11 environment.

The material that follows takes an interdisciplinary approach. No doubt it will offend purists in a variety of fields—economics, sociology, political science, public policy, and management theory among them. Most of my guides along the way cross over disciplines with aplomb. Such boldness helps us gain insight into man-made structures such as organizations.

One such bold fellow is Professor Don Hicks, who cochaired my dissertation committee at the University of Texas at Dallas. Don remains unafraid to challenge boundaries in academic disciplines. He takes on conventional wisdom no matter how controversial. One day the world of public policy will catch up to him. I would like to thank Professor Euel Elliott, also a cochair on my dissertation committee. Euel helped me get started down the long road to bringing this book to press. Thanks also to Dr. Kathleen Trask, former advisor to the Ministry of Commerce in Afghanistan. She read over a very rough first draft of the manuscript in Kabul and offered much useful editorial guidance for which I am grateful. Don McCubbrey of the Daniels School of Business in Denver provided research suggestions that strengthened the book's arguments.

I owe whatever insights I may have garnered with regard to outsourcing in large measure to Peter Bendor-Samuel. Peter served as my guide and mentor for a year as CEO of the Everest Group. Peter possesses an instinct for outsourcing, and I hope his instruction has rubbed off on me, at least a little.

I would also like to thank Curtis Russell at PlainSmart, who championed this project tirelessly. Palgrave editors Aaron Javsicas and Julia Cohen were instrumental in getting the final manuscript into shape.

Most important, I would like to thank my wife, Renee, and four children—Matt, Rachel, Taylor, and Jack—for their patience and indulgence. In one form or another, this project spanned a period of over ten years. Through it all, my family always proved supportive of my research and work. Their love and understanding carried me through it all. I remain deeply grateful to them.

FOREWORD

Since I entered the world of outsourcing and business transformation several decades ago, the market has changed dramatically. But one thing has not changed: executives are still wrestling with the challenging dilemma of how to be more efficient, more competitive. However, to achieve these goals in the twenty-first century, new organizational structures and governance will need to be in place to drive performance in new contexts.

As this book's subtitle indicates, *The Market Benchmark* looks at what is happening today—the fundamental change now underway that will have an enormous impact on organizational management. External and internal business pressures in today's world of fast-paced priorities can gang up and cause executives to make decisions with wrong consequences. In essence, Mr. Tunstall discusses in this book the organizational governance principles that must take precedence over the pressures of business, showing readers what is important in planning for and reacting to business demands.

I can assure you that the issues that Mr. Tunstall brings up in the latter part of this book—discussing how to reshape our organizations to be able to live in this new world—are, in fact, taking place in today's leading-edge companies. At Everest Group, where we advise many of these companies around the world, it is clear that the next frontier for competitive success requires companies reorganizing and restructuring themselves to take advantage of the new way of doing business, which Mr. Tunstall describes. As he points out, it is different, and it is painful.

This book applies equally to people who have already taken the step of outsourcing and are struggling through the inevitable subtleties of how to align their organizations in an outsourced world, and to people who are thoughtfully considering outsourcing and want to understand the deeper implications of organizational impact.

For the thoughtful reader, the book presents an important set of issues to both reflect and take action on. Mr. Tunstall describes business as changing to an incentive-driven services structure. It looks different. It is componentized and highly subject to measurement. It depends on alignment of vision, capabilities, and incentives. This type of structure will require more organizational sophistication, new skills, and new governance.

Contrary to what readers might like, there is as yet no handy formula for operating in this new way of doing business. This is not a book that provides the steps to take and the things one must not do. It grapples, rather, with the principles at the core. It also helps readers understand how this situation has evolved and why an incentive-driven services structure is inevitable.

He points out the inertia and drag on performance that has resulted from autonomous business units shielded from real scrutiny compared to market forces and other dysfunctional behavior. He then moves to a discussion of the historical drivers of change and outsourcing. Today's situations then bleed into the historical context, and he shows how the changes led companies to evolve to new structures. He addresses how the transaction alternative for outsourcing to buy a service rather than doing it in-house determines where management draws organizational boundaries, which then determines how the organization is run. With services provided by external companies, the enterprise complexity increases, necessitating new and improved management structures.

Mr. Tunstall summons readers to think about some of the challenges of new organizational governance structures and the new rules that apply in a service economy. Ultimately, for instance, in-house departments will need to be governed with as much rigor as outsourcing partners. He brings up questions surrounding the fact that there will need to be greater coordination of people, defined outputs, better frameworks to harmonize relationships, and the gain or loss in competitive advantage as transaction costs go up or down.

He discusses the challenges of governance at length, as it applies to both internal and outsourced relationships. At Everest Group, we find that governance encompasses issues all companies now struggle with. Its importance cannot be overemphasized. In fact, we find that perhaps as much as 70 percent of the potential value of an outsourcing relationship leaks away when appropriate governance is not in place. As Mr. Tunstall points out, outsourcing is a valuable tool in the new way of doing business, but it can result in failure if not managed well.

When should an organization move an activity or service to an external provider? What constitutes bad management internally and externally? What are the potential measures of an organization's value? How should market benchmarks be used? How long does a best practice remain "best"? How can leaders do a better job of forecasting and scenario planning? How can management better understand where to grow the organization?

Drawing on benchmarks, Mr. Tunstall's book points out the need to make sense out of these and other dilemmas within the context of the new ways of doing business.

At the same time, he makes it clear that there are no simple solutions to these new decisions in running a business. He points out the fact that these new organizational structures and governance models require changes that take time to develop and discusses things that must be put in place to enable the changes. Contracts will require more fairness and more give-and-take, he writes; and they must be better at defining intangibles. In the new organizational structures, intellectual property rights can become an important factor.

The book will force you to consider the viability of your own organization in the light of the new business world Mr. Tunstall describes. Like many things of subtlety, the author does not give readers a clear formula but, rather, identifies the principles from which we must shape our respective solutions.

By PETER BENDOR-SAMUEL, *CEO of the Everest Group and author of Turning Lead Into Gold: The Demystification of Outsourcing*

INTRODUCTION

The modern organization in the service and information economy (or new economy) remains a black box in many ways. Its inner workings often appear something of a mystery. Even still, few executives seem to grasp how the organizational whole becomes greater than the sum of the individual parts. Layers of bureaucracy shield department heads from market forces. This enables dysfunctional behavior that should have been cast aside long ago to permeate organizational hierarchies. Sometimes a simple case of inertia gums up the works. Taken together, these insidious factors impose a drag on organizational performance at many levels. We can expect to see changes ahead as a result.

Having said that, let us give credit where it is due. There can be no doubt that the large corporation remains a formidable force even though its history spans a little more than a century. The sole examples of effective large organization for millennia consisted of governmental, military, and religious institutions, all of which often intertwined.

Then, something big changed about a hundred and fifty years ago. The introduction of mass production techniques broadened the scope of the large organization in a fundamental way. Economies of scale drove the accumulation of larger profits that enabled enterprises to grow like never before. The structure of organization underwent a transformation from rigid hierarchies to more flexible ones. But hierarchies have remained for nearly a hundred years.

Starting around the mid-nineteenth century, small proprietorships grew into larger ones. Greater scale precipitated the development of domestic corporations. Multinational corporations later sprang up to tap foreign suppliers or markets. The increased economies of scale in manufacturing-dominated economies in turn required larger management hierarchies. These changes extended well beyond the boundary of the firm as the division between work and leisure for most people grew starker.

The vastness of the large organizations produced societies very different from the previous ones. Sizeable urban centers became far more common.

Dispersed rural populations began to concentrate in the cities, where the residents worked in the factories. The day-to-day routine of the average person was forever altered. Management made changes as well. One-off managerial styles gave way to more systematic approaches.

In the early stages of this organizational growth, management still relied on a rigid hierarchy that was a direct offshoot of the family patriarchy. As a governance model, hierarchy demonstrated drawbacks for many types of organizations. The rigid top-down structure often made these ever-larger firms unresponsive to the market because a small team controlled most or all management decisions. Sometimes a single person ran everything. This state of affairs changed when innovative management created something new. It is what we know now as the divisional organization. The new type of organization separated the Finance and Strategy functions from Operations. Business units were given more autonomy in decisions, but budgets remained in control of top management. It became necessary for executives to create formal strategies. The articulation of long-term vision became part of their jobs.

The divisional organization governance suited the manufacturing era well enough. In fact, management style modeled itself after the simplicity of divisions. The nature of mechanization also guided management techniques. Measurable outputs of material things made operations straightforward. The more difficult to measure service or overhead component seemed an afterthought because it comprised such a small percentage of total costs.

The turn of the twenty-first century has changed all of that. The advent of the service-dominated economy now signals a historic transformation. Organization and management will undergo a revolution in the information age that got started over two decades ago. The drivers of this change include four key recent developments:

1. The increased quantity of information contained in products.
2. An emphasis on services instead of physical goods.
3. Greater availability of outsourcing options.
4. Lower transaction costs.

The market benchmark is the catalyst that will force changes on present governance systems. It will challenge organizational management. We can expect some painful adjustments in the process.

Management styles have been refined over a century to support an economy based on manufacturing. Now they attempt to support an information economy with only partial success. All this will change. New managers will at last exploit the implications of this transition that will still take decades more to play out. The new service economy will be componentized. It will be readily subject to measurement. There will be more external interfaces than ever in and across organizations. This environment will challenge managers like never before. Successful managers will either bring new styles to the game or overhaul existing mindsets.

Huge pockets of inefficiency remain, that stem from organizational structures designed for the manufacturing era now in decline. The emergence of flexible technologies will catalyze changes in the rules. More to the point, the new environment will require a rational, well-grounded management practice that, at least to date, still too often escapes current practitioners. However, organizations can no longer house hidden inefficiencies because global competition will render such enterprises obsolete. The next generation of executives will employ outsourcing. They will take systematic approaches. Management will be more disciplined and will insist on real evidence before making decisions. Technology will be better utilized. These factors taken together will redefine organizational structure. They will drive performance to new levels.

The definition of effective management will never be the same. Old school styles will be history. Every function an organization chooses to undertake in the very near future will be subject to the market benchmark. It may not always ensure greatness, but it will certainly demand minimum standards of performance.

Definition of bench·mark

a: a point of reference from which measurements may be made
b: something that serves as a standard by which others may be measured or judged
c: a standardized problem or test that serves as a basis for evaluation or comparison

Merriam-Webster

CHAPTER 1

THE HIGH LEVEL FRAMEWORK

There's something wrong with the world. You do not know what it is, but it's there. Like a splinter in your mind, driving you mad.

—Morpheus in "The Matrix"

The Beginning of the End

There has been only one fundamental shift in the way organizations get managed since the inception of management theory. Over a hundred years of study has produced just one epoch. The run-up to that first pinnacle was great while it lasted. So, let us celebrate the old school boys for just a moment.

The old school traditional manager came of age in the new suburbs or hip urban settings in the early 1960s. Management of the mechanized organization had at last reached its zenith. The hangover from the Great Depression on the downside of the Roaring Twenties was long gone. World War II had ended. Peacetime ensued. The backdrop for this golden age consisted of a relatively stable prosperity in the industrialized countries.

In the lingo of operations research, we would call such an event a steady state process. Consistent but routine improvements in management technique had been ongoing for decades after the widespread adoption of the divisional form of organization. However, most of the improvements centered on better production methods rather than management styles. You remember the photos from the early 1960s, if you were not actually part of the workforce then. Managers donned thin black ties. Crew cuts reigned supreme. Executives consumed two martinis at lunch if the opportunity presented itself. A decade earlier in the 1950s, William Whyte's seminal work *The Organization Man* described a prototype that celebrated what is now the old guard of management.[1] The world was a different place. And as is the case with the culmination of all great successes, inertia kept things from changing too much. Why not? If you were in the right circles, life was lots of fun. Beirut garnered high marks from the jet set. Arnold Palmer traded green jackets with Jack Nicklaus at the Masters tournament in Augusta seemingly every other year. The rest of the white-collar world longed for an afternoon on the links to conduct business deals. The refined erudition of Sean Connery's James Bond and Roger Moore's Simon Templar supplied the ultimate role models of good taste and charm.

All good things must come to an end. Management styles at the time hinged on the dominance of the industrial and manufacturing economy that dated back nearly a century. The need for new styles became imperative as the number of jobs in the service and information economy overtook manufacturing.

By the early 1980s, the baby boomers that had transformed culture two decades before began to transform business as well. Tom Peters got things rolling on the management front when he coauthored *In Search of Excellence*.[2] A revolution in information systems had been underway even earlier when VisiCalc spreadsheets provided the killer application for Apple computers. Though not apparent to most practitioners at the time, old management styles had begun a long slide into irrelevance. Michael Maccoby took a stab at the new managerial mindset in *The Gamesman*.[3] According to Maccoby, *The Organization Man* would be replaced by *The Gamesman*. The gamesman took risks in the interest of sport and tended to be somewhat one-dimensional, perhaps even a bit soulless. The gamesman's family was often a casualty of his immersion into his work life. Coworkers tended to get branded as either winners or losers. This kind of management style was not sustainable. A better roadmap will be needed for management in the information economy. While *The Gamesman* signified a period of experimentation, management theory still has a long way to go in order to find success in the information age.

So where are we now with regard to this great transformation? We are right in the middle of it.

Take note however. The reasons for the eventual collapse of the old guard will not constitute the usual suspects. Free wheeling, former hippie, WOW![4] managers might have catalyzed things, but the fundamentals run much deeper. The new rules involve a practice that we are now very familiar with—outsourcing. More specifically, the outsourcing of service functions. And while this may seem unremarkable, it is a fairly recent development. Service outsourcing combined with the unrelenting pressure from markets to seek out new niches will have a huge impact on organizational governance before we reach the next great epoch. Modern organization, and the managers who run them, will undergo radical change. Fresh governance options will drive new, innovative enterprise structures. These changes in governance will also forever alter the type of management style required to lead. A great journey lies ahead for all students of management.

If you want to cut to the chase, it boils down to some basic tenets that too many working managers still fail to employ. For starters, managers and executives must be more skeptical about what is "known." In addition, leaders have to understand that feedback must *always* get a hearing, even if not acted upon. Most importantly, managers will have to understand the fluid nature of services far better if they want to effectively manage them. They will come to terms with the fact that while the corporate and organizational hierarchy will not go away entirely, it will be transformed into something new. The ability to outsource services means that the market will strip down the old organizational forms and make them more transparent. What they get reassembled into, will change not only how organizations interact, but how managers and executives do as well.

Our insight will come by way of extrapolating from history. In order to do that, we have to pause for a moment and gaze over our shoulder. We cannot appreciate the whole story as a simple snapshot. The road begins with important contexts about the evolution of management and organization since the mid-1800s.

First things first. Let us talk about the scope of management activity and the range of institutions that are affected. The definition of what managers manage is broader than we might assume. While such a definition would include businesses, the list would now also be expanded to include to non-profits and government agenies. The universe of modern organizations that goes beyond business firms has done a lot for us as a society in the past hundred years. The modern organization constitutes a formidable entity that adapts itself better than other institutions. It manages change as part and parcel of its structure.

Of course, the precursor to a broad-based definition of modern organization remains the corporation. Just look at the way both government agencies and nonprofits try to emulate business all the time. The corporation takes its place as one of the brilliant organizational forms of the twentieth century. It is an exclusive club that includes only the nation-state, the military, and religious institutions. These comprise the short list of durable mechanisms to harness large quantities of collective effort.

Where does our story begin? The old style business firm traces its existence to the earliest days of merchants in public markets, perhaps as far back as antiquity. Such a categorization would include single proprietorships though it was not until centuries later in the mid-1700s, that one of the first great economic observers documented any systematic information on the subject. It was Adam Smith who detailed the role of how government compliments the market. He also offered us a philosophy of business organization. His two great works consist of the more familiar *Wealth of Nations*,[5] along with the less well-known *Theory of Moral Sentiments*.[6]

Almost everyone has heard of the 1776 classic *Wealth of Nations* by Smith. Far fewer people are familiar with *Moral Sentiments*, published earlier in 1759. It lays out a functional view of ethics that compliments Smith's views on enlightened self-interest in *Wealth of Nations*. Smith devoted significant time to the exploration of ethics in order to understand the economy. Business should always be bundled with ethics. That remains as true now as it did over two hundred years ago. Why? Because otherwise you may be apt to get absurd analysis by economists that view a crook who takes your wallet as a transfer of wealth. Or executives who loot pension plans as creative cash managers. Smith (as well as most of the rest of us) would call these actions outright theft. The public, in fact, regarded Adam Smith as a moral philosopher prior to the publication of *Wealth of Nations*. They knew him afterward as the great political economist. We should try to think of him as both.[7]

These works by Smith complemented notions of individual rights from the European Enlightenment. Together they planted the seeds for the scale economies that fueled industrialization, first in Britain, and later in the United States. This resulted in the enormous material prosperity we see around us in the industrialized world. It was in fact the rise of successful large organizations that served to increase society's wealth as never before. The framework that combined liberty, individual rights, property rights, and open commerce enabled enterprises to organize in a big way. Ambitious firms took advantage of the increased pools of capital from the banking system in order to grow. Organizations expanded for the first time not by grant of governmental monopoly, as with the British East India Company. Rather they exploited the economies of scale in competitive markets. The only way to manage these complex activities efficiently was with large enterprise structures.

There was a problem though. Firms continued to adhere to rigid hierarchical structures even as their scale and scope increased in the late 1800s (figure 1.1). These top-down frameworks dated back at least as far as the Renaissance. They varied little from the very same ones used by the small proprietorships. Such unwieldy organizational structures suffered from a lack of imagination. A fundamental change became necessary.

The explanation for this proves simple enough from a modern perspective. Rigid hierarchy demands a certain type of leadership not easy to

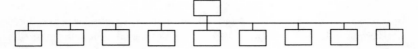

Figure 1.1   Rigid Hierarchy

sustain. Effective control over an ever-larger organization takes lots of attention. Many managers today would be aware of this style. We know it as extreme micromanagement. The trouble is that almost nobody can pull this off. No matter how gifted, one individual can do only so much.

Some organizations recognized the need to move away from the control-oriented hierarchy as early as the 1920s. The one or two man show just could not keep up. Foresighted executives ceded operational responsibility to line management. General Motors (run by Alfred Sloan from 1923 to 1956) represents the most famous example of this first fundamental transformation of the corporate structure. Many other organizations soon followed GM's lead. Incredibly, this first sea change carried organizational management through the end of the century.

The success of these innovative companies left little doubt that the structure of organizations could produce significant improvements in performance. The techniques to manage organizations also evolved as technology advanced. These principles remain as true today as ever.

Yet organizational structure only tells us so much. We need to know more, though that is easier said than done. A lack of systematic knowledge about the inner workings of organizations continues to vex practitioners even today. Researchers struggle to chip away at the edges. Academics burrow into selected niches. At least with manufacturing, the moving parts were made of metal. The now, people-dominated service-side of organizations introduces a whole new level of complexity.

Not that mechanisms of governance do not provide attractive topics to economists as they hunt for new things to research. Look at Ronald Coase and his work on transaction costs. It was Coase who first questioned the impact of transaction costs on where organizations draw their boundaries. His insight was a real watershed event. The structure of the firm (also organization) began to interest economists a lot more after his 1937 *Economica* paper was published.[8] As well it should. The firm represents a mainstay institution. We see the evidence of large companies all around us every day. Their trademarks adorn billboards. Their pitches get piped in from television, in print, on the web, on other products. They take the form of cool new products and new services. Corporations truly do blend into the fabric of everyday life. They are everywhere, all around us. We see them when we go to work, to school, and when we turn on our television. In most cases, they hardly rate a second thought, except maybe when they advertise during the Super Bowl. Otherwise, we just take them for granted.

Seems a little odd when you think about it. The large firm is a relative newcomer compared to government, religion, or the military. How could it become so integral in the span of just a hundred and fifty years? The reason is that there are some things armies, religious institutions, and governments just do not do as well as the modern corporate organization. The modern organization serves customers better and has become an essential engine for economic growth for one thing. Even critics of corporations embrace them for the jobs they create and the tax revenues they generate. Nonprofits serve their donors and stakeholders to fill in gaps that other institutions fail to fill.

Economists charted the first real progress about analysis of the firm or organization. Yet early, even economists viewed the firm as a black box— inputs in, outputs out—for many decades. What happened in between simply got reduced to a production function. For manufacturing environments, this was often enough. After all, economists cared about the final tangible output relative to what went in. The inside of the firm remained otherwise opaque to them. Nowadays we can see the weakness of the analysis if all the activities performed within the organization stay behind as independent or exogenous variables.

The curse and the blessing of economics is that it has always tried to boil things down to the essence. Given all the variables economists have to deal with, the use of parsimonious models provided the benefit of simplicity. All of the moving parts inside organization presented the unpleasant prospect of introducing too many messy variables into their elegant equations.

Even still, economists struggle to come up with numbers about how to define a lot of the pieces. How do you quantify the way people interact inside the organizational box? You can get a feel for it if you spend enough time on the office. Even so, it is very tough to measure in an objective fashion. Try to put a number to interorganizational effectiveness and calculate that back to sustained market performance.

Let us take an example. Entrepreneurship labored under the same ignominy for a long time. There used to be just three key components in economics textbooks that fueled economic growth. No more. Economists now recognize entrepreneurship as a fourth key essential resource needed to create wealth—right alongside land, labor, and capital.

Likewise, awareness of the need to better understand the cogs and wheels that turn inside organizations generates continued interest among economists, management theorists, and day-to-day practitioners. This book will try to shed some light on what goes on inside organizations in a service-dominated economy. One thing that will become clear is that the market benchmark will force the modern organization to be sliced and diced into completely different forms. All the pieces that remain hidden from researchers and society will get exposed to market forces.

The importance of the modern organization manifests not only product markets, but equity markets as well. News of them fills the financial pages. Once again, we see evidence that large organizations permeate our existence. Why they work so well—and sometimes do not—generates lots of questions. As well they should. Continued improvement in societal well-being depends on an answer. So let us dive in. The first question we might ask is what we should focus on, in our search for those answers.

In order to get a micro-level perspective, we have to stand back to view the bigger picture. We will see, for example, that enterprise structure drives the management behavior that is permitted inside. Structure of organization remains important because it dictates how information gets channeled up and down. Management behavior or style determines how well the information then gets put to use. Success or failure of an organization remains highly dependent on effective management. So how can we find out more about management style? Here we will encounter one of the first hurdles that block our way—the limits of research into management practice.

What Research Cannot Tell You

What characteristics comprise good governance of the organization? How do we get a peek inside the black box? What activities should a firm or organization undertake, particularly those in the service-dominated sectors? What does core competence look like? More to the point, why do we not understand more about the structure of an effective organization? What limitations do we encounter when we try to find out?

Part of these answers can be found in the landscape in which organizations operate. Put another way: How does the market influence the shape, size, and function of organization?

Transaction costs highlight a key component of what an organization looks like, along the borders. Transaction costs get charged to organizations by the marketplace for the performance of some activity. It takes time to search for a supplier. Contracts must be negotiated and so on. On the other hand, sometimes management can save on those costs when they do not use the market. It is along these boundaries that we can often figure out why a given activity is on the market side or the organization side if we can understand the costs on each side. You invoke transaction costs when you buy something in the market. You do not when you make that item on your own from scratch. Use of the market sets up an altogether different cost structure than work inside an organization. Each option offers advantages and disadvantages.

Why is this important?

The available alternatives at any particular moment in time drive decisions about where management draws the boundaries of the organization. These boundaries, in turn, make a huge difference about how the organization runs. These alternatives are also very dynamic—they change all the time. Relative costs in one area or another begin to come down as the market produces innovation. New opportunities surface. Incentives may shift in other cases so that one form of organization gains advantage over another. Current business models can move out of balance. Pressure builds for a correction as these conditions change. What used to be too expensive to purchase on the open market now becomes affordable. Previous in-house expertise gets too pricey. Internal interactions may start to look dysfunctional for some reason. So, what approach should managers take to make decisions about organizational boundaries and structure?

Let us talk about why it is hard to get more specific. The issues that surround the boundaries of organization dog economists in the same way that sociological research gets hampered. It can be tough to see what goes on inside the black box. Ethics highlight just one example. Researchers would like to probe into every aspect of human interaction that occurs inside organizations, but they cannot.

The Stanford Prison Experiment demonstrates this dilemma. In an unusual sociological research project, college students took on a couple of different roles. Some became prisoners. Others became guards. Philip Zimbardo, the project director, planned to run the videotaped experiment over an extended period as a sort of a game. Zimbardo was forced to cut the whole thing short. The viciousness with which the participants assumed their roles just plain got out of hand.

So we cannot put people in a test tube. We cannot shake them around to see what happens (though as researchers and practitioners, we might like to). We need to be a little more creative to gain insight into organizational mechanics. Manipulation of human behavior to produce useful results comes with limitations attached. Not all doors remain open to social science researchers. This contrasts to "hard" sciences such as physics. These are very real issues.

There is more.

The impact of observation on human interaction can also cause problems. Such scrutiny may flaw the validity of any research conclusions about the behavior of human beings in experiments. The subjects know that someone watches. Visual inspection of inanimate objects in the world of physics, for example, does not often affect the outcome. It can change everything in social settings. This Hawthorne effect means that observation can alter the outcome of an experiment. The Hawthorne effect informs us that research into how an organization works might create an artificial environment. Objective examination of the inside of an organization often proves tricky as a result. Consultants sometimes attempt to furnish this type of analysis in the course of their work. However, such convenience samples have limited value. The truth is that regular systematic research on organizations remains elusive.

So why do organizations not run many internal behavioral experiments? Organizations conduct activities to accomplish a particular end result. Firms run a business. Nonprofits have a set of social goals to pursue. This means they produce goods and services that can be resold at a profit, or conduct various operations on behalf of their stakeholders. An organization usually considers research into itself as a distraction. So firms and other organizations do not often carry out true experiments within their boundaries. The advance of the state of knowledge of the enterprise itself shapes up as an incidental concern from the view of management. That leaves us with a heavy reliance on tangential or anecdotal information to try to figure out how service firms work. These limitations make direct organizational analysis dependent on voluntary participation. Not an ideal situation from a research standpoint.

So what are we left with? Researchers and practitioners do have tools at their disposal. Surveys of one sort or another may be used to obtain data. Theory can help. Algorithms also provide insight. Too often, these come to us on a piecemeal basis and prove unsatisfying. Let us talk about why.

The use of surveys attempts to draw out objective information by selection of some sample. Key topics for management theorists include governance structures and organizational best practices, although almost any topic is fair game. However, it must be said that researchers rely on a few overused methods that include:

- Personal interviews (or case studies)
- Mailed surveys
- Financial data or government statistics[9]

Each has drawbacks. Questionnaires, for example, suffer from low response rates. Senior executives in large companies receive several of them each week, most of which end up in the trash basket.

Both personal interviews, as well as questionnaires, become subject to possible bias on the part of the respondents. Senior officials will put a positive spin on outcomes that result from their own decisions. Employees, fearful of retribution may hold back their candid comments. The condition of anonymity may help, but it provides no guarantee that we will get the whole truth, nothing but the truth.

A report of what looks like sincere bad news to researchers may be vulnerable to bias as well. You will not get the straight story if disgruntled managers or employees furnish the information. As we all know, the truth can be shaded in a lot of ways.

Response bias also comes as baggage with personal interviews or questionnaires. Response bias affects the willingness of respondent to take part at all. What does this mean? It means that any systematic or nonrandom characteristic of those who refuse to participate can flaw the study's results. An entire team that worked on a failed project may refuse to provide information. An attempt to draw conclusions in such a case will lack crucial perspective.

Then there is public financial information or government statistics, which can offer us a much more representative sample. Because more organizations get polled, the data tend to be much more systematic. That is fine as far as it goes. Unfortunately, the collection process does not allow for customization. The desired information for the particular research project may not get tracked or documented by statisticians at all. Many times you cannot even draw inferences from the data. In such cases, these sources provide little value. Lots of data does not always mean useful data.

Other approaches include theory, which can serve as worthwhile incubators to formalize ideas. However, in the end, these apparent brainstorms may or may not offer important insight, no matter how enthusiastic the management guru. There may simply turn out to be a lack of evidence to support a thesis.

Algorithms work okay for a program inside a computer. Each method (theory or algorithms) can be helpful though both must also be tested in the real world to be of any use. A production line in a manufacturing environment represents a deterministic setting. In other words, everything that happens in the process can be predicted with great precision. As such, a manufacturing environment is well-suited for testing algorithms. Operations research produces many useful job shop scheduling models that improve assembly line efficiency. These tools work fine in a machine-based system. Yet algorithms do not predict with precision what *people* will do inside the closed environment of an organization. Situations vary. At the risk of stating the obvious, people are not machines.

Some activities outside the firm better lend themselves to analysis due to greater visibility. Motives are less tainted. Take the application of auction theory by regulatory authorities, for example. The use of auctions helps maximize the revenue from telecommunication spectrum in a consistent fashion. The actions of players in a transparent (market-based) setting tend to produce more dependable results.

The field of experimental economics remains quite young otherwise. Significant examination of the firm or organization still lies ahead for that discipline.[10] These limitations in methodology should not dissuade us from attempts to gain insight into the nature of organization. They do tell us that tackling the assignment will not be a trivial task. The world of human interaction demonstrates complexity yet can nonetheless be understood.[11] Fundamental rules do indeed exist about successful organizations that can be inferred in a variety of ways. These rules can be employed in a systematic manner. The need to understand these basic rules remains essential for management in the service economy with its many people issues.

As we can see, there are a host of research methods available, yet most have drawbacks. Direct real-time observation may be flawed. Surveys prove problematic. Algorithms remain too sterile. Should we give up? Not at all. We will, however, have to be judicious about where we pull our evidence from, at least until service measures become better developed. One way to illuminate the new economy involves the use of historical context. The past can help us see the future. Economics can help too. The discipline of Adam Smith can shine light on both human motivation as well as cost analysis.

Let us start with a few economic fundamentals applicable to management. The information economy makes some general trends appear clear. Transaction costs continue to go down for a variety of reasons that will be explained later in more detail. Suffice it to say that this decrease in transactions costs comes as a direct result of the employment of information technologies or IT. While perhaps a long time in gestation, IT tools now permeate all types of enterprises and constantly liberate productivity at every level.

Lower transaction costs mean that the use of providers outside the organization to obtain services looks a lot more attractive all the time. The use of external providers can often get you a better deal if it means that you can buy more things at lower overall cost. You can also make a profit on other items that you choose to sell. This avalanche of new choices will cause the boundaries of most organizations to begin to shift or re-form in different places. Interfaces will change. Organizations will revisit what to do on a regular basis. Management will also get a better handle on what not to try to take on.

As the transformation continues, medium-to-large enterprises will become more transparent to the outside in response to the realities of the new economy. The impermeable boundaries will get porous. The stiff borders that worked okay in the manufacturing era will not cut it as we go forward. This will change the rules for competent management over the twenty-first century. The figurative mechanized manager hit his/her prime in the early 1960s. It will come as no surprise then that his/her computer of choice went by the nickname of Big Iron. His/Her foundation started to give way in the 1980s. Now he/she is old school as the world has changed around him/her. Sure, we still see the remnants of his/her style everywhere. Time will change that too. Our old school boy will start to fade away like all good soldiers.

Larger organizations now enter a new era. While all of their successes in the twentieth century stand acknowledged, they remain old news just the same. The shift will necessitate the design of new methods of governance. New management styles will be required. The rules of manufacturing structures will give way to information structures. The mindsets of the mechanized managers must instead wrap themselves around the needs of a service-dominated economy. Research and better measures will catch up, but it will take decades for that to happen.

Management and Myths

Successful organizations do not seek to survive. They look ahead. They peek around the next corner. They live to make their competition irrelevant. You might say that they recreate the landscape in which they compete. This can be referred to as value innovation,[12] or strategic innovation,[13] or any of a number of other names. You want the *Reader's Digest* version? It means you must identify underserved markets to then exploit the opportunity.

The world of the competent professional manager represents an exercise of experimentation. Some bets pay off. Others do not. Managers employ many different avenues or methods to find success. Not all of them involve rocket science. Seemingly mundane approaches can be used to gain competitive advantage or create new markets just the same as technological breakthroughs. Such unremarkable tactics include operational strategy. Others rely on inventive organizational structure.

Managers play the key roles in the overall process of the exploitation of innovation. Yet what are their credentials? They only have a finite, if varied set of tools with which to work. Personal insight based on day-to-day practice represents the most common management tool used almost everywhere. Experience does count—there is a difference between knowing the path and walking the path. Yet that know-how comes in a sporadic fashion because it arrives from different sources. Most managerial knowledge is limited to first-hand experimentation that takes a period of many years to accumulate. Managers may augment their own first-hand knowledge with an awareness of direct competitors. They may look across industry lines or functional boundaries. Often they consult mainstream management books and periodicals.

Graduates of business programs get trained in key functional areas as an additional benefit. This group possesses more formal education from the use of case studies as a tool of analysis. Well, at least it simulates actual experience.

Even so, much management theory too often gets compiled on the basis of anecdotal evidence that becomes subject to frequent reexamination. A well-known example of this remains the management handbook entitled *In Search of Excellence*.[14] It hit the shelves in 1982, and plaudits followed for years. The book intended to identify companies with timeless culture that conferred sustainable competitive advantage. *Excellence* sure served to shake management up. That much is true. It did hit a few snags though. Several of the companies cited in the landmark book began to falter not long after publication. Even one of the companies cited in Jim Collins' book *Good to Great*,[15] Fannie Mae has lost much of its former luster because of an over-valued, mortgage lending, portfolio combined with overstated earnings.[16]

These examples suggest that systematic evidence of sustainable organizational success will be hard to come by. Transferring research findings to the workplace would be a welcome start. Yet, the unit of analysis—the company or organization—will always be dynamic. Any good organization evolves. No assurance of long-term success exists for anyone. Markets morph. Technologies progress. Regulations change. What determines success will be something of a moving target. What works today may not work tomorrow. Cookbook answers to strategy will find themselves destined for mediocrity. Sometimes they result in outright failure.

At the same time, effective management of change in large organizations must be a deliberate process of governance. An organization comprises a significant number of employees. These roll up into various departments. A whole host of functions gets carried out in the course of operations.

Executives keep their hands full as they manage the many pieces. They reconcile multiple stakeholder interests. Customers must be served. Shareholders assuaged. Owner soothed. Donors coddled. Regulators satisfied. No one benefits if the organization tries to change directions on a whim. A medium or large organization requires a more deliberate approach to strategy.

The balanced scorecard, for example, provides a useful management tool because of its focus on a stable set of broad indicators. The scorecard considers more than just profits or revenue. It tracks fixed categories that can be measured. These include:

- Financial data
- Operational measures
- Customer satisfaction
- Internal process improvement[17]

Managers direct their activities to serve the organization's larger constituency. Specific components of the above indicators can be redefined over time, though they should remain static in the short-term. The balanced scorecard takes the first steps at a systematic approach to management and the use of measures that is particularly helpful in a service-dominated economy.

Part of an organization's stability comes from rules. We often refer to these rules as bureaucracy. Some bureaucracy is necessary. Good bureaucracy can make organizations successful. It enables them to change or to service their customers better. They can accommodate their many stakeholders in a systematic fashion.

Bad bureaucracy demonstrates an unresponsive demeanor. Sometimes it acts in an arbitrary fashion. It serves customers or other stakeholders as a by-product of the organization's operation.

Spotting good or bad bureaucracy can be a challenge. A "useless" form or process step may be the key to effective crossfunctional communication. It may provide an important audit trail to meet regulatory requirements. Certain elements of bureaucracy could serve as the means to track a useful measurement to benchmark against competitors.

It is often difficult to tell which is which. And yet, managers with all the answers often swoop in on situation and render judgment post-haste. Shoot-from-the-hip analysis about such matters, too often proves incorrect. There just are no silver bullets. No magic. No pat answers.

There *are* other things. Frameworks or structures of knowledge do exist though they take more time to acquire or more effort to assimilate. Robust frameworks give information its utility. Any hope of systematic organizational success means that you have to understand these more elaborate knowledge stocks. A solution or "fact" presented inside an organizational setting need not get accepted at face value. Yet, it often does. Whatever we think we know, may be irrelevant. So it should always be fair to ask how we know what we know. Those with the answers or solutions should not be afraid to repeat them. They should not be annoyed if someone asks for a clarification once in a while. Are there facts or just suppositions? Sometimes suppositions are all that is available. Fair enough. They should be treated as such—not as facts.

Managers should insist on this type of disciplined approach. Sociologists refer to it as epistemic correlation. In other words, is there cause and effect? Is the effect systematic? Does A make B happen? Or is the relationship reciprocal? Maybe sometimes B or even C causes A to occur. That is okay too. It just means that you do not have cause and effect. You have unanswered questions. So continue your analysis. Experiment. Dig into recent peer-reviewed journals to see what hard data can be offered from people who spend their careers researching organizational management issues. Such beneficial rigor often lays bare, incorrect assumptions.

Destructive, false beliefs may take the form of urban legend or myth. They consist of shared views that are specious or erroneous. Yet, people inside organizations often accept them without question. Effective management *refuses* to tolerate these fictions, although of course, situations in real life can make this hard to do.

The use of facts as a defense against poor judgment may not be so simple in an organizational setting with its attendant hierarchy. As we all know, charismatic or headstrong leaders can remove the doubt of the faithful in a heartbeat. A senior manager on a mission often intimidates all but the most vocal of critics. Those who decline to acquiesce to the browbeating get dispatched.

Jeffrey Skilling, at Enron, simply dismissed employees who criticized the company's business proposition. It just took a roll of the eyes from the big boss. That was it. Career over. Lots of smart people waited in line to get into Enron at the time anyway.

Skilling hailed from McKinsey and Company before he went to Enron. McKinsey used to like to do road shows of the Enron business model. Both Skilling and McKinsey helped transform Enron from a sleepy oil and gas company into an energy trading powerhouse. Jeff Skilling was McKinsey's poster child. The famous consultancy often gave presentations to senior management in other organizations. McKinsey remained eager to demonstrate to prospective clients how to revamp a tired business model with enough consultants. Clients could go light years ahead of the competition just like Enron did. Of course, that was a long time ago. McKinsey folks do not like to talk much about Enron anymore.

The late Ken Lay, who helped found Enron, tended to patronize stock analysts that asked too many questions during conference calls. Closer examination revealed that lots of good questions did indeed fail to get asked or answered at Enron.

Such systemic failures of analysis reside at the heart of dysfunctional organizations. Communication paths get shut down along with the ability to acknowledge reality. This lack of fact-based decisions surfaces as a key cause for organizational failure on many levels, in many settings.[18]

You Can Get There From Here

It is really hard to see the scope of a changing landscape while living in the middle of it, as we are now. Not that we do not try. Business leaders, forecasters, and politicians attempt to discern the future all the time. Sometimes they get blamed for looking backward or they may fail to see some unexpected trend. It must be said that the use of the past to instruct the present can shed light on many issues. Patterns of history do indeed repeat themselves. Larger business organizations trace their foundations back about a century and we can learn a lot from past precedent.

The problem with a view from the rearview mirror tends to be twofold. Managers often make a superficial analysis that fails to take full appreciation of the lessons of history. People look back a year or two maybe, a decade at most. You have got to go back farther than that to capture the robust panorama of the past. The other problem is that people are nostalgic. We remember the good; we downplay the bad. We must look for long-term patterns in an objective fashion if we want to use history as a guide.

Migration to a service economy does not signify the first such upheaval for industrialized countries. A similar transformation happened once before (though not in our lifetime). Yet, even as you read this, critics continue to bemoan the current economic climate because of the loss of the manufacturing base. Even more, nostalgic folks still claim to regret the loss of an economy dominated by agricultural jobs. This assumes that most of us would prefer to live or work on farms. That is nonsense. Most people do not want to live on a farm. The amenities of cities, of neighbors, of so much to do in close proximity, augur well for community living.

Even fewer of us want to *work* on a farm. Not that it matters. A productive economy only needs about 2 percent of the population employed in agriculture.[19] Such work remains unnecessary even if people wanted to do it in the first place.

So let us see what history can tell us.

The path that our agrarian culture took, will look a lot like the road that manufacturing travels down. The agriculture industry culls jobs with regularity even today. Manufacturing now, does that as well. Between 1995 and 2002, 22 million manufacturing jobs disappeared across the globe.[20] Although the G7 industrialized countries lose manufacturing jobs—so does China.[21] During the 1995–2002 timeframe, China lost 15 million manufacturing jobs, which was actually a higher proportion than the worldwide average of 11 percent.[22] Yet economic growth and job growth continue across the world economies. All of this signals the transition underway—one that will occur whether we like it or not.

It is true that work at a fast food counter qualifies as a function of the service economy. Of itself, this observation tells us nothing. It does not inform us, for example, that the service economy also drives the development of sophisticated IT systems architecture. Likewise, for improved accounting tools (particularly in the aftermath of Sarbanes–Oxley). Greater use of broadband technologies and their attendant job base would qualify as well. These are all components of the new economy.

The Dallas Federal Reserve performed an analysis of the nature of work in the early phases of the transition to a service-dominated economy by looking at the 30 best and worst jobs from a *Jobs Rates Almanac* ranking of 300 occupations. The list highlighted only working conditions in order to emphasize the relative quality of the work experience. Wages were removed for purposes of the analysis in order to emphasize the quality of the duties performed on the job.

Higher growth good jobs included ones like financial managers, mathematical and computer scientists, biological and life scientists, medical and health managers—even painters and sculptors. Jobs going away include coal miners, farmers, and textile machine workers.[23] The better jobs in terms of working conditions—most of them in services—will clearly be a growth industry as compared to many relatively unattractive jobs. Yet, services still too often, get a bad rap from pundits and the media.

A storm brews unlike any in over a hundred years. The last such transition can prove instructive in order to help us cope with the one underway now. Many economies transitioned from agriculture to manufacturing in the late 1800s. Work changed. Organizations transformed. Sources of profit migrated to different parts of the value chain. And society adjusted as it always does. Changes in the nature of work caused population settlement patterns to follow, in the wake of urban industrialization. Political power shifted for generations as the economy took on an altogether different character. Not for decades did the realities set in. The pervasive transition impacted all segments of society.

Let us examine this first transformation further from the standpoint of incentives and behavior. Family farmers faced greater competition as automation along with increased scale imposed higher levels of productivity on agricultural businesses at the beginning of the industrial era. The farm environment proved grueling enough already. In response, many workers chose to move to the cities. Jobs in the industrialized economies migrated away from agriculture toward more value-added endeavors such as manufacturing where wages were higher. Political power followed the urban constituencies. Towns and cities increased in population as rural areas ceased their period of rapid growth. These changes caused consternation. The shrinking rural population rebelled against industrialization. New skills came into demand. Old ones were rendered obsolete. The economy drifted between boom times and panic or even outright depression. Modern organization went through growth pains along the way as well. It took a long time to restore the equilibrium that we became comfortable with, in the years after World War II. We should not be surprised to see an untidy transition this next time around. In fact, we can use this knowledge of the past to peek around the next corner in our time. What will an economy, that goes from manufacturing to services, look like?

Some people will indeed wait tables. Some will work in retail outlets. Yet there will be other types of jobs that look a little more glamorous. Skilled workers will develop information and communication technologies (ICT) that drive productivity improvements. Much of this will be enabled through the digitization of information. Ubiquitous and rapid transmission of voice, data, and video will lead to innovative applications that exploit these tools. Workers in growth industries such as biotechnology will make substantial use of ICTs also. They will catalog vast amounts of information for instant retrieval across the planet. They will decode the raw data that produces new cures for illness. Still others will create knowledge that enriches our lives or develop entertainment that provides welcome diversion. Everyone will feel the effects. Many of us will be active participants in the transformation. The learning curves across such momentous eras appear steep to the people who must live through them. The assimilation of new knowledge presents a formidable challenge in many ways. Old habits die hard. People who got comfortable with the world set up in a certain way are loathe to see it change.

An information economy will drive the redefinition work processes. We can look back once again at history to get an idea about why. In the early days of industrialization, a new widely available power source—electricity—replaced manual labor or steam power in factory environments. But did management immediately employ the most optimal approaches to take advantage of this new power source? No. Management simply retrofitted the new power source into existing processes. Executives did not launch into a business process reengineering (BPR) exercise to rethink the workflows prior to implementation. The term BPR did not even come into general parlance until the 1990s, when authors Michael Hammer and James Champy published *Reengineering the Corporation: A Manifesto for Business Revolution*.[24]

When electricity was introduced to factory environments, a central electric dynamo powered an entire facility through an inefficient system of belts to turn the machines. All it did was allow managers to replace an even larger steam engine. A real rise in the productivity in manufacturing settings required management to employ smaller, decentralized, electric motors (along with lots of wall sockets) that came along later.

Service industry productivity gains will also lag in their impact. One recent example brings the point home. Organizational management essentially air-dropped stand-alone PCs into all sorts of business environments in the 1980s. The deployments produced uncertain benefits in terms of overall economic productivity. We realized the limitations of such automation only in retrospect. We now understand that networks hold the real key to liberation of the gains from stand-alone processing power and the applications they drive. This holds true across an organization or across the globe. This process of discovery in the new economy will be similar to our previous foray into manufacturing. Progress will center on thoughtful management, just as it did a hundred years ago.

Management theory, as a guide of any sort, was in its infancy back then. Even still, it spends far too much time on the manufacturing process relative to services. We have a lot more ground yet to cover. Modern day enterprises will need more useful tools than those available now. The few timeless lessons applicable to a service economy that may be gleaned, should indeed be savored. We have to take our insight from wherever we can find it.

Management theory borrows from other older disciplines that include economics, sociology, political science, and even biology. Schools of management trace their roots back no farther than the late 1800s. Harvard Business School was founded in 1908 and received some criticism at the time for a lack of rigor.

Economics boasts a much longer lineage. It goes back to at least 1776, when Adam Smith published *Wealth of Nations*. The French physiocrats (who exerted a significant influence on Smith) theorized about a *laissez-faire* approach to economic policy even before that. Mercantilists advocated export promotion through trade regulations.[25] The Mercantilists, to their credit spent time in contemplation of trade issues even if they did miss the mark. The physiocrats were a product of the French Enlightenment. They fared better perhaps because they attempted to employ a scientific approach to the study of economics. This kind of fundamental rigor continues to provide the field with respectability even today.

Management theory came very late to the party. Even today, it remains more of a practitioner's art than economics. Still, economics provides a good point of departure for a journey into the nature of management. The two fields relate to each other well. Economics maintains a one-hundred and fifty year head start. Both disciplines cover much of the same ground. It was economics that recognized the obvious weakness in the treatment of the business firm as a black box. The theory of transaction costs arrived and remedied that shortfall.

Organizations are not black boxes. What happens inside is not magic. The idea of a black box may be simple but it sure does not provide much edification. Any notion of a black box to describe organizations provides only marginal value.

The concept of transaction costs begins to deliver an explanation about where managers choose to draw organizational boundaries. It also helps clarify what operations they undertake as well as why. This principle still remains underappreciated.

Managers, strategists, and economists often work under the assumption that progress in society occurs through scientific innovation, faster processing chips, and new production equipment with higher capacity. Such a perspective masks the fact that how we organize—in and of itself—can also have significant impact on productivity and output. Techniques to leverage organizational capabilities comprise a central theme of management theory.

Of course, the study of management does try to take regular steps forward. New management books proffer innovative new approaches all the time. The most well-known early management theorist was Frederick Taylor, who conceptualized labor as an augment to automation. Taylor examined workflow efficiency in manufacturing environments around the end of the nineteenth century. He used time and motion studies to get data for his analysis. These kinds of analyses did not tap the full range of human potential though they did benefit from measurement. At last it made hard data available to management. The increased use of meaningful measurements of this sort describes exactly where management will be headed in the future.

Manufacturers have become very good at the implementation of measurements in the past hundred years. Statistical Process Control (SPC) took manufacturing to new levels of improved performance. Services have not received anywhere near this kind of attention from SPC. It is fair to say that a comprehensive view of service organization management did not exist as the twentieth century came to a close.

Overall, management theory still consists of a set of individual pieces in a lot of ways. A production function here, a human resource strategy there. Core competence, financial wizardry, corporate strategy, operational excellence, customer intimacy, marketing razzle-dazzle all come to us one or two at a time. There is no unified field theory.

There also exists a plethora of acronyms developed around various technology-driven process improvement tools. Software companies intended the tools to support one or more of the above functions.

Integration remains a challenge. The applications often compete or overlap with one another. Let us take a moment for a sampling:

- ERP (Enterprise Resource Management) served to make operations inside an organization more streamlined.
- SCM (Supply Chain Management) came on board to extend ERP functions to partners outside of the enterprise in order to coordinate external relationships.
- CRM (Customer Relationship Management) attempts to provide the glue to hold the ERP and SCM pieces together from a customer-centric standpoint.

Other related three letter words abound.

- CMM (Capability Maturity Model) helps set rigorous standards for software development.
- ITO (Information Technology Outsoucing) enables organizations to off-load the management of technical services and processing platforms.
- BPO (Business Process Outsourcing) allows organizations to off-load noncore functions and processes, much like ITO.
- KPO (Knowledge Process Outsourcing) represents an emerging type of outsourcing that targets more value-added service functions such as paralegal work or engineering design.
- B2B (Business-to-Business) relates back to supply chain (SCM) issues that speak to the relationships outside organizations.
- TQM (Total Quality Management) tries to provide a methodology to improve processes from beginning to end. TQM is not unlike CMM for software, though many people prefer to use 6σ (Six Sigma) over both TQM or CMM (the author included).

Confused? The bad news is that there are many more ingredients in the business and technology acronym soup that management must be conversant with. To keep track of it all remains a challenge. The trouble is compounded because each discipline or practice tends to view management issues through their own prism. Some practitioners see ERP as the center of the universe. Others latch onto TQM, or CMM. While each set of methods and tools can be useful, they can also demonstrate a variant of the garbage can theory developed by Cohen, March and Olsen in 1972. That is, they are a *solution* looking for a problem.[26]

So, management theory still searches for a center. It has yet to achieve a commensurate level of maturity with other academic or scientific disciplines. Enough lack of systematic theory exists to leave a lot of room for debate in the meantime.

As a result, individual judgment for management becomes part of the trade as with other practitioner arts. Take medicine or law. No two patients are the same. No two cases are identical. No two organizations are alike either. Yet management does differ from medicine and law in one key respect. Good management does not center on the individual. It is a team sport, where the teams can get really, really big.

The best doctors, the best attorneys often achieve a fair degree of celebrity. The best managers or executives work behind the scenes—people unknown to you.[27] Individual celebrity in management, almost always serves to bolster an outsized ego more than it does to steward an organization. Some few recent books on management provide insight on management in the new economy. They begin to demonstrate that systematic approaches will move the discipline forward.[28] One day, management theory will catch up to the transition underway. In the meantime, we can certainly chip away at the edges.

We will see why it is important to understand the role of four key components in the decades ahead:

- People
- Information
- Services
- Transaction costs

Management theory can often be criticized for being too anecdotal. It seems subject to wholesale revision every few years, as fads come in and out of fashion. Flavor-of–the-month management is no way to run an enterprise. Yet a coherent picture starts to take shape even now.

The Disconnect Between Theory and Practice

Management books and predictions about the future abound. The biggest issue that remains unresolved is putting sound technique into practice. Managers and executives are besieged from all directions from consultants, vendors, and gurus about how best to go about transforming their organizations.

Why is it taking so long for markets and outsourcing to substantially alter old school management styles? Because there is no critical mass of practitioners yet. Some blame a lack of evidence-based management on the failure of business school programs to educate managers on the use of applicable scientific research that is available in abundance.[29]

Whatever the reason, managers and executives are still poking around the edges. Service workers are experimenting with alternative career choices, but on the whole, most people are still stuck in a mindset that dates back to the industrial era. Almost as if living inside the movie "The Matrix," most people do not seem to want to be unplugged.

So in the meantime, those brave pioneers will have to work within the existing hierarchies and do a bit of evangelizing. Some worthwhile advice comes to us from a recent work that exposes some of the pervasive myths and fallacies that afflict management practice. The authors employ a variant of the Hippocratic Oath, which admonishes physicians to "First, do no harm." Stanford Business School professors Jeffrey Pfeffer and Robert Sutton propose that if nothing else, managers should slow the spread of bad practices by deferring action when organizational directives are not based on rational evidence. It is at least a first step. Besides, in many cases, it will be self-defeating to attack the formal management structure head-on.[30] In other words, resistance is not futile.

Part of the problem we face in bridging theoretical notions with the real world is that no one knows for sure what the organization of the future will look like. One of the oft-used examples is the Hollywood movie production model, where specialists come together for a project for a finite period of time and then disband. Every time someone is involved in the production of a particular film, they get to list it on their resume. The industry comprises a results-based set of occupations by virtue of the fact that the outputs are visible and readily measured. The movie industry inspires great passion both within, as well as across the mainstream population. Relationships are highly collaborative and the industry is consistently innovative. Yet, it is also very much a system based on rules of engagement.

Because of its worldwide popularity, Hollywood is forced to be transparent. Mistakes as well as successes receive lots of attention. No doubt, there is favoritism and nepotism in the industry; many working relationships are based on friendships. Luck does not hurt either. But in such a results-oriented industry, where box office receipts and critical reviews get widely circulated every day, a poorly performing artist will not continue working, no matter who they know or are related to. Organizations could do worse than to emulate such a model that inspires creativity and is a global exporter.

The consulting industry offers another model of what many organizations may look like in the years to come. The rise of the independent contractor means that pools of workers can shift from project to project, industry to industry as demand changes. Key indicators of success are utilization percentages and customer satisfaction. As Internet services become more sophisticated, individuals can hang out their own shingle online, making the brand name that most people identify with their own—not that of some larger company or organization. By the same token, organizations will outsource not just to other companies, but also to growing pools of individuals.

More people work at home, a throwback to the days before industrialization. Here again, we see the trend toward results-based performance because working from the home means traditional monitoring by supervisors is not feasible.

Existing government structures and incentives are also impeding the transition that markets and outsourcing will drive in terms of changing work styles. For example, corporations in the United States receive a deduction for the costs of health insurance, while individuals do not, unless they are 100 percent self-employed and are not eligible for coverage under a spouses plan—yet another remnant of the industrial age. As the need for change becomes more apparent, tax laws and government expenditures on infrastructure will reflect those changes.

Now that it has become painfully clear that the traditional corporation is unable to provide even an implicit guarantee of employment the way it once did, a more independent workforce will continue to emerge that requires appropriate support mechanisms.

Look at how local libraries are becoming a part of the workforce infrastructure in the new economy. In the past, libraries were mostly card catalogs, books, and periodicals. Now the traditional book sections of libraries are being overtaken by computers that support basic applications, electronic media, and Internet capabilities. Schools in some states are fulfilling a similar function during off-hours that democratize access to new economy technologies—the new tools of the trade.[31] Internet cafes, Starbucks hot spots are all manifestations of the same trend.

Again, these trends imply increased transparency, a requirement for collaboration, and a focus on results—not the micromanagement that many managers remain comfortable with. As time goes on, it will be increasingly difficult to conduct business with a hierarchical mindset or hierarchical organizational structure. The old school boys had their day, but the market benchmark in the service economy will force that to a conclusion. Management theories that deal with services are indeed making their way to reality. It is just a matter of time.

CHAPTER 2

GOVERNANCE OPTIONS

Where the Organization Ends

Organizations of course have a choice about what sorts of activities they take on. It is now pretty clear that core functions should not be outsourced. Even so, many organizations struggle to define their core competence well enough to serve as an actionable guide. The nature of service functions can make it hard to separate core from noncore functions. Any direct comparison of performance measures between two governance mechanisms continues to present problems to management. Activities within the organization often do not lend themselves to any one-to-one market comparison.[1] Sometimes this occurs for good reasons. Often, a new business idea, in its formative stages, will not find market support. An activity that an organization performs far better than anyone else should be retained within also. These types of decisions are easy to make.

Some of the other reasons managers use to keep functions in-house are not so good. In fact, department heads may work very hard to keep their operations shrouded in mystery. They are happy about the larger organization's inability to compare their operations against the market. The failure to subject all parts of the organization to the market benchmark raises some very basic questions about governance. Why does the management have no objective rationale about what gets done in-house? An attempt to keep people employed in unproductive jobs should not be the basis for the decision.

So how can management approach this in a systematic manner? There is no one-minute answer for management. The alternatives span a wide continuum.

Let us start with pure buy decisions for commodity goods on the spot market And consider the example of office supplies. Few organizations choose to produce their own pens, paper, desks, and chairs because of the scale. Makers of such items need lots of customers in order to be profitable—certainly more than a single firm or organization. Supply chain requirements also make external producers more efficient. So, most organizations logically choose to purchase such items off the market. This kind of quick analysis works fine for simple items.

The alternatives become fuzzier with services. A host of issues must be considered when the discussion about commodity goods ends. Services are different. They comprise an extensive menu of intangible outputs. Consider the aspect of labor. An organization has various options such as managing contractors in-house, domestic outsourcing, offshoring (offshore outsourcing), and so on. Another option is that an organization can enter into a joint venture. Management can select various sorts of partnerships with any number of other types of organizations to meet its needs. It can make an outright acquisition, which is known as vertical integration. This will be discussed later.

It should be obvious at this point that no best single answer exists that applies to all cases. Otherwise all organizations would use it.[2] Outsourcing cannot always guarantee success for any function. It would suggest an odd conclusion if it did: that the role of organizational innovation or the organization itself would be unnecessary. Every function could be contracted out to an individual in the marketplace. The market would make the organization obsolete. This does not project a realistic scenario. You cannot outsource everything.

Okay. Then what does get outsourced?

The nature of the outsourcing business comes to us by way of increased market competition as a sort of arbitrage. Outsourcers got started by harvesting easy solutions to resell like low-hanging fruit from a tall tree in a giant orchard. This has been underway for some time. ADP (Automatic Data Processing) did it with payroll functions in the 1950s. Outsourcers already perform many of the simpler functions that enterprises require. Basic data processing is one. Janitorial services is another.

These functions suggest just the tip of the iceberg. Organizations will continue to evolve in the service era to better exploit the more elaborate menu of outsourcing options. They will restructure and employ better measurements. Organizational management will learn from mistakes so that there will be fewer blunders as the practice matures.

Outsourcing, the decision to relocate a function or operation outside the boundary of the organization must be regarded as a tool. It can lower costs, improve performance, or both. That is the good news.

So then, what is the bad news? The potential downside always remains a possibility. Outsourcing can drain organizational resources. It can result in failure. Sometimes outsourcing is not the right approach even if managed well.

The decision about whether to perform a function in-house presents a dynamic set of options. Since the landscape constantly changes, organizational function can never reach perfection. The nature of competition makes all improvements relative, always in comparison to something else. Something better will always come along sooner or later.

Let us get some semantics out of the way before we go on. What do we mean when we talk about markets? The definition can seem a little abstract without a context. It may be useful to think of the market for our purposes as the collection of all the "other" organizations, firms, or even individuals who operate in a competitive environment. Taken together, they represent a constant potential to offer superior alternatives. "Best Practice" probably does not describe what the market is very well. What is best today might not be so great tomorrow. Instead, "leading" practice provides a better description of what the market can offer to forward-thinking managers at a given point in time. The next innovation that will make current options obsolete threatens organizations at all levels, and at all times. Few things ever stay the best for long.

The breakthroughs now come from everywhere with ubiquitous global competition at hand. New ideas percolate in people's heads every minute of the day. Creative teams in organizations domiciled in countries scattered across the globe develop potential breakthroughs as you read this. These advances by external organizations increase the number of new options for management. Technologies now enable loose-knit or flexible organizational structures. Managers can shape their own hierarchies to exploit opportunities. Key factors used to shape organization include:

- People
- Techniques
- Environment
- Culture
- Technology

Managers now need to be in a position to use all of the above factors. Notice that people are once again perched at the top of a list of tools or concepts that deal with the service economy. What other resource within any organization could manage to pull everything together?

Organizations retain a wide range of choices for governance in the new economy. Expertise hired one individual at a time can serve to develop a particular competence inside. Entire divisions can be outsourced. Or anything in between. The dependency rests only on the lack of imagination by management or sometimes by the available alternatives in the marketplace.

The nature of the boundaries across organizations can be mapped along a continuum. Many cannot be classified by textbook extremes of vertical integration or pure spot market contract. A simple dichotomy just does not capture the full set of options a service economy presents.[3] The choice of organizational structure can be visualized as a range of possibilities in figure 2.1, the Market-Hierarchy Continuum.[4]

Some organizations now operate as loose confederations. Others should use a more centralized control structure.[5]

Airlines retain numerous interdependencies. Planes, crews, and customers must be brought together at specific times every day. Significant constraints from field operations, remote support staff, pilots, and crews require a single system approach to the entire network. Optimal performance in a competitive industry depends on it.

The use of new technology to enable alternative forms of organization represents nothing new. Large firms experimented with organizational structure since their rise at the start of the twentieth century. E.F. Hutton's great insight that led to its premier position in the brokerage industry for decades revolved around the power of communication technology (in a low-tech way).

Hutton had expanded to the western United States in search of new markets in the late 1800s. The company found that the geographical separation presented an obstacle. Hutton could not communicate the buy and sell orders of its California client base fast enough. Traditional broker age firms anchored themselves in New York near the major exchanges. Hutton needed something along the lines of a real-time communication system that spanned the continent in order to service its client base.

Telegraph companies at the time refused to risk the investment needed for a transcontinental link that would provide an uncertain return. So Hutton financed a portion of the cost to complete the telegraph to the west coast, which prodded Western Union into finally building it. The link solidified Hutton's regionalized operational structure. Hutton's access

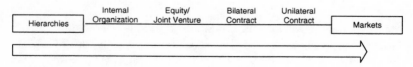

Figure 2.1   Market-Hierarchy Continuum

Source: Adapted from Oxley, Joanne E. "Appropriability Hazards and Governance in Strategic Alliances: A Transaction Cost Approach," *Journal of Law, Economics, and Organization,* 13:2 (October 1997) 387–409.

to almost instantaneous information gave the company an unrivaled advantage over west coast competitors. Hutton was able to tap a very lucrative market for a long time.[6]

Organizational structure can be exploited in tandem with technology for competitive advantage then as now. A broadened scope of operations extended the geographic reach of Hutton's operations. This helped establish good customer relationships. The use of communication technology bridged the physical separation between the stock market and its west coast offices. This solution ensured that Hutton's customers received superior service. These innovations also restructured the brokerage industry. The story of Hutton's use of technology to restructure its organization sets the stage for a similar transformation in the twenty-first century that will cut across all industry lines.

Efficient Transactions

The recognition of transaction costs dates back to the first part of the twentieth century. Many management handbooks touch on the concept with different degrees of emphasis. Transaction costs intertwine much more with services than physical goods, so we should expect them to become even more significant in the future.

Gains to be tapped from manufacturing now operate on something that resembles a steady-state system. The regular efficiency with which national economies produce goods boggles the mind. It may surprise you to learn that the increased efficiency in manufacturing now results in a constant reduction in the number of jobs on a worldwide basis.

A similar push for efficiency in the service functions of world economies looms large, even though the number of jobs will still increase. Both, transactional efficiency, as well as the total number of transactions must increase in order for the economy to continue to grow in the service era.

Put it another way, transaction costs must continue to go down. This means that the market will pay less every day for each transaction. The only way for an organization to make up the difference will be to process more transactions. The ability to interact with increased productivity on a global basis depends it.

The use of closed electronic systems to decrease transaction costs has been chronicled extensively as far back as 1989, by Malone, Yates, and Benjamin.[7] Now with the widespread use of the Internet, the systems are open.

People and organizations all over, want to conduct more exchanges all the time. Other folks want to sell us stuff as well as buy things. This adds to the pressure for increased transactional efficiency. Many people with poor to average educations now chase employment all over the globe. The last thing anybody wants is for the cost of doing business to get in the way. Sure, politicians or journalists may serve up rhetoric against lower costs because they can drive wages down. Such statements make headlines but do not address the underlying dynamics of globalization, expanding markets, and outsourcing. Impediments to legitimate commerce may benefit workers protected in jobs that have become obsolete or grossly inefficient. The rest of us will be stuck with an economy that has fewer jobs to go around.

The story is more positive than negative, but let us not sugarcoat things. The good news is that more transactions will increase efficiency along with the ability of the economy to create innovative jobs. The bad news is that many of the impacts will be disagreeable to many, at best. Change can be painful.

Is there an alternative? Not really. Executives, along with the managers they direct, will be forced to take advantage of lower transaction costs in order to reshape their organizations. Global competitiveness demands it. These efficiencies will improve economic well-being in the longer term in the same way that lowered manufacturing costs does. That is all to the good news. Even so, significant upheaval awaits us in the meantime.

The path ahead appears clear, unless for some reason higher priced goods suddenly get wildly popular. This does not seem likely. So then the question arises: Do we benefit from transactional efficiency other than in the form of lower prices (which may also bring lower wages in the process)?

The answer is yes. We benefit. Let us discuss why.

Transactional efficiency enables specialization. Significant specialization means that many of the jobs performed in the industrialized economies command high wages. Specialization produces few benefits to anyone in isolation. Standards of living increase only when specialization gets combined with the ability to trade. An economy requires transactional efficiency in order to facilitate trade. Inefficiency leaves you with stagnation. We cannot improve our lot in life very much if we cannot trade.

Transactional efficiency can be increased in other ways as well. The use of money lowers transaction costs. It increases the number of transactions possible in an exponential fashion. The economy would not have grown very much if society relied on barter as it once did. Imagine the inefficiencies involved in the attempt to match up buyers and sellers with precise sets of goods for millions of exchanges. Instead, sellers are glad to accept a generalized asset—fiat currency—what we call paper money or coins backed by the reputation of the government that issues them.

Even eBay, the online trading system, could not survive on a barter system. There would be no incentive to operate. Forget the fact that it would be a lot harder to link up specific buyers with sellers even with the help of the Internet. The barter system would preclude the easy ability to charge a transaction fee. eBay does not bring all those people together as an act of goodwill. It intends to turn a profit on the deal.

Money is an instrument of stored value. It introduces an enormous amount of flexibility into an economic system. Stable national currencies better enable organizations to grow. They also encourage activities like outsourcing. Money lowers comparative transaction costs in a big way while it also enables greater specialization. Outputs can be converted into generalized assets. The use of electronic currency accelerates this potential. Easier ability to transact means more outsourcing and hence more specialization.

The concept of generalized versus specialized assets often surfaces with outsourcing. Specialized assets—if the specialization serves a useful purpose—represent the most important reason that organizations exist at all. Markets, in the form of outsourcing, often cannot make use of specialized assets. There just are not enough customers to sell to.

When specialization provides economic value to society, it often occurs when industries or companies are young. Markets have not matured enough.

On the other hand, specialized assets or proprietary standards that are used to extract profits or tolls from customers—well that is another story. If intended to benefit only a single company, nonutilitarian specialization provides limited or no benefit and is on the way out.

Gains from specialization in the new economy that also comes with industry standards will be enormous because of the ability to enhance ever more discrete knowledge or technologies. Management will be able to mix, match, repackage, or incorporate the pieces into new forms. No single firm (or organization or country) can hope to keep up with all of this complexity in isolation. Increased specialization complements decreased transaction costs. Together, they will result in greater numbers of transactions.[8] Deals across organizations will be easier as well as cost less. Managers in organizations will have more interaction with the outside.

This will drive different management behaviors. To work with other organizations requires skills different from those often demonstrated by traditional managers. Internal departments can be managed by whim. Outside companies will eschew such caprice. Old authoritarian management styles will prove ineffective. Even laughable. Disorganized one-man shows will give way to shared rationales. Greater collaboration will become a must. Collaboration improves coordination. It also helps managers avoid dumb mistakes. Decisions, in isolation, very often produce tragic results because useful feedback often does not get factored in—and the bad decisions do not become obvious until later.

We can see that outsourcing will increase cross-organizational interaction. As such, it heralds the advent of modular organizations.

The story does not stop there.

The next step should seem logical enough. The same discipline that seeks structure with external organizations will very soon turn itself right back on the guts of traditional organization. Interdepartmental relationships will start to change because of this logic. That is where the real fun will begin.

Imagine in-house departments managed with as much rigor as expected from an outside company. Perhaps the real question is: Why have we not gotten there already? A deeper look into the increased interplay across organizations will help explain why management in the new economy will be so different. It will highlight why the change will take some time. The rules of engagement across organizations can help us understand the problems (and benefits too) that occur inside.

Transaction efficiency demands three prerequisites:

- Individual autonomy
- Secure property rights
- Secure and predictable contracts

Individual autonomy drives creativity necessary for innovation. Secure property rights provide sufficient motivation so that people can expect to keep the majority of what they earn. The ability to contract wraps a nice bow around everything. It is the icing on the cake. Secure contracts ensure that all parties can operate with confidence that agreements will be enforced. Secure contracts enable exchanges. Contracts unleash productivity and increase standards of living.

Work inside an organization entails the forfeit of some portion of each of the above bulleted items. We lose a little individual autonomy. We may give up some intellectual property rights. Most of us work on the basis of somewhat vague implicit contracts as opposed to explicit ones. The reasons for these differences will tell us about where a contrast exists between the market and organization. More on that later. For now, let us continue to explore how markets will impact relationships across organizations. Transactional efficiency across organizations depends on autonomy, property rights, and secure contracts. What are the mechanisms to get those things? Aside from the court system, it seems that we need lawyers for starters.

Lawyers do aid in the establishment and definition of property rights and contracts—at least up to a point. Where that threshold begins, remains uncertain. Research into metrics suggests that there should be just so many attorneys on a per capita basis. If we could find the right mix, this would optimize societal transaction efficiency. The occupational function of lawyers appears to place a drag on the economy after that proportion breaches some saturation level.[9] Many attorneys would even agree.

In their traditional roles as client advocates, lawyers do not create much in and of themselves. Rather, they comprise part of a framework that enables impartial enforcement of the rules by the judicial system. Lawyers provide the most benefit (from an economic standpoint) when they improve transactional efficiency. Contract costs affect transactional efficiency. These costs depend on the legal environment. Effective contracts lower transaction costs as long as outcomes remain predictable. That is the key. It cannot be a crapshoot to rectify discrepancies. Inequities must be addressed on an impartial basis otherwise contracts provide little value.

Transaction costs increase whenever the economic system invokes the judiciary or outside arbitration for contract enforcement. Outlandish tort verdicts wreak havoc on attempts to plan for the future from a business standpoint. Unpredictability in any number of venues (political, judicial, legal enforcement) causes investor enthusiasm to wither. Entrepreneurs withdraw. The best scenario in terms of transactional efficiency involves an explicit contract with unambiguous terms. This lowers uncertainty. The costs to do business can be estimated in advance. Both the buyer as well as the seller retain recourse if either believes to be injured.

We most often think of contracts as formal vehicles. Agreements that have been put down on paper are explicit. On the other hand, lots of agreements that affect our day-to-day lives are implicit. For example, contracts with at-will employees inside organizations. Others include contracts outside of the organizational framework that rely on brand or reputation.[10] Implicit contracts can work okay under the right circumstances. We have reached to the point that they often suffice for the purchase of tangible products. For instance, consumer goods like soap, toothpaste, and so on. Such simple transactions imply simple contracts.

Things get a bit more complicated for services. This makes explicit contracts for the intangibles essential. It is also more of a challenge to define those intangibles. Purchases of complex services defy easy definition. This explains why many activities end up inside the organization. The flexibility of implicit contracts often favors the placement of such hard-to-define operations within organizational boundaries.

Does that mean that complex operations cannot be outsourced? No. Organizations can and do contract on the outside for some of their more sophisticated needs.

First things first. An organization should try to define relationships with explicit contracts, if at all possible, when it does go to the market for the acquisition of complex services. Why leave anything to chance or interpretation if you do not have to? Having said that, it may not always be possible to do so. Sometimes the challenge remains just too great. In these circumstances, shared financial risk may be required as an alternative to an explicit contract. This can serve to assure better alignment of the motivations of both organizations.

This raises a question. We see that lower transaction costs allows management to make use of the market. Does transactional efficiency only impact relationships between organizations? Not exactly. The decrease in transaction costs works its magic both within and across organizations. Sometimes the first stage of improved transactional efficiency often occurs within organizations. A good example would be data communication networks. Management first pioneered large-scale networks inside organizations with suppliers such as IBM, Fujitsu, and Toshiba. As late as 1992, these in-house networks constituted, by far, the most dominant form of data communication for enterprises. The potential scale economies encouraged the deployment of even bigger cross-organizational networks over the Internet. Offerings from companies such as Cisco, 3Com, and Bay Networks focused on internet protocol (IP) standards that complimented in-house networks. IP products leveraged the local area network environments inside organizations along with the personal computers attached to them.[11]

In other cases, the market will force efficiency on internal organization. We will see this more and more in the years ahead. So the debate between the use of internal organization or outsourcing gets hazier as the rules change. The answer will not be determined by a one-line rule in a management handbook. Each alternative offers advantages and disadvantages.

The basis for optimal organizational governance will be contingent on goals, plans, and opportunities—in a word—context. Or as consultants are wont to say, "It depends."

Let us look at an example of how important context is. Acronyms provide a good way to do that. What is an SME? In the training world, it is a Subject Matter Expert. In marketing contexts it is Small to Medium-sized Enterprises. A CD? Compact Disc for music and software. Certificate of Deposit if you are talking about banking. For shipping purposes, COD means Cash On Delivery. For Crime Scene Investigators (CSI), it is Cause Of Death. PMS? In the hotel business, it is not a women's issue—it is the computer that runs the facility, also known as the Property Management System.

So, context matters a lot in a specialized, information-intensive world. The decision to outsource will always depend on context. If there is a rule of thumb for managers, it is that outsourcing for all manner of service functions has become a lot more viable. The market benchmark lurks in the background, ever present, always ready to foment change.

New Management Styles

The options that organizations now possess to direct internal or external resources grow all the time. Information and Communication Technologies (ICT) rewrite the rules for the management control of operations. The abundance of choices creates opportunities to organize around all sorts of activities.

New and improved structures will be required of enterprises as complexity and scope increase. This means more granular outputs, more market segmentation. Organizational outputs will get broken up into multiple components. There will be greater coordination of people. All of the pieces get harder to keep track of in the process. The result will be, the development of improved methods to define outputs of all types, by managers. Better measurements will come out of all this. Functions that seem abstract or difficult to define must be captured too.

We need to remind ourselves that the office place we knew in the twentieth century went out the window well before the end of the last millennium. The new enterprise will not be our father's organization. Technologies grow more complex. The need for expert skill sets to manage the activities also increases. Renaissance men and women will go out of style—instead, the modern organization demands specialists.

Of course, leaders cannot specialize in all areas they manage. But the proven ability to specialize in some area or another will inform technique about collaborative relationships between specialists. In the end, executives cannot be afraid to dive into the details when necessary. Once again, old school dilettantes will be history.

Too many people compete in the market for generalists—organizations will soon find themselves in the same boat. Organizations cannot hope to be experts in every function that must be carried out. Other than traditional internal organization, new forms of governance will be required. Organizations have to plan to off-load significant functions where competitive advantage cannot be maintained. This will be the way modern enterprise manages increased complexity. More complexity leads to more specialization. This leads to more outsourcing. The cycle becomes self-reinforcing.

Interfirm relations will become integral. It will be impossible to run an organization without them. Individual product or service components will be grouped, regrouped, integrated, packaged, and resold to ever-diverse market segments. Contractual relations become inevitable as part of the deal. No organization, just as no country[12] or individual can demonstrate comparative efficiency for everything.

A revolution is underway. The contractual frameworks that serve to harmonize relationships will be more paramount than in the past. Effective coordination of both external suppliers and internal resources will force the use of management control mechanisms. Process interfaces will be critical.

So what are the rules of engagement? How are conflicts resolved? What are the penalties for nonperformance?

It will be regular measurements that provide the stair steps to evaluate results.[13] Also, the usual rules that pertain to employer-employee relationships will be irrelevant as a result of this transition. Internal departments along with external organizations will be judged on definable outputs along with individual employees.

A case of a non-G7 country demonstrates how these new rules will generalize even to the most rudimentary settings. Consider the case of the Da Afghanistan Bank (DAB), the central bank of the fledgling democracy in Central Asia. Donor organizations work to establish greater security in the post-9/11 environment. Building physical infrastructure constitutes an important function as well. There also continues to be substantial effort by the international community to establish an economic infrastructure as a foundation for commerce. These important efforts include reliable land titling to guarantee secure property rights. An overhaul of the legal system is in the works to ensure enforceable contracts.

The goals of the DAB remain similar to other central banks throughout the world. These include the promotion of sound monetary policy, creation of a country-wide interbank payment system, and establishment of a strong supervisory function to oversee the commercial banks in Afghanistan. The DAB maintains over 70 branches in the country. The Central Bank in Afghanistan functions as the lender of last resort. It also fulfills the role of commercial banker of last resort. Many remote areas of the country will not justify the establishment of a commercial bank for some time to come, if ever.

To support its expansive operation, the DAB issued about 400 computers to its employees in the three years after the expulsion of the Taliban. Various donors include the Asia Development Bank, the World Bank, and the United States Agency for International Development. These agencies provided computers to support the central bank's policy goals.

The fact that the literacy rate in Afghanistan continues to be among the lowest in the world, means that people must be trained. This will remain a challenge for some time. Even so, employee performance issues may not be as different as one might imagine.

A team on the ground designed a crude experiment intended to gauge how well the bank staff utilized their computers. International advisors along with the DAB IT staff undertook periodic spot checks of the offices. The selected employees constituted a convenience sample. A true experiment would have entailed selection of the subjects on a random basis.

Nonetheless, the spot checks revealed that many bank employees spent their time on a variety of activities. Everything from instant messaging to the settlement of international payments. They surfed the web. They listened to music on CDs. Some managed the bank's portfolio. A few played Solitaire. One fellow even worked through basic calculus integrals in a notebook (not using his computer at all). The nonrandom sample may not have been representative, though we found ourselves intrigued anyway.

A superficial analysis could suggest that this behavior demonstrated widespread shirking and employees goofing off. Yet, information economy employees in the developed countries with computers on their desks do the same thing. This simple experiment, in Central Asia in a country at the bottom of the worldwide literacy ladder, suggests a couple of possibilities.

One centers on the issue of perceived performance. Such activity in the G7 countries (or anywhere else) might cause people to get behind in their work. They might stay late at the office; they might need to push deadlines back. This often impresses bosses as examples of employee "dedication," whether in Kabul, London, or New York.

Management often sees some last minute scramble to finish an assignment as a sign of real energy. The actual cause for the late night heroics might instead be the result of many wasted daytime hours. Long hours or slipped deadlines may signal disorganization. Perhaps a lack of planning. Maybe just plain procrastination. Contrary to popular belief, it does not represent prima facie evidence of an overwhelming workload. The case does not measure up to our sociologist's standard of epistemic correlation. We lack demonstrable cause and effect. Such scenarios suggest that many traditional gauges of performance no longer cut it. In and of itself, face time in the office proves almost nothing anymore.

Productivity in a service environment derives from the establishment of measurable outputs that must be tracked. To try to manage employee activities minute by minute wastes time. It is the relevant deliverables that furnish useful criteria needed to assess employee performance. These provide the keys to organizational success when linked with strategy.

Such result-oriented gauges became the norm in manufacturing settings years ago. Tangible outputs define employee or departmental contributions as well as serve as the basis for rewards. It is true that in a manufacturing environment you often have to be on-site. Fair enough.

In a service environment sometimes you do, sometimes you do not. The decision should be based on the merits, not an old school manager's idiosyncrasies.

Of course, there is no doubt that the assessment of useful service outputs is harder to make than manufactured products. There is no historical precedent to economies dominated by services. Traditional service measures—such as they are—do not do a very good job at defining the contribution of an activity to the organizational mission either. Individual or departmental productivity often gets tracked by such tired indicators as hourly wages, hours billed, annual salaries, revenue by department (if applicable), perfect attendance, or the typical tripe that ends up on annual performance reviews.

Who can say whether an employee surfing the Internet demonstrates a waste of time or an attempt to add to his or her knowledge? The employee might use the Internet to seek out industry data. Is instant messaging in Afghanistan a needless social activity or a modern day tool to improve real-time communication links within the banking system? Any of these guesses could be correct.

More to the point, our experiment may highlight the failure of DAB management to establish solid individual performance targets. This speaks of the competence of the bank management at the operational director level. It does not necessarily reflect on the willingness of employees to execute bank policy.

In modern organizational environments, we understand little enough about the creative process. Management that attempts to apply crude, heavy-handed methods to mold employee behavior will backfire. The issue instead, should center on why management does not expend more effort on the establishment of goals. People are people. No one works well with somebody over their shoulder.

Employee actions should be directed to activities and outcomes tied to organizational goals. As with outsourcing, performance should be punctuated with rewards and consequences. By the time the current transition from manufacturing to service takes its course, it will be a new day. The traditional measure of clocked hours in an office will be irrelevant, no doubt to the dismay of the old school boys.

New Options, New Rules

Measurement still eludes many service industries for reasons not hard to understand. Measurement of tangible objects by comparison, presents no great challenge. A dining table has specific dimensions, a certain quality of design. Its construction consists of a particular type of wood or other material. It will support a finite amount of weight before it breaks.

The measurements remain far more difficult for services. A service exhibits extreme transience. The opportunity may be lost if you forget to establish measurement mechanisms in advance. The dining table, by comparison, is not going anywhere. It can be measured and tested at leisure.

To measure the speed with which a call center answers the telephone requires advance planning. Otherwise you get left with estimates or impressions. Customers put on hold for four or five minutes may complain of twenty-minute waits. Sure, four or five minutes on hold constitutes a long time by service industry standards. Even so, five minutes does not add up to twenty minutes no matter whose clock you use. Sometimes customers can be as unrealistic as any mismanaged organization.

Older types of service organizations have done a good job refining measurements over the years. Consider the hotel industry as an example. Average rates per occupied room, by market segment, by total available rooms on a daily and period-to-date basis have been standard information that operators have collected for decades. Profit and loss (P&L) statements can easily be generated on a property-by-property basis. Customer feedback gets solicited regularly for the premier chains in order to ensure high levels of guest satisfaction.

On the other hand, newer service functions are still in the formative stages. Operations that make use of large-scale information systems, for example, may seem to work well, though no one really knows why. The knowledge management to capture organizational intelligence and learning are recent tools, but they still have a long way to go.

Outsourcing pioneered the use of measurement for services. In order to work with other organizations you really do need the outputs to be well defined upfront. Outsourcing contracts no longer start out as a handshake between two executives, as once was often the case. Smart executives will not touch those kinds of deals anymore. Well-defined agreements with explicit measurable outputs comprise essential elements of outsourcing arrangements. The same principles of measurement will soon enough be applied within organizations. One might wonder why this has not been done already.

The discipline of the measurement of services inside organizations has not happened yet for one simple reason: managerial work-arounds. Hands-on management still allows our ubiquitous unorganized, yet vigilant manager to put out fires all day long. You have seen him/her. You have probably worked for him (or her). Most of us have. This type of manager can throw an entire department into chaos to pull together a last minute presentation for someone upstairs who asked for it two weeks ago. Late night heroics are due to nothing more than poor planning and procrastination.

Sometimes disorganized managers bemoan a lack of data that would help them operate more effectively, but in the final analysis, that "is" management's responsibility. Rather than blame the organization for the problem, competent managers and executives will insist on implementing mechanisms that report the metrics they need.

Managerial work-arounds employ minute-by-minute approaches to cover a multitude of sins that can hide shoddy management practice. Failure of governance due to a lack of a systematic measurement will become apparent only when the individual leaves.

This highlights a key difference between the way outsourcing gets managed as opposed to internal management. A good outsourcing deal requires structure. That explains why metrics of performance (and enforcement of service levels) for outsourcing remain more sophisticated for outsourcing. Micromanagers inside an organization can get away without any sort of formal metrics for years—even an entire career. In-house operations remain in physical proximity. They allow for hands-on control over all of the factors involved. Managers can bird dog projects in ways that make up for a failure to plan or the lack of performance metrics. The close oversight covers a multitude of sins.

Monitored formal metrics will become essential to effective management.[14] Service components now dominate the majority of the economy. This implies that the use of the appropriate systematic measurements along with service levels will be just as important for internal operations as external ones. Services will establish the sort of rigor that has been typical of manufacturing environments for decades. Sophistication in methodologies improves all the time even though measures for many services remain elusive. Service delivery exhibits inherent flexibility. More human interaction infuses processes. Service measurements benefit from frequent reexamination in order to ensure their relevance.[15] Organizational operations will have to increase the use of internal service levels. These benchmarks, along with the interfaces on the inside will look an awful lot like those for outside suppliers as the demarcation of organizational boundaries becomes harder to find.

Implicit measures everywhere are on the way out. Even so, some theorists suggest that incompleteness often represents an essential feature of a well-designed external contract.[16] Why would any organization use implicit service targets? Once in a while, management does not have a choice. Ideas in formative stages may preclude comprehensive contracts. Often, these new ideas form the basis for the creation of an organization. Figure 2.2 illustrates this cycle. Managers can use the advantages of organization to develop new offerings to society.

The need for external governance becomes more critical only later as the organization grows. The limits of managerial capabilities come into

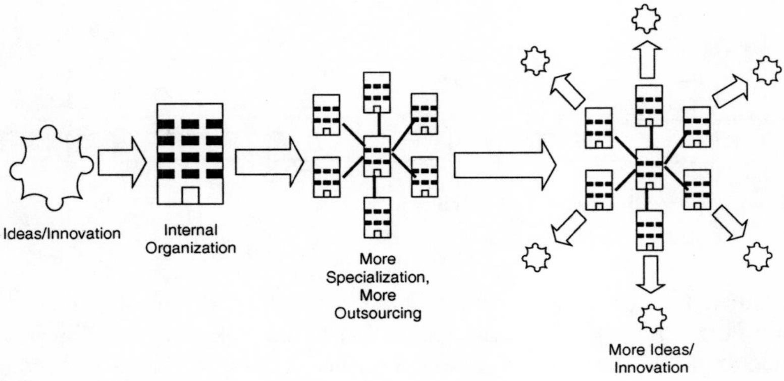

Figure 2.2   Outsourcing Evolution

play. Inefficiencies creep in because people just cannot specialize in too many areas. Management is forced to look at other options in order to stay competitive. Outside suppliers develop offerings that support organizational functions or outputs over time anyway. Outsourcing represents one alternative. Partnerships or joint ventures can be employed as well. Use of these options spurs the creation of other innovations as resources get freed up. The cycle continues all over again with the development of new firms.

Yet, doing things in-house still remains the default option for most organizations. Management takes on service functions themselves if any doubt exists. The decision to keep a function inside the organization, too often gets made for the wrong reasons. It rests on a desire to retain control rather than to better innovate or to remedy a lack of market options. The issue revolves around comfort zones. Given the choice, managers always prefer to take on new activities for their departments. Internal management also enables closer day-to-day supervision. Such a continual feedback system is high maintenance. It burns up lots of management resources. Comparisons with outside alternatives become very difficult to make.

The constant micromanagement integral to this approach also acts as a severe impediment to succession plans. Ironic that managers operating in this fashion often receive kudos for their work ethic. Even as they receive plaudits they hold up a house of cards. No one seems to understand that their long hours stem from a lack of solid measurement mechanisms. The entire department or system may very well collapse when they leave.

Old-fashioned internal organization will give way to more effective alternatives. The divisional organizational form (figure 2.3) replaced the rigid unitary organization. It enabled GM to overtake Ford in the mid-twentieth

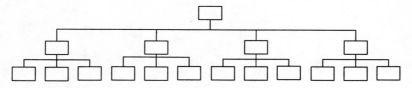

Figure 2.3   Divisional Organization

century. It spurred the growth of thousands of large divisional firms. The introduction of the divisional organization in fact represents the first great transformation of organizational structure since the advent of industrialization, perhaps even since the inception of the business firm.

New forms of governance are set to change in the new economy in a similarly dramatic fashion. At last, managers will come to terms with the pervasiveness of the service component. Consequences combined with clarity will be required for interfaces between internal departments just the same as across organizations. Organizations will be more assiduous as they scrutinize what functions to take in a world of increased specialization and interconnectivity. Service outsourcing will be high on the list of potential alternatives. Leading practices continue to improve through refinement even if management's ability to optimize the outsourcing of services still has a long way to go. The rules will change and it would be best to get ahead of the curve.

Reputation, Relationships, Results

There is a story that gets retold periodically in business newspapers or magazines, which demonstrates another current managerial dysfunction. It is the tale of a manager who systematically reengineers the department's functions to the point where they can be reassigned elsewhere or eliminated altogether. When these results get reported upline, the organization rewards the enterprising manager by laying him or her off. This hardly seems like an equitable resolution.

In fact, such managers should be rewarded by organizational leadership. As we enter a new era of management styles, these are the kinds of managers who will be placed in charge of other departments so that they can be unleashed to repeat the process. In a constantly evolving economy, value will not be found in bureaucratic, turf-warring managers making themselves indispensable. Successful managers and executives of the future will consistently demonstrate the ability to make measurable contributions, and then make themselves obsolete.

It is these kinds of changes in existing mindsets, that will present the most significant challenges to old school managers. Other changes will come as well.

For example, people farther down or outside the traditional hierarchy will take on some of the functions previously associated with the larger organization. The rise of the large organization of the twentieth century saw a huge emphasis in the use of branding for the outputs. The main inputs to the service organization of the twenty-first century, which are people, will make use of a sort of soft branding also.

In effect, three things will determine how the organization of the future will operate: reputation, relationships, and results. What does this mean for organizational structure? We can look at the kinds of changes that are possible across society in order to get an answer.

Communities of people do not have to be based on geographies any-more, but rather common interests. Communities that were limited to neighborhoods, cities, states, or nations can link globally to over six billion people. The spread of leading practices, once inhibited by geography, will cross borders more rapidly than bird flu.

Common interests can be further subdivided, made more granular. Once again, more specialization will be the order of the day in both work and leisure. Accessibility and democratization of knowledge tools will combine with the ability of people to react, to learn. More information is out there in cyberspace every day, and people are using it.

People will be members of more associations of common interests. Companies and other organizations will, in fact, start to look like more associations as well. Many managers and employees will identify with more than one organization on a part-time basis, as opposed to a single organization on a full-time basis, which will serve as a way to improve the flexibility and utilization of resources. This becomes more feasible as the expectation of transitory working relationships gets more ingrained into the social fabric.

The responsibility of funding and management of benefits like health-care will migrate away from organizations, to either the individual or the government. It makes no sense for the traditional organization to continue to administer such functions. The uncertainty of the employment contract, with its regular and periodic layoffs does not provide a suitable foundation for many traditional benefit programs like health insurance and pension plans.

Certifications will figure more importantly as a credentialing process that will augment or substitute for formal degrees. Assigned office space is an expensive fixed cost that will give way to hoteling and shared use of resources.

The meaning of status will change. For example, title inflation now makes monikers that once sounded impressive almost meaningless. Vice presidents in many organizations are a dime a dozen. Hang out a shingle on the internet and call yourself CEO. Titles just do not convey a track record. A list of successful campaigns or projects will be the new currency of prestige.

New technologies will provide improved logistical support. Not only will more transactions be possible, but many transactions will be shorter. How many brief emails do you receive and respond to every day? People will be able to focus on the things in life that are most important. Figuring high among these will be leisure activities and a focus on longevity. Such priorities of time and interest will be underpinned by technology (all those gadgets), communications (the ability to linkup anytime, anywhere), and process (the know-how to create solutions and make everything work together).

The ability to store, retrieve, track, manipulate, and analyze more pieces of data, as well as the availability of more people to do it means that is just what will happen. The available intellectual capacity and computing power remain faced with too many unanswered questions.

There will be less reason to waste time than ever, and less tolerance for doing so. The bar will be raised for in-person meetings, whether to close a business deal or to provide updates to working groups.

The discipline of outsourcing is, in part, a response to the lethargy of many organizations. Too many marginally managed establishments were allowed to survive because the inefficiencies were not apparent. Outsourcing promotes transparency, flexibility, competition, and efficiency.

The idea of a largely self-contained organization will be replaced by a greater emphasis on the quality of the individual in terms of reputation, relationships, and results. Organizations will center on these very things. Organizational form and the corresponding borders that tend to come as excess baggage will become secondary to a focus on rapidly deploying resources to get the job done.

CHAPTER 3

ORGANIZATIONS OVER TIME

Why Havoc?

Mankind has used the power of organization in the form of a governmental/religious hierarchy as far back as the days of the pyramids in Egypt. Individuals could not rival such a formidable force derived from collective effort. The issue concerned the need for large amounts of manual labor unavailable in another form for the Egyptians. With no electric cranes or bulldozers at hand, the pharaohs pressed the slave population into service.

The world's need for manual labor has continued to decrease relative to the needs of knowledge work as the centuries have passed. The automation of material production techniques drove most of that reduction in demand for labor. Since there are more workers than ever now, all of that productive effort got shifted somewhere else. Where are the new jobs coming from?

The next wave of jobs will come to us in the form of the digitization, transmission, and application of intellectual capital. Organizations today require increased specialization because of more complex individual components. This characteristic of modern economies drives the creation of teams of subject matter experts. These work groups integrate output as subcomponents for intermediate producers or for end users.

Organizations remain important for the same reasons as always: the coordination of effort to produce what individuals alone could not. Synergies or economies must exist. The lack of scale or scope begs the question of why an organization would exist at all. There would be no need for firms or organizations if market coordination could achieve the same level of output. Yet organizations do exist for a variety of good reasons.

Specialization enables increased standards of living. So does scale. One person cannot do everything no matter how gifted. The ability to share expenditures such as general and administrative, selling, advertising (SG&A), and research and development (R&D) costs provide examples of economies found inside the boundaries of the organization.[1] Proof of the economies embedded in organization reveal themselves through financial measures, among the more mature of management disciplines.[2] Consider relative revenue and profit. If a firm's revenue falls by 10 percent, profitability may fall much further, say by 20 percent. Scale economies that drive organizational efficiencies cause this to happen.

Certain fixed cost investments lay the foundation for every organization. This changes everyday of course, as more costs become variable in the new economy. All costs would indeed be variable if an enterprise could do a simultaneous match up of levels of effort and materials for a given product or service offering. In effect, applicable resource costs would be incurred at the moment of the transaction.

The old joke goes that all costs are variable in the long term. This alternative, idealized market would mean that all costs become variable even in the short term. Everything could be purchased on the spot-market. Companies like Dell work to further refine this kind of approach every day with Just-In-Time (JIT) production models enabled by superior Supply Chain Management (SCM) to some extent. Computers do not begin the assembly process until a customer places an order. Suppliers maintain most parts inventories, not Dell. Componentization of products makes this more achievable.

Even so, firms still possess coordination benefits that make their existence necessary even if most fixed costs become variable. Organizations have unique advantages for governance that markets cannot always mimic. Relationships in organizations demonstrate more stability than the market. Organizations can build learning and trust more easily. They can develop a shared language. Market transactions tend to focus on a few key attributes like price or reputation (or brand). Markets may boast efficiency but it is not all happy times. Markets also demonstrate opportunism as many researchers and practitioners have learned.[3] One must be cautious. You have to know what you want.

Markets offered limited options for services and service functions in many ways over the past fifty to hundred years. That changes every day now. The market supplies more and more things that organizations used to produce and provide just for themselves. As a result, managers and executives have to work to adapt to these new realities. Management in turn, must be very careful about what outputs it seeks to create or reproduce within. No one should want to reinvent the wheel in a competitive global market. There is too much chance of coming out on the short end of the stick and wasting lots of organizational resources in the process.

The logic of the organization no longer emphasizes a portfolio of products or services, but rather a portfolio of capabilities and relationships.[4] Large organizations contain lots of stored potential that can be liberated with good management. The result of this change portends important implications for organizational structure. Organizations will become much more selective about what activities they choose to conduct in-house. They will need a disciplined approach that defines the nature of the interfaces with other organizations. A tough evaluation of measurable outputs will be the best gauge to decide which functions should be performed inside the boundaries, as opposed to across them.

Management Authority

The implications of the actions of senior management propagate far and wide as an organization becomes larger. The late, great Peter Drucker, in one of his last columns indicated that one of the most critical attributes of an executive-level manager now consists of sound judgment.[5] A single mistake by a front-line employee will not put substantial amounts of a company's resources at risk. A strategic misstep by a CEO can flush millions of dollars of company resources down the tubes. It can put a firm years behind its competitors. Senior managers in large organizations command vast pools of resources that consist of both people and capital. These resource pools carry inherent inertia. It is always possible to engineer some level of flexibility into a firm's systems though you have to plan for that if you want to pull it off. You will need to plan to spend some extra money too. Infinite capacity or flexibility just might mean infinite cost too.

There will always be inertia in organizations. It can be a good thing when it provides stability. At the same time, inertia also constitutes a set of choices—for good or ill, right or wrong. Once the senior management charts a course, the path that the large organization pursues will reflect those choices. Inertia builds until executives signal change in another direction. The change will take a while. Nothing happens overnight. It is up to top management to ensure a proper course. Strategy has to be prudent.

The larger the organization, the less senior management can administer minute details of an operation.[6] The job of senior management should be to survey the landscape and act thoughtfully. We rely on executives to articulate a strategy. They must set the direction that the organization should take. In a large organization there are lots of other projects that need guidance for strategy development. For efforts already underway, the role of the executives will change. Once the strategy has been set, the presumption should be that it is sound unless the market has changed in some way. With the implementation phase, oversight should consist of exception management while progress gets monitored with good measurement methodologies. Attempts to maintain control at the departmental level will blind senior management to storms on the horizon. They will be below deck micromanaging while their organizational ship breaks apart.

Business historian Alfred Chandler studied the divisional organization at length. He argued that innovation in organizational structure stems from overloaded top executives. The workload reaches a point where organizational effectiveness started to decline. They redesign the organization to better channel information flows once they realize they cannot deal with the huge volume of decisions. Chandler identified this as the primary reason organizational structures shifted away from the now-dreaded, stiff hierarchical models in the early 1900s.[7] The reasons should seem straightforward enough. Inflexible, top-down micromanagement approaches cannot appreciate the detail of day-to-day operations. It explains why successful organizations restructure often. The old organization charts just do not cut it anymore.

Managers now must tailor organizational structure around the needs of important constituencies, which then enables a better upward flow of information patterns. The success of the organization in a competitive environment will depend on senior management to deploy its entire pool of resources in an effective manner. This will be true department-by-department, function-by-function. The organization suffers when management at any level makes faulty decisions on a systematic basis.

A large organization in the new economy does not work like a mechanical device though they are still often managed that way. The emerging modern organization is more like an organic entity that can run on its own as long as it gets fed. You can even leave it unattended for a while. It will not work too well if you do though. An organization requires competent leadership to thrive. This seems like a simple enough proposition. But in hindsight, it is not.

Breaking Up is Hard to Do

The stability achieved by a large organization over the years enables management to take calculated risks. That stability can also allow a mismanaged organization to run well beyond its useful life. Management's ability to tap large pools of resources accumulated through years of successful operation can cover a multitude of sins. Organizations that underperform the market waste societal resources. All of these people or materials could be put to more productive use. The macroeconomic downside of mismanagement for large organizations can be significant.[8] This has implications for the use of societal resources. No wonder that more scrutiny is now placed on management performance from all manner of stakeholders.

Market signals need to get matched to specific aspects of an organization's operations. This lowers the odds that the organization will waste limited resources and act as a drag on the economy. As a result, we will be better off on the whole. Having said that, if you want to improve organizational performance, it means you have to understand it first. The idea of an operational black box remains antithetical to notions of a well-run organization. Comparisons of individual functions cannot be made. We do a pretty good job with manufactured items but services or information still contain many elements of the black box.

"Overhead" or SG&A comprised a small percentage of the overall product cost in the manufacturing era. Outlays on service (or information) did not matter so much years ago. Now service and information *are* the products. They must be managed with as much rigor as that of a modern manufacturing process. The best avenue to gauge service performance across the board relies on the market to keep things honest.

How do managers ensure that governance choices impose market forces across the organization, while still maintaining necessary structure?

Governance, along with its attendant bureaucracy can be a double-edged sword. Governance mechanisms can enable. They can also get in the way. Coordination becomes harder as organizations grow larger. This constituted one of the key challenges for management over the past century.

Let us look at a company that has charted some new ground in the service sector. Microsoft manages growth with simple rules of governance. Product groups maintain thresholds of 400 people. Functions must be compartmentalized in order to make this system work.[9]

Microsoft executives faced some hard choices during its period of rapid growth that started in the late 1980s. Microsoft senior management enlisted partners to administer training functions and established program standards rather than attempt to develop internal training groups. The company refused to get into the customer training business as IBM had done two decades earlier. This modular approach also proved measurable.

Conflicts must always be reconciled as the organization grows. Internal scale economies may be superior to anything the market can offer. Proprietary capital can provide sustainable advantages to an organization. The difficulty of coordination will often be overcome inside the organization than through the market. Outsourcing is not always the right answer.

Some say that the new economics of the Internet, which lowers transaction costs, will reduce the average size of organizations. While this dynamic may be at work, it tends to oversimplify the analysis way too much.

Remember that with outsourcing, the work still gets done by somebody or some organization. It just gets done somewhere else more efficiently. You have shifted the work to specialists, you have not eliminated it.

It is true that lower transaction costs can reduce the size of organizations. Cheaper transactions make outsourcing more feasible. Less expensive contracts means you can get more of them. More contracts imply that more companies will go to the market for services. The demand for services increases because more deals can be made. This in turn implies more companies like outsourcers.

The increase in the number of new companies implies smaller ones as well. This analysis is fine as far as it goes. However, decreased transaction costs also changes the nature of how organizations choose to structure themselves altogether. The boundaries may shrink, but more to the point, they may also re-form in different places. Sometimes the operational advantage will accrue to the organization. Sometimes it does not. It depends on the nature of the transaction and the service provided. Organizations take on different structures in the process. Management will employ creative new practices. This push and pull will reshape the governance of enterprises in the new economy for decades to come.

The ability to pursue all kinds of interorganizational ventures comes straight to us as a result of new communication technologies and the lower costs associated with them.[10] Not so long ago, email was possible only within the organization—if at all. Now it follows us everywhere.

Remote communication was limited to telephone calls or hard-copy documents in the days before email. Maybe faxes. Otherwise you were left with in-person contact.

A lot of coordination depended on physical proximity until the last decade or two. There was not much opportunity for cross-organizational development of products or services unless you worked in the same building as everyone else.

Some things have not changed in that regard. In-person contact may still be important in certain situations. Some big deals will not get closed any other way.

However, for the bulk of activities, this is changing because technology now ensures that different rules apply. The transmission of digitized information in standard formats to almost anywhere, can provide a substitute for face-to-face conversation. For uncomplicated issues, email can be a lot more efficient than a ten-minute in-person or telephone conversation on the subject.

It may turn out that external factors such as rising gas prices will also force some of the issues of dated management styles to come to a head. The high cost of so many mindless commutes to the office makes it all the more probable that employees will force management to rethink established customs.

Some old school managers do not seem to have figured out that the new landscape will require them to change. Many old boys still resist the use of such technologies. It has got be that the new tools take them out of their comfort zone. An insistence on in-person meetings often functions more as a personal preference than a desire to make optimal use of organizational resources. Good managers do not indulge themselves at the expense of other group members or the greater good of the organization. The conversion to streamlined communications processes will be inevitable. Organizational structure will shift along the way in order to remain competitive.

Telephone interaction introduced a century ago now takes a back seat to more efficient ICTs. Fax machines are destined to be declared obsolete wherever scanned documents can be sent by email. That is not to say that the telephone will not still be important. We just have to keep in mind that it serves as one of many communication mechanisms in a growing arsenal. The way that work gets done because of these changes will drive alterations in operational structure.

Call centers highlight perhaps the most obvious example of how organizations have begun to restructure to gain efficiencies. These large units operate with ever-greater scale. Their scope now covers a wide range of functions—from sales to product support. These type of activities used to pull lots of organizational resources because they required significant amounts of labor that were often expensive. Further, the resources were often hidden inside the SG&A line on the income statement. These resources were drawn both formally and informally from departments across organizations.

Now predictive dialers augment call functions. Computer assisted support provides call center staff with everything from customer history to technical troubleshooting tips.

Technology changed the nature of this organizational sales and support function because new tools increased efficiency. Technology also enabled service outsourcing because the functions could be quantified, compartmentalized, and stripped from the corporate body. The economies gained when organizations outsource such functions to specialists will be perilous to ignore. Organizations that do eschew these tools, find themselves at a cost disadvantage relative to competitors. Political constituencies can agonize all they like over the prospect of outsourced functions, but as will be discussed later, the end result remains more or less inevitable. The market benchmark will continue to drive changes about where the organization ends and external governance begins.

The First Wave

Once again, it will be instructive to see how far we have come over the last century. The multinational firms got off the ground in a significant way about fifty years ago. Things kicked off right after the end of World War II. The large corporation that required professional managers dates back another fifty years to around the end of the nineteenth century. It may seem odd that agriculture still employed a majority of the world's population just a hundred years ago. Perhaps more startling: In 1900, the second largest occupational category in all developed countries comprised domestic workers in the form of live-in servants. The number of these live-in servants continued to grow until the outbreak of World War I.

Let us go back a bit earlier. The majority of factory workers in the mid- to late-1800s worked in small craft shops. Each of these facilities contained no more than twenty or thirty employees. Brand identity was nonexistent. Industrial workers migrated to factories that employed hundreds or even thousands by 1900. These industrial workers constituted the largest single group in every developed country by the 1950s.[11]

The Industrial Revolution sparked the transformation from agriculture to manufacturing and set the stage for rise of the divisional organization. In Britain, the Industrial Revolution got underway around 1760. Demand for skilled workers increased as the economy switched from manual to mechanized production. This provided a radical shift to the model of the skilled tradesman that had been in place for centuries. What had consisted of manual work done in a decentralized fashion now segued into mass production. Industrialization brought with it economies of scale and marked a major change in the types of skills the economy needed. Hundreds of inventors complemented thousands of entrepreneurs in just a few years. These became the occupational groups in demand, along with even more nimble-fingered factory floor workers.[12]

Before 1900, few U.S. businesses needed a full-time administrator or an organizational chart. A more formal organizational structure began to take shape later, after the establishment of large transportation links such as canals and railroads. This framework served as a model for other growth industries as well.

After 1850, industrialization resulted in migration to the cities. These population centers fueled growth in the demand for food, clothing, housing, heat, light, and other products that could be produced on a large scale. Whereas farmers could produce and trade in their own locale for many of these items, urban dwellers did not have this option to fall back on. The city folk depended on the broader marketplace. Factory output began to increase to serve these new markets. Firms expanded across regional geographies. Families, as it turns out, ran many of the growing enterprises. By the 1890s, as the companies grew, these family businesses needed full-time professional managers. They employed salaried administrators to focus on the operational considerations of the separated units.

Over time, people became more interested in these businesses now managed by professionals. By the onset of World War I, academics were publishing books and articles on industrial organization. Analysts seemed fascinated with the structure of large-scale enterprises.

Supply chain activities of firms increased in size. Sometimes this occurred through vertical integration. In other cases the enterprises went to the market. Either way, this increased the number of functions required of managers in order to administer a firm. The companies that were able to better manage these various components developed their organizations on a national scale.

At first, companies structured as holding companies served well enough. Later, however, more comprehensive controls became necessary, such as a central headquarters staff. The larger business firms also began to create a corporate brand identity as they established national footprints. The organizations developed ever more formal rules of governance as they got larger. The heads of member firms managed the separate enterprises. At first, they operated as a sort of loose confederation under the auspices of holding companies. Over time, these confederations ceded control to an executive office under a more formal corporate structure. This led to the development of what we now refer to as a professional manager. Unlike the patriarchs who had managed family businesses, professional managers often held little or no direct stake in the firm. (This sets the stage for the timeless issue of the divergent interests between principals and agents, discussed in the next chapter.) The professional manager constituted a new breed of executive whose characteristics remained something of a mystery.

Management in the late 1800s and early 1900s, went through a period of experimentation. Executives struggled with the decision about what to control or what to leave to the other parts of the organization. Consolidated organizational structures with a central headquarters enabled top-level management to dominate most operations. Firms could standardize processes as well as consolidate material procurements. In order to further decrease uncertainty of supply inputs, firms often resorted to vertical integration. The addition of an extended in-house supply chain increased the complexity of the management of internal activities.[13]

As executives of these manufacturing companies tried to come to terms with the management of increasingly disparate operations, they borrowed from other industries, since they had few precedents to guide them. We may recall from history that the railroad constituted among the earliest examples of a large firm. The development of the line and staff organization by railroads established a clear definition of rules for communication. The line and staff functions made complex manufacturing and distribution operations more manageable.

By the 1920's, this centralized structure had become pervasive. The use of basic functional departments like Accounting and Operations served as the model for all large firms. The structure performed well enough up to a point, but things got bogged down as the scope of operations continued to grow. The fact that a small headquarters staff still made many decisions constituted a major weakness. In addition, vice presidents at headquarters tended to be knowledgeable just in their own area. Cross-departmental training at the senior management level was unheard of. MBA programs or formal business training of any kind did not exist. This inflexible form of governance suited certain industries well enough. The line and staff organization proved very workable within static industries for a long time. For example, many manufacturing and food processing companies continued to use this rigid organizational structure until about 1960.

While companies with a finite set of existing products experienced less pressure to find new organizational tools, by comparison, ambitious firms could not be so complacent. In order to pursue a more complex strategy of related diversification, they adopted an alternative framework consisting of semiautonomous divisions. These separate business units organized themselves either by regional geography or along related product lines. Long-term strategy then became the exclusive responsibility of the central staff. Headquarters delegated day-to-day decision-making to the operational divisions since they resided much closer to the customer. A few foresighted firms employed this new divisional form of organization prior to World War II. The most notable included General Motors, DuPont, Jersey Standard, and Sears, Roebuck. The rapid spread of the divisional organization occurred after World War II because it provided firms with the ability to diversify into related areas. GM made use of different divisions to produce tractors and airplane engines as well as several brands of automobiles.[14] The design and use of the division organization was a watershed event that remains unrivaled in the annals of the modern organization. On the way to the next epoch, management has undertaken some experiments with mixed success.

The Short-Lived Conglomerate

From the 1920s until the 1960s, the divisional organizational was in ascendancy. Firms used the structure in manufacturing-dominated economies to combine lower costs with increased product variety. The emergence of service-dominated economies changed all that. It is not a coincidence that the divisional organization model peaked at about the same time as mechanized manager.

The conglomerate form of corporate governance surged into prominence around 1960 with the tactic of unrelated diversification. Harold Geneen at ITT popularized this quaint experiment. In some ways the conglomerate approach mirrored the holding companies of the late nineteenth century. The theory of this type of corporate governance rests on the idea of "good management" as its core competence. The approach suggests that general management expertise in and of itself can oversee any number of disparate businesses. While the divisional firm enabled growth through "related" diversification, the conglomerate sought to grow through "unrelated" diversification.

In less than a twenty-year time span, ITT acquired hundreds of diverse companies. These various entities spanned a wide spectrum of industries. Yet the approach always contained one main common element: a centralized staff management system. Geneen, in common with other chief executives in the 1960s and 1970s, believed that they could achieve organizational success with this type of corporate structure. The approach combined capital infusion with strong general management expertise at the divisional level. The executives who ran these conglomerates believed that any type of company in any industry could flourish with these ingredients.[15] Or so the theory went.

Diversified conglomerates still looked viable until not too long ago. This is not the case anymore. A modern classification of "good management" would refuse to accommodate superficial general managers who are a mile wide and an inch deep.

The unrelated diversified conglomerate provided little more than a distraction from the disciplined advance of management science. In place of the conglomerate have marched enterprises that insist on a rigorous definition of core competence. Put another way: organizations must specialize.

The conglomerate started its downfall a mere twenty years after it came into vogue. Raiders challenged corporate managements of bloated firms through the use of the leveraged buy-out in the 1980s. While all types of firms were subject to takeover, conglomerates made particularly attractive targets. The reach of the raiders extended to any company whose share price remained undervalued by the market.

The large diversified conglomerate reappeared briefly in the 1990s with Tyco, which maintained a portfolio of four unrelated enterprises. It showed some promise for a while until company management came to realize that investment analysts disagreed. Tyco announced plans to split up the four units in January 2002.[16] While it was abandoned three months later amid a lukewarm reception by investors at the time, it was revived again in November 2005.[17] The market continued to price Tyco's stock below the aggregate value of the individual businesses. The parts were worth more than the whole—the exact opposite of good organization. Effective organization must gain more through collective effort than can be otherwise achieved with smaller units or individual effort. Otherwise management should use the market. Period.

The unrelated conglomerate approach still maintains adherents though one might wonder why. GE provides perhaps the sole example of sustained long-term performance of the companies that used the conglomerate structure. Every other instance of unrelated diversification has resulted in mixed or average results over the past thirty years.[18]

Perhaps conglomerates made sense before the widespread adoption of portfolio theory.[19] One school of thought suggested that the conglomerate structure benefited investors. Because companies could smooth out earnings, they could ride out recessions or industry downturns in a more stable fashion. An investor who owned the stock would see less volatility. This just might make sense if a person could only afford to buy the stock of a single company.

Of course, that is not the case anymore. Investors can now diversify their portfolios with ease through investment vehicles like mutual funds. Corporations do not need to structure themselves to accomplish the same purpose. In fact, the opposite argument could be made. More unrelated diversification by a firm makes it harder for investors to understand all of the various components. Senior management will not have an easy time sifting through all of that complexity either.

The implications of such a broad collection of businesses could in fact require a full-time team of analysts to wade through. Who could articulate the strategy in any cogent fashion? How can management make reliable forecasts about where future income will be derived from the disparate operations? On what basis does management determine if organizational structure is optimized?

The conglomerate as an organizational form flies in the face of any concept of transparency. The opaqueness hamstrings investors because they can't structure a portfolio that reconciles levels of risk with expected return based on their individual needs. They don't even know what levels of risk they have taken on in some cases.

Indeed, perhaps the greatest advantage of the undiversified conglomerate may accrue to company management. Executives can use the earnings fluctuations of the diverse businesses to offset one another. The conglomerate approach lets management smooth out reported earning streams in order to avoid share price fluctuations. It appears more likely that management takes advantage of the conglomerate structure to create our familiar black box that no one can see inside of. While the company looks rock solid from the outside at least for a time, further analysis often uncovers a real mess on the inside. Once in a while, even General Electric receives unflattering reviews for its reported earnings when subjected to scrutiny.[20]

The conglomerate organizational structure maintains some significant hurdles when viewed from an objective standpoint. The ability of management to find economies in the course of the management of a bunch of diverse companies must be considered a questionable approach to strategy.

In the early 1990s, the concept of core competence started to drive discussion about governance models for organizations. It portends implications for the entire gamut of organizational functions. Core competence rests on the theory that organizational capability should be based on a consistent set of characteristics.[21] These capabilities might appear very confined at first. But they are not. Realization of core competence often results in the ability to produce distinct end products. 3M Company considers one of its core competencies to be the design, production, and marketing of thin materials laden with information. This translates into such disparate end products as optical CDs and Post-It notepads.

How a company defines core competence remains embedded in its strategy. It should be difficult for competitors to replicate. As such, core competence defies conventional definitions. At a minimum, the concept serves as a guide for management to evaluate on a regular basis, the functions taken on by the organization. The theory also implies noncore functions should be outsourced.[22]

Of course, the issue of what to outsource or what to produce in-house may always be a topic for debate within organizations. It is just that now, the pressure is ratcheting up. That is a healthy discussion to have because the old rules have changed. No part of the organization will be immune for much longer. Core competence provides the means to ask questions about how to better focus. The market benchmark provides the criteria to evaluate the choices.

CHAPTER 4

THE BLACK BOX EXPOSED

Elusive Transaction Costs

Transaction cost theory leads to all sorts of interesting questions about how management directs an organization. It determines what functions either get outsourced or managed in-house. Transaction cost theory particularly shines in the context of the transition from a manufacturing-dominated economy to an information-dominated one. Most or all costs associated with information can be classified as transaction costs. In fact, much of the essence of transaction costs could be defined as services or information. They must be considered a central theme in an information economy (see figure 4.1).

You will always incur expenses over and above the stated cost of what you purchase if you conduct business on the market. That is the price of doing business. The market furnishes no guarantee that it will be the most economical choice. This explains why management often prefers to bring functions or operations in-house. Sometimes market transaction costs do indeed get pricey. Internal governance can serve as well or better than the market under the right circumstances.[1] Let us go back to first principles to better understand why.

Ronald Coase won a Nobel Prize in Economics for his work on transactions costs. In his famous 1937 paper on the subject, he asks why firms exist at all.[2] Coase comes to the conclusion that transaction costs associated with market alternatives can be expensive indeed. According to Coase, organizations exist to economize on transaction costs. Of course transaction costs can look a lot like management costs as we will see. A general categorization follows:

- Search
- Information

- Bargaining
- Decision
- Policing
- Enforcement

The costs of going outside the organization to acquire inputs constitute the same costs associated with the management of many internal processes. This applies even more for the new economy. Coase points out that costs associated with the coordination process differ across coordination mechanisms (markets or organization). The impact of the choice between hierarchy (operations conducted within the organization) or the market matters a lot.

The common make-or-buy decisions that organizations wrestle with, demonstrate just one aspect of this calculus. The differences between the market and internal organization must always be compared.[3] No absolute benchmark will ever exist because the alternatives change all the time. The challenge for management will be to select among imperfect alternatives. Management has to choose the best mechanism to coordinate a particular set of transactions at that particular point in time. They will be limited to whatever the market can offer or what they can develop themselves.[4] These decisions remain crucial. The ability to economize on transaction costs operates as the primary driver for the choice of one form of organization or governance structure over another.[5] Superior governance mechanisms can define competitive advantage for a decade or longer as we saw with E.F. Hutton. What provides the more economical or effective solution in-house for an organization today may be better or cheaper to outsource tomorrow as technologies and processes are constantly changing.

Having said that, there will be patterns we can discern. The ability to outsource becomes more viable as a given market evolves. It starts like this: Organizations begin to produce some product or service in-house because of a lack of available suppliers. No one in the marketplaces can offer them

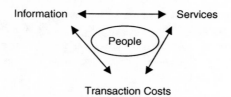

Figure 4.1 Inseparability of People, Information, Services, and Transaction Costs

what they need. Once the competence is honed, these internally produced products and services translate into external business opportunities because other organizations see the value.

Companies create solutions on the inside to solve problems in response to a void in the marketplace. The solution is unique at first but becomes commoditized over time as knowledge of that process becomes more diffused. A competitor may emulate it. Sometimes employees leave the organization and take knowledge capital with them when they do.

Airline yield management systems offer one example of this pattern. American Airlines first developed their revenue optimization systems for internal use. They proved quite successful against aggressive competitors. Later American built a separate business called Sabre that sold the yield management systems to other airlines. The unit became so profitable that American was able to spin off Sabre to the benefit of the airline's shareholders.

The in-house capability will transfer to other organizations one way or another. As the number of customers grows, so does the number of suppliers. The market often becomes a superior alternative, if given enough time. Indeed, the market works particularly well for more mature services as transaction costs come down. It is not hard to see why. Competition pounds on service providers in the marketplace day in, day out. More providers come to the marketplace as entrepreneurs seize new opportunities.

This trend continues to accelerate. We can now expect to see new market entrants come from almost any country on the planet. The industrialized economies no longer maintain a lock on high-end services or products. The aggressive forays by China, India, and others signify the shape of things to come.

Managers beware. The abundance of new suppliers of all kinds puts a lot more emphasis on the cost of transactions across organizational boundaries. Lower transaction costs increase productivity. Economical transactions also increase opportunities for companies. Higher transaction costs impede interorganizational linkages. Put another way, it means that pricey transactions make it more expensive to do business. This translates into a comparatively stagnant commercial environment. This scenario is not good if you want to increase standards of living. We will live a more prosperous future if we continue to lower transaction costs.

The Internet, along with its complimentary ICTs, continues to push transaction costs in one direction—downward. How do we know this? We do not know for sure, in the sense that we can document specific savings. We do know that communication costs have come down, which power such tools as the Internet and such applications as universal email.

Otherwise, we have to infer lower transaction costs in a variety of ways. This task remains problematic though people try it all the time.

Economists would love to track transaction costs. It is hard to do so for a variety of reasons.

Let us look at some of them. One problem is that transaction costs are bundled up with a lot of other stuff. They can be tough to measure—tough to even identify. A lot of service industry value stays linked to transaction costs. Who can say when one ends and the other begins?

A simple example may help. Organizations used to identify prospective suppliers through paper-based systems like the yellow pages. Now this process can be performed much faster over the Internet. We identify suppliers anywhere on the planet with ease. How much do we save because of that? It is indeed hard to say.

Few studies document the aggregate time savings by organizations or societies in any systematic fashion. Economists employ indirect measures or proxies to track overall productivity.[6] One proxy we can look at, is the use of self-service check-in for airlines. Forrester Research found that it cost the airlines US $3.68 to check-in passengers with human agents while the self-service stations cost only US $0.16 per passenger.[7] Replacing cashiers with self checkout stations tell a similar story as do bank tellers with ATM machines. These tell us about productivity. They do not shed light on direct transaction costs though they will certainly follow similar trajectories.

Let us start with what we can infer. It appears that transaction costs started to come down fast sometime after the introduction of ICTs in the 1980s. In 1994, global network computing with the Netscape IPO got things started. The upshot meant much easier procurement of both goods and services from external sources. No one wants to make everything themselves anyway (though where the line is drawn regarding what to make and what to buy does not yet receive the attention from management that it deserves).

Transaction costs vary by type of organization. Smaller firms in emerging industries will tend to be more specialized. They will use proprietary standards so we can figure that higher transaction costs will apply in these cases. Transaction costs also vary across different types of industries. Such costs will be lower in mature or regulated industries. Sometimes this results from the domination of monopolies or cartels.[8] More mature organizations change slower than markets populated by many small firms. Search costs are lower. Industry standards have been put in place. Transaction costs decrease because of this more predictable environment. Markets start to look a lot like organizations.

Service industry efficiency has caused transaction costs to come down a great deal. Services used to be wrapped up inside organizations so that it was hard find them in discrete bundles that could be measured. They have become much more visible in the last few decades to the benefit of entrepreneurs who always keep a lookout for good ideas. Market entrants can seize on these opportunities to form new businesses. Service outsourcing is a new growth industry. Everyday, entrepreneurs try to peel off functions that large organizations perform for themselves. These enterprising capitalists make a market in the form of outsourcing, where no market existed before.

This means that the delineation between market on the one hand, and organizational function on the other, will become very hard to map as information or service infuses every aspect of commercial interaction. The market now fulfills the same role as internal managers in many cases. Both act to synthesize information in order to ensure its accuracy. Both can increase overall productivity. Both can stimulate commerce.[9]

Why are the rules for transaction costs different in the new economy? Simple. Because many professions associated with service industries *are* transaction costs. This would cover almost every occupational category except those associated with the actual process of direct production or transportation.

Transaction-cost-oriented functions include those performed by lawyers, financial institutions, entrepreneurs, managers, clerks, police, intermediaries, federal, state, and local government.[10] The list gets longer all the time as manufacturing becomes more efficient and sheds workers every day worldwide. New jobs will have to come from somewhere else.

Where? From the service sector.

Service occupations will increase as the role of information grows in the new economy. Let us look at a real life example. The job of many salespeople is to disseminate information. Transaction costs constitute the bulk of services performed by both the public as well as private sectors. This starts to explain their importance. Strategic management too often fails to recognize the impact of transaction costs on organization. The subject incorporates economics, management, and organizational theory in a useful way that will forever alter the rules of governance.

Transaction cost drives discussion about the following items in a more systematic manner:

- Vertical integration
- Outsourcing
- Diversification
- Joint Ventures
- Divestitures

Even so, transaction costs still do not inform debate to a sufficient degree. When contemplating mergers, for example, management now instead looks for redundancy. Organizations try to capture market share without always considering long-term shareholder value. Managers shore up the balance sheet with financial maneuvers while executives work to increase tomorrow's share price. These kind of initiatives intended to increase shareholder value, need to encompass more.

When discussions about the scope of the enterprise or its structure get underway, management should focus on how to create effective inter-company linkages, not engage in vague discussions about synergies. The word "synergies" means lots of things to a lot of different people. The value added (or taken away) through these linkages will become the focus of better measurement and they are easier to get your arms around than synergies. To do this, analysis will require a good understanding of the implications of transaction costs. Sound decision-making will depend on smoother interorganizational interfaces so that information can be traded more easily. Successful organizational design will reflect the realities of the new economy by capturing measurements oriented toward transaction costs.

Why do transaction costs not rate much attention yet? Traditional accounting functions combined with a preoccupation of financial treatments deserve much of the blame for this. What gets measured gets recognized.

Of course, transaction costs generate questions about the structure of organization where the boundaries should be drawn even if they do not receive systematic measurement yet. These represent important issues for management. What sort of things cause transaction costs to change? Several factors affect governance structures:

- Rate of growth of demand
- Elasticity of demand
- Technology
- Production techniques
- Complexity of a product, expected life
- Social cohesion
- Cost to borrow
- Degree of development of the stock market[11]

The cost of a transaction on the inside, relative to the cost of one in the marketplace goes up or down as changes occur in one or more of the above areas. New technology introduced to the market often requires outside expertise to implement, so outsourcing will be more expensive at that stage. When ERP first hit the market, expertise to implement the software was scarce and expensive. New technology developed on the inside can be managed better in-house because that is where the proprietary expertise resides. Outsourcing from a supplier will make sense only if cost is a secondary consideration. Typically this occurs because a new technology is only available from someone else and cannot realistically be developed in-house on a competitive cost basis.

Outsourcing can make sense at any number of stages during an organization life cycle. A company's fast growth may require outsourcing in order to achieve a rapid scale-up. Larger organizations can use outsourcing to shed bloated functions. Perhaps a shift in core competence has altered organizational priorities. Insourcing, or brining outsourced functions back in-house remains an option as well. This dynamic ebb and flow causes firms to gain or lose competitive advantage, based on their structure.[12]

Let us look at other factors. The need for social cohesion augurs for the use of hierarchy or organization because the pieces and the players may have a history or work well together. Likewise, internal financing will look attractive if it costs a lot to borrow on the open market. Management has to consider several factors when it designs an organizational structure. In the same way that products or services that can now be mixed or matched, so can the individual functions or components of the organization. No two successful organizations will be designed the same way. Like an organism in an environmental ecosystem with its many niches, if two organizations find themselves in competition for the identical niche, only one will likely survive the contest.

This explains why a formula for what functions to perform in-house remains elusive. If you want to break all the rules, you first have to know what they are. No seven-step guide will give you the answer on a single white sheet of paper. While that would be nice, it is not on the menu of choices.

Bill Gates once referred to or coined the term friction-free capitalism.[13] No such thing can or will exist. Transactions in a market economy have costs associated with them. It does not matter how efficient they get. While they will continue to decrease on an individual basis, transaction costs will never reach zero. That is because much of the value added in a service economy is wrapped up part and parcel with transaction costs. The best we can hope for is to reduce relative transaction costs.

It will be those lower transaction costs that lead to more choices in the marketplace. Lower transaction costs provide a competitive alternative to internal organization. The standing option of outsourcing provides a way to keep service functions cloistered inside organizations honest. This fundamental principle will drive organizational productivity in the new economy.

The Perils of Agency

Agency costs mirror transaction costs in a lot of ways. What are agency costs? We know that transaction costs occur across organizations. Agency costs, by contrast, get expensed inside—if only you could see your accountant for details. Unfortunately he or she may be part of the problem.

The concept of agency costs derives from principal-agent theory. Principals ran the companies in the days when sole proprietorships dominated business. These were the guys in charge who had skin in the game. However, many proprietors just could not manage their companies once business growth reached a certain point. As we have discussed previously, this made the use of professional management more common—essential in fact. Professional management now remains the norm today for organizations of all types: firms, nonprofits, and government agencies. Professional management maintains a strong—although not uniform—track record as an adaptive governance mechanism.[14] These hired hands brought higher degrees of competence in administration with them. Alfred Sloan at General Motors best typified this new style of management. Sloan went head-to-head with Henry Ford in the early days of the automobile industry. GM returned consistent growth and profits under Sloan's leadership as compared to Ford's. Sloan demonstrated that an innovative organizational design combined with savvy management could provide the key to success in the manufacturing economy. GM's divisional structure proved far superior to Ford's top-down hierarchical organization.[15]

Widespread employment of professional managers was not without a potential downside. Principal-agent theory or just plain agency theory alerts us to the possibility that managers (agents) in an enterprise may not share the same goals as the owners (principals). While professional managers often do provide competent administration, they may also lavish themselves with generous perks. Why would they do that? Because their reward systems are in conflict.

The sole proprietor or company owner will be motivated to build the overall value of the firm. This motivation will generally be shared by the great mass of shareholders (or principals) of a corporation. However, the interests of management may be inclined to diverge. Of course, there have been attempts to match the interests of agents with principal better, by using incentives ranging from bonuses to retirement plans.

Stock options were widely issued in the 1980s and 1990s in order to try and create greater alignment between principals and agents, owners and managers. This served as an attempt to reconcile some of the differences in reward systems. The results have been mixed. For one, the use of stock options tends to mask or understate the true costs. In addition, stock options often provide managers with an incentive to focus on near-term share prices. Executives can boost share price at the expense of the long-term benefit to the firm. So as it turns out, there are no silver bullets here either.

Principal–agent theory can be a useful guide to align individual motivations with those of the organization. Let us see why.

The nature of the divergent motivations between proprietors and managers traces its roots back about a hundred years. Proprietors owned the business. Their compensation often came in the form of some share of the residual profits at the end of the fiscal year. Managers received a salary. They got paid regardless of whether the business made or lost money. The proprietor's interests retained close alignment with that of the business. So the proprietor tended to keep tight control over expenses in order to maximize the firm's profits. On the other hand, generous executive salaries or perquisites supplied more significant motivations for many of the agents. The overall performance of the organization often became a secondary consideration. These hired guns could very well be satisfied if business operations only returned adequate or even lackluster profits.

Further, executives constitute just the most egregious examples of agents in action. The big boys happen to be more visible because they figure prominently in annual reports and their salaries are reported on securities exchange filings. However, the effects are far more widespread. Agency costs permeate all organizations. They exist at every level throughout.

Governance in the service economy must find a way to manage these costs. The trick will be to avoid the imposition of excessive burdens that would obviate any benefit, which is easier said than done. Attempts to control agency costs too often result in the use of a very ineffective tool: monitoring.

In its simplest form, monitoring consists of the stereotypical manager who looks over the shoulder of workers. The manager may walk the shop floor or stroll around the office to ensure that no one shirks. Going up one level, the manager also must be monitored. He or she has a boss who performs a monitoring function as well. Monitors report to other monitors, and so on and so forth ad infinitum. So we travel up the organizational hierarchy until we reach the CEO's office. The CEO may also be chairman of the board. The board makeup often consists of cronies appointed or nominated by the CEO. Other company executives besides the CEO, may be board members also. The Securities and Exchange Commission in the Unites States hopes that Sarbanes-Oxley will remove some of this favoritism at the board level. We will have to wait and see.

Monitoring, in the crude manner of the traditional manager serves as a blunt tool. It adds to costs and can cause at least as many problems as it solves. And it does not contribute to direct output. Not only that, it can be implemented in a very clumsy manner.

Monitoring takes a variety of forms beyond measurement or observation. It manifests itself through structural functions such as budget restrictions. Compensation policies play a role as do operating rules. Monitoring can be made so complete that nothing gets done without oversight by one or many layers of hierarchy.

This in fact describes the problem of excessive bureaucracy. Some bureaucracy provides for much needed order in the form of prudent rules. Too much leads to excessive burden on the organization. So the trade-offs associated with agency costs must be balanced against the costs of monitoring.

If, as it appears, that agents (workers, managers, and executives) do not always act in the best interest of the organization, it begs the question: Why could that be?

The answer relies on the assumption that individual motivation derives, in large measure from self-interest (as we hearken back to Adam Smith once again). The classic techniques of economics can prove beneficial, if we accept a general notion of self-interest. Structured use of the principles of competition serves as a good place to start. Incentives can help us direct behavior. Also, consequences provide very effective tools. Taken together and used intelligently, these tools can redirect inefficient behavior of managers and other employees that would otherwise drive up agency costs.

Most markets have the potential to be competitive. The labor market for managerial talent is no exception. The challenge for governance will be to find the measures that serve as the best proxies for long-term organizational success. Good governance will ensure that the proxy measure correlates to executive management rewards or penalties.[16]

Dashboards can help with monitoring. Yet these tools remain in relative infancy. Dashboards cannot yet provide a comprehensive measurement apparatus for organizational performance. Too much of internal organizational does not get measured against the rigors of the market on a regular basis. For your consideration, the most debilitative manifestation of agency costs lies directly ahead.

The Internal Monopoly

Many functions that an organization performs can be purchased in the market. The decision about whether to go outside for services does not often receive a rational hearing. More often than not, the organization refuses to employ the market benchmark in a systematic manner.

Organizations cling to functions out of tradition. There may be political pressures. Management might maintain too broad a view of core competence.

The truth is that any function performed inside an organization qualifies as a potential de facto monopoly. The activities in this internal monopoly might be better visualized as a mini-economy.

Let us consider what this means in more detail. Every organization maintains a set of little businesses referred to as departments. Sometimes we call them functions. In other instances they are known as activities. These little businesses operate in a self-contained environment that can be shielded from market forces. Someone with the proverbial budget ax may come along once in a while to chop off an arbitrary 10 percent or 20 percent from the expense line, but otherwise the department escapes any real scrutiny. Application of market comparisons remains rare. The relative cost or quality of many internal services may not be known to anyone. Most department heads learn to game their budgets in anticipation, when the time comes to tighten their belts. They bulk up on resources. They pad budget allocations when times are flush.

Of course not all departments have the ability to do this. Functions or departments situated close to customers will tend to be more exposed to market forces. This also holds true for activities close to the direct production of tangible goods, services, or other customer outputs. These types of activities run pretty well because they often link to core competence. That is not so surprising.

Yet many of the service economy functions do not fit into this category. As one explores deeper into a large organization, the picture starts to get very hard to discern. One finds a raft of personnel that operate far removed from market forces. These departments remain intertwined with other activities, hidden inside forests of procedures or mountains of policies.

The pattern should look familiar to those who have worked in large organizations. Managers submit departmental budgets that get aggregated repeatedly as they travel upward toward senior management levels. After enough levels of hierarchy, an army of accountants cannot sift through the morass. Significant inefficiencies get masked in the process. These tucked away departments continue to get away with what an economist might call rent-seeking behavior. People get paid without adding any real value to the organization.

The managers who run the internal monopolies game the system like professionals. This tendency does not discriminate among different types of organizations—it applies to both government and private enterprise.

The reason this rent-seeking behavior still occurs is because of inadvertent accounting weaknesses peculiar to modern service organizations. Accounting systems designed for manufacturing environments now serve to protect these functional backwaters from scrutiny.

Let us look at the stark contrast between how services are treated and the cost allocations for traditional manufacturing. In the 1950s, direct manufacturing inputs constituted the bulk of most firms' costs. Materials could be linked to the final output. Overhead comprised a small portion of total costs. So allocation was easy.

A lot of things have changed in the past fifty years. Overheads did not matter so much in the pre-service era. Now they are crucial.

Overhead consists of an ever-larger bucket of functions, even in manufacturing firms. Some of these functions are as follows:

- Accounting
- Finance
- Information technology
- Human resources
- Legal services
- Building maintenance
- Landscape work
- Housekeeping/janitorial
- Transportation
- Marketing

Such categories are now a big part of the new economy. They should serve as a value-added part of an overall process. Yet the old artificial borders between departmental silos that derive from limitations in management theory designed for the manufacturing era remain in place. Too often we think of these functions as cost centers.

The above functions and others take up an ever-larger share of overall costs. The question arises as to who manages these areas if the organization does not outsource them? The internal monopoly, that is who.

Okay, so now we are starting to get an idea about where to find the culprits for large chunks of organizational inefficiency. What then? Executive management might like to slice suspected laggards off the organizational body with the precision of a surgeon—either to outsource or hold up to the market for comparison. If only it were that easy. You run into systematic problems when you attempt to streamline the internal monopoly with a blunt instrument. If you shoot from the hip to fix it, you will probably hit your foot.

Why?

Standard functions still tend to be treated or classified in a nonstandard way for accounting purposes. Information technology expenditure may be mixed up with SG&A expenses. Differentiated functions that add real value find themselves combined with commodity processes. Big batches of disparate functions get reported up line in broad categories of expense items. This makes meaningful comparisons with external alternatives tough.

Calcified organizational culture also may be the culprit. "That is the way we have always done cost allocations" perhaps sounds a familiar refrain. A simple case of inept management could be the cause. Senior management might not recognize the magnitude of the problem. Where does the root of the problem lie? Let us just say that departmental cost allocations in such instances would have to be described as arbitrary at best. In the worst case, they look absolutely irrational.

Another problem also deals with measurements. Sometimes they may be applied in an improper manner. Maybe they do not get applied at all. While there are remedies, tools like activity based costing (ABC) continue to receive too little attention. ABC is important because it allocates levels of effort (and thus costs) to specific products or services. It provides an accurate identification of actual costs that makes sources of profit and loss become clear. The view can be seen at whatever level management decides.

ABC has yet to receive widespread adoption despite its ideal application to the service economy. The result is that reporting tools like the P&L statements portray a view of things at very high levels of aggregation. Resource consumption at the level of individual product, service, or process simply cannot be gauged at all in most organizations. Yet, inefficiency in any support area relative to the marketplace now represents a liability. In effect, the organization has allowed costs to get out of line.

This failure to understand an operation at a more granular level explains why senior management imposes indiscriminant enterprise-wide cost reductions in times of trouble. It is a tribute to their lack of knowledge about the cost structure of their own organization.

To highlight why this is true, let us look at a common scenario. When an organization outsources some activity, executives and managers often gain unexpected insight in the process. They learn the true cost of the service their organization had consumed all along.

Like many in-house functions, the services received, seemed free prior to outsourcing. Management just did not understand that clean demarcations for services may be artificial. The untracked costs across departments avoided detection until an external provider began to send monthly invoices for them. That gets their attention.

Consider the IT support function. The formal IT staff may not be the only ones in an organization tasked with providing technical assistance. Individual departments often fund their own people to provide some level of IT support. When all of the resources employed in the activities are relieved of that responsibility, the outsourcer picks up the slack. To add insult to injury, the in-house department will be inclined to find makeshift work for the superfluous resources in order to protect their budget dollars. Overall costs can actually go up when senior management fail to grasp its true cost structure.

Resistance to outsourcing comes not only from populist pundits such as CNN's Lou Dobbs, but very often from management at various levels within organizations. Sometimes management chooses not to outsource because it believes a function can be performed in-house at lower cost. That is indeed possible. By the same token, managers will not know for sure if poor internal measurement mechanisms may mask the true costs because the analysis will be flawed.

Good measurement will lead to better understanding of where an organization adds value and where it does not. Not that improved measurement should be taken as an invitation to micromanage. Instead it gives management choices because in-house functions can be realistically compared against the market. Competition can be simulated, which is where the market benchmark will take us.

Let us look at how the market has evolved in its treatment of the traditional external monopoly. Economics textbooks characterize monopoly as the ability of a firm to set its own price for some good or service. Antitrust law dates back over a century. Antitrust agencies target these large firms that dominate entire industries. Yet, the tools used to combat industry-wide monopoly have varied over the years.

In some cases, the courts have used forced divestiture to break up AT&T. The local telephone companies (Baby Bells) still operated as regulated monopolies after that. In other instances, Public Utility Commissions have imposed rate-of-return pricing or price caps on the Baby Bells, which are not really very effective tools. Why? Rate-of-return pricing means the company is guaranteed a profit based on its investment. This makes it virtually impossible for the operator to lose money. At the same time it encourages excessive capital spending.

More recently, price caps have been employed to better effect because they motivate companies to aggressively manage their costs. That is because the operators can pocket whatever profits they make within the price-capped fees they charge. Unfortunately, price caps could also be termed price fixing, albeit with an endorsement from government. That is because telecommunication equipment suppliers compete in an innovative, aggressive market. Phone service providers can charge end users a government guaranteed capped price, while the cost of equipment inputs goes down at the same time. Such generous compensation schemes come at the expense of the public. Forced divestiture, rate-of-return pricing and price caps often do not do much to lower prices or improve service.

So, what does work?

Regulators are now inclined to see the market as a way to impose discipline on industry monopolies. Deregulation of the telecommunications industry, for example, lowered prices a lot faster than price caps. The same was true about deregulation with the airline industry. One wonders how health care might be affected in a more competitive environment.

For all of government's efforts to micromanage the telecommunications market, it was competition from many directions that prodded complacent incumbent telephone companies to get more efficient in a hurry. Even after passage of the U.S. Telecommunications Deregulation Act of 1996, some critics had argued that the Regional Bell Operating Companies maintained a tacit agreement to limit competition. In exchange for the telcos staying out of the entertainment delivery market, cable companies would not get into the local telephone service market. But markets and competition are funny things. One way or the other, they usually get the animal spirits moving.

Once the telecommunications market in the Unites States was deregulated, cable, satellite, DSL, and wireless technologies spurred the old telcos into action like no regulator could. It is funny how we are so often amazed at what can result from a little competition. We should use this lesson to inform the management of the plethora of internal monopolies inside organizations. Exposing in-house departments to the rigor of outsourcing is one way to replicate competition.

Of course, there will be politics and personalities to content with. Managers of the internal monopoly wring their hands when they come face-to-face with budget reductions. They wail and gnash their teeth if only for show. Sometimes they even speak in tongues. For sheer entertainment value, few other things compare. Just the same, any savvy department head also understands how to pad a budget. The managers who run the internal monopoly know the players, the rules, the customs, protocols, and the processes better than anyone else.

This explains why the long-heralded zero-based budgets produce limited gains. Zero-based budgeting treats every annual budget as a blank page—in theory. It is supposed to require each department or program to rejustify its existence.[17] The reality differs quite a bit from this scenario. Personalities come into play. Histories factor in. Simple inertia cannot be separated from the process. So no one starts back at zero.

The market benchmark can cut through the gamesmanship of departmental budgets, but it is not magic. Even the market benchmark can be misused if not applied in an objective manner.

Let us consider a common example. Sometimes an information technology (IT) department head will be directed to request bids from outsourcing firms. Senior managers undertake this activity for a variety of reasons. Perhaps they need to assuage the board of directors. Maybe the executives wish to gauge comparative efficiency of an in-house IT function. The idea at least represents a good start and that is fine as far as it goes. However, when all is said and done, once the initial evaluation process is complete, the report up line must still be viewed with a jaundiced eye.

This is because traditional management mindsets will often render us with a predictable outcome. The results of such an analysis come back too many times like this: The department head will indicate that an outsourcer would be no more effective than current in-house operations. (Surprise!) This revelation often coincides with what the in-house IT group predicted beforehand. Here again, motives matter.

These in-house comparisons are worthless without an objective third party or executive-level sponsor to oversee the analysis. Why? Because most department heads will not be pleased to lose control of their operation. This means that senior management will invite trouble.

Sometimes even executive management may not be up to the challenge. Too often such internal reports will get accepted at face value.[18]

How do costs get so far out of line for internal monopolies? Sometimes organizations lavish resources on support functions. Unneeded headcount gets added. Perhaps available cash flow prompts purchases of top-of-the-line laptops or networks. It could be that management sees limited alternative investment options. These types of inefficiencies highlight other manifestations of agency costs. Management abrogates its duty when it spends capital rather than pays it out to shareholders as dividends.[19] Such behavior conflicts with the best interest of the owners or principals.

Objective analysis ensures the placement of meaningful measures of performance. This includes the path up through the organization or across organizational boundaries from the external service provider. Information has to be unbiased. Management must drill down as far as it takes to construct an accurate picture if any doubt exists. Comparisons will only be meaningful if done on the basis of apples-to-apples. Indirect as well as direct costs must be considered in order to understand the value (or lack thereof) of the internal monopoly.

The internal monopolies that defy measurement should be flagged as the areas most in need of reform. It will not be easy. These departments or product groups keep the rest of the organization from knowing too much about them almost as part of their design. The managers in these departments often conduct ill-defined processes. Hands-on oversight props up blatant disorganization and mismanagement. The great irony, of course, is that these managers are perceived as hard workers. No doubt they also demonstrate a keen acumen for organizational politics. Internal monopolies become entrenched for nontrivial reasons. Any attempt to address their shortcomings requires a deft touch. To test this theory, just ask a few too many questions to the managers of such departments if you are in doubt about this. The response will either be hostile or reek of condescension.

Executive management should be wary of the internal monopoly in general. External comparisons must be sought out often from many sources and examined from different angles. The value added or detracted from any organizational function has to be clearly understood.

Many organizations steam ahead in the other direction despite these issues. New functions, departments, projects—even entire companies—get added with regularity. The tendency of management is to continue to build internal empires. Government organizations share in this guilt as much as or more than private enterprises. Look at the ever-larger role of public service employees in many countries. Few people would argue that most government agencies are operating at peak efficiency and would not benefit from market-based reforms. Yet, like the internal monopoly, governmental monopolies persist. In the private sector, vertical integration demonstrates how old school managers transform an external organization into another internal monopoly. Such a strategy must be viewed with caution no matter how popular it is with investment bankers. The purchase or development of related businesses up and down the supply chain may provide certain advantages in the early stages of industry development. The extra pieces of the business to be managed can lead to severe drawbacks later on as well.[20]

Let us take just a few notable examples of management that tried to use magic to build bigger organizations. Sony acquired Columbia Pictures for US $3.4 billion in 1989 and took a US $2.7 billion hit on the deal. Matsushita acquired 80 percent of MCA for US $6.5 billion in 1990. They sold that stake in 1995 for US $5.7 billion. AT&T acquired NCR for US $7.5 billion in 1991 only to divest it five years later in 1996 for

US $3.46 billion. Novell acquired Quattropro and WordPerfect for US$1 billion in 1994. The two companies got sold for a whopping US $181.5 million less two years later. Quaker acquired Snapple in 1994 for US $1.4 billion. They sold it at a huge loss in 1997 for US $300 million. Even GE purchased an 80 percent stake of Kidder, Peabody in 1986 for US $600 million with Jack Welch at the helm. In 1994 they sold it for US $670 million.[21] All this sounds okay until you find out that they also absorbed US $917 million in losses from 1986–1994. This is an expensive theme that recurs all too often. The jury is still out on the acquisition of Compaq by Hewlett-Packard, but changes in organizational structure have already led to the resignation of CEO Carly Fiorini, who championed the deal. The pending merger between the two telecom giants Lucent and Alcatel has all the earmarks of a problematic union in the making as well.

A lot can go wrong when an organization acquires a supplier, distributor, or competitor. The insulation from market pressures often results in a loss of incentive to productive efficiency. The purchase or development of a downstream distribution channel expends a lot of organizational resources. It may do little more than add overhead to an organization's cost structure.

Sluggish Management

Some predictable things begin to happen as organizations grow. The activities become more numerous, more complex. Bounded rationality—the ability of one person to assimilate a finite amount of information—comes into play. A single person can no longer manage operations. This sort of problem for large organizations dates back at least a hundred years.

In order to management ever larger spheres of influence, delegation becomes an imperative. However, this can mean that market signals from the outside get diffused as they wind their way across departmental or divisional boundaries in a tortuous fashion. The organization may fail to react as the market changes.

Bounded rationality, combined with diffused market signals, can be serious impediments to organizational performance. The market signals that serve to discipline smaller organizations through competition become hazy as the organization grows. Decreased efficiency can often be the result.

There are a variety of factors that can cause this to happen. Excessive bureaucracy creeps in. Internal politics combines with a lack of common objectives to take management off track. Use of firm resources for personal reasons can drain an organization as well.

Economist Harvey Leibenstein (1922–1994) referred to these types of agency costs as X-efficiency factors.[22] The name X-efficiency itself suggests difficulty in the identification of these factors. They would be more at home with self-help books than economics texts. Synonyms might include motivation, work ethic, or get-up-and-go. X-efficiency factors remain a challenge for sociologists to measure, much less bottle up to power organizational progress.

X-efficiency factors contrast with the more traditional economic focus on allocative efficiency. Economists use the term allocative efficiency to describe how management tries to best marshal the factors of production. These include better processes or more efficient coordination—both of which are a key focus of this book. X-efficiency factors are interesting because they are clearly an important element in the definition of organizational success, yet defy measurement.

Bill Gates has referred to the X-factor as the need to maintain a sense of urgency. If that sense of urgency gets lost, managers and employees may be inclined to rest on their laurels. The attempt to create an atmosphere of urgency or crisis presents a real challenge to management as an organization grows. Success breeds complacency. The triumphs tend to be taken for granted after a while.

Compare such an attitude with that of start-up organizations. These small shops can and do run on pure adrenalin. The fear or excitement may very well be one of the fledgling organization's initial competitive advantages.

On the other hand, to maintain motivation over a period of years or decades in a large organization, requires more than infectious enthusiasm. It requires the institutionalization of something akin to the X-factor.

Before we look for a remedy, we should try to understand what gets in the way of the X-factor.

Organizational inefficiency occurs for a variety of reasons. One stems from the ability of employees to mask the true costs of some function. Managers may oversell their role as coordinators. Workers fail to share knowledge about how an organization works in any meaningful fashion. All of these constitute examples of agency costs.

This information asymmetry benefits those employees who understand the details. They know more than either supervisors or owners. These front line or back-office employees increase their in-depth knowledge of particular task expertise. Not all of this know-how gets passed along to the benefit of the enterprise.

Workers instead choose to use their knowledge to accomplish personal objectives. Employee goals, not in synch with those of the organization, result in a loss of potential organizational efficiency. Getting employees aligned with organizational objectives will always be a challenge for managers. All the same, it does not relieve managers of their responsibility to make that happen. As much as possible, the collective knowledge of managers and employees should be captured to harness for the benefit of the overall organization.

As the world gets more specialized, the increased complexity of functions makes it easier for employees to increase agency costs as well. Of course, this is not true for every function.

Look at a well-understood activity like basic facility maintenance. Such work can be scoped and defined with ease. Landscape services do not require high-end labor skills. Low barriers exist for market entry. Keen market competition keeps the cost of this function priced very much as a commodity.

However, other occupational categories that contain aspects of technology or information systems will prove a little trickier. The average layperson does not understand the intricacies of higher end IT functions like programming or system design. Many managers struggle with these types of things too. As such, a disconnect often occurs between technicians and organizational management.

The trend toward increased complexity will only continue to increase. This means that the management of the people involved in technical activities will not get easier over time. The new environment demands workers with more in-depth knowledge. Further, there will be a wider range of applications over which to manage. As a result, any attempt to oversee or monitor on the basis of first-hand knowledge just takes you down a black hole.

Leibenstein's results demonstrate how managers can assuage the effects of information asymmetry between managers and employees without having to become expert in all areas. Key principles based on Leibenstein's research center around motivation and productivity:

1. Smaller work units will be more productive than larger ones.
2. Work units made up of friends are more productive than those made up of nonfriends.
3. General supervision produces greater efficiency than close supervision.
4. Units given more information about the importance of their work demonstrate greater proficiency than those given less information.[23]

Leibenstein shows us that universal rules do exist to improve organizational performance. It also reinforces the futility of trying to micromanage employees. Micromanagement remains an old-school practice that is both expensive as well as unproductive. Relevant competition, combined with market-based comparisons provides the most objective means to gauge organizational performance. A market-based approach also serves as a better framework for motivation.

What this means for management is that you have to focus on outputs instead of processes to get an organization to operate effectively. The emphasis on outputs will also depend on solid measurements revisited on a regular basis.[24] Incentives must accompany these measurements. Linking meaningful results to rewards and consequences will be critical. It is why more people start businesses in market-based economies than socialist states. It is why people establish organizations in order to accomplish some social goal. The prospect of benefiting from one's own work effort is the basis for the great gains in material prosperity in the industrialized world over the past two hundred years.

What Makes People Tick

Trying to predict how people will react in a given situation seems to befuddle many managers. Some very basic rules still have not sunk in. Perhaps managers do not want to face the issue realistically because the organizational bureaucracy suggests otherwise. Their retreat may consist of being obtuse in the name of the corporate good. Has a department manager ever tried to explain a company policy he or she did not buy into? Or did not really understand the rationale?

Managers would do well to take into account some basic rules about human behavior in order to find success in the new economy. Styles that could pass muster in the manufacturing era will not withstand the stress of a knowledge economy.

It might be useful to think of things in terms of the oldest whine by the stereotypical Hollywood actor to the director: "What is my motivation?" The complaint has validity. Information about a character's history enables an actor to see through the lines of dialog in the script. Major life events that shape the character helps the actor empathize. The actor can then act in a similar fashion as the characters they portray.

When you get right down to it, an organizational setting is not too different from a Hollywood production. A read on the other character's motivation can be quite useful. Good salespeople understand this. They know that everybody harbors a few hot buttons. You can spur all kinds of action if you know which ones to press.

Even though such information is useful and fun, it is best to remember that a prudent manager will be circumspect in its application. Like all benevolent monarchs or superheroes, good managers know that the power to press someone's hot buttons should be used only for good.

To gain an understanding of what drives a given individual does not mean you must become a Method actor, a psychoanalyst, or even a sales representative. You do not even have to know a person's deepest secrets to predict their reaction in a given situation in an organizational setting or economic system.

What do you think will happen, for example, if you drop bags of money out of a helicopter onto a busy city street? It is a safe bet that most people will stop to pick some of it up. Would you not?

The fact is that the majority of employees do not bring too much of their personal baggage with them to an office that exists inside a system such an organization. It is not a free-for-all—it is a system based on rules.

Contrast the behavioral norms within an organizational setting against what people might do at the end of a Tequila party. Who can say the kinds of bizarre actions that might result? But that is off-hours.

The rules change when we get to work. The nature of the large organization tends to discourage such indulgences. The atmosphere of a purposeful corporate environment makes it a bit easier to understand what drives individuals as a result. Attempts to engineer process transformation become more feasible because of these constraints.

Let us look at one great constant. Most people do not like change because it is often painful. The assumption that people will be averse to change should always be our de facto assumption. Most of the time, we will be right.

Sure, there will be exceptions. No one minds moving into a bigger office with a better view. Likewise, there may be some small organization out there populated with nothing but change-addicted rocket scientists who thrive on unpredictability from one moment to the next.

Most of the time, the reality is different.

More often, organizational change gets implemented because of the need to dislodge the inherent inertia. Enterprises continue to look for ways to become more efficient in response to outside pressures or because of proactive management. This holds true even more as we enter a new era of global competition.

So the more probable scenario for change unfolds a bit differently than people might prefer. What if you were asked to move into a smaller office or one without a window because costs need to be better managed. Suddenly the prospect of change does not look so appealing anymore.

Almost any kind of change can set people off. Simply rearranging the office furniture in order to improve workflow efficiency will cause someone to find something to complain about.

Again, not everyone reacts in the same way to the same situation. That is a little too naïve. People are different and it can take time to get to know them a bit. Sometimes you do need to ask a question or two to get a pulse check. Even so, there are useful generalizations that can be made in most cases.

Members of the internal monopoly that face no external competition will act in a pretty consistent manner. They will not appreciate an in-depth analysis of their operation. Department heads own their turf and will defend it. Organizational bureaucrats almost always seek to expand their empires. Few employees will volunteer to take one for the team and accept a layoff.[25] It does not matter how efficient the organization becomes in the process.

Acting in the service of the greater good will not be the best predictor of what people will do in a given situation. That is human nature. Successful programs for change, take into account such innate, consistent motivations. Good managers plan for them.

When an organization outsources some function, senior management should expect employees to be concerned. In the absence of formal communication, the rumor mill will fill the vacuum with unproductive speculation. So management should be proactive in planning for the transition and communicating options and impacts to affected employees. Those who will not be affected should be informed as well. Otherwise all sorts of unproductive activity will result and detract from the business at hand.

Organizations will have to be more effective despite any individual's reluctance to change. Competition will remain the operative comparison because that is the new reality. You cannot wish it away. It will be management's job to direct workforce motivation toward improved performance in a constructive manner if it is to face off global competitors.

It is not hard to see that changes are occurring all around us. New organizations start up in the first place to fill an unmet need of society. Competition operates as a response to the ineffectiveness of established organizations. Everyone must innovate to survive in a business setting. Organizations will have to move toward greater efficiency.

Otherwise, the unattractive alternative will be to atrophy a little at a time. The most ineffective organizations will wither away altogether in the end.

Competition in the form of the market benchmark serves as a way for experimentation to find its way into practice. A new offering can receive a real world evaluation. Companies in a competitive industry are granted no guarantee of a fair rate of return. In fact, a company in a competitive environment gets no guarantees of profitability of any kind. An organization in a competitive environment will soon find itself out of business if costs get too far out of line with market prices. Those that make use of the market at all levels on a proactive basis will be in a better position to thrive.

Hard Choices

Nothing focuses the mind like live ammunition. What holds true in a military setting applies to business as well. The final group of bidders in a tender focuses much better after a buyer pares a large number of competitors down to a few. Employees reluctant to learn new skills while still employed, find new motivation after they get downsized out of a job. Two mice in a maze see that someone has moved their cheese and—well you get the idea.

We all hate to give good people bad news, but sometimes that is what we need to hear. Lessons from competitive markets suggest that adversity stimulates innovative thinking. The importance of why motivation drives degree of effort cannot be underestimated. Competitive pressures from outside organizations lead to better performance because of the rigor of the market. The absence of such pressures encourages employees to become apathetic. It allows service to suffer or costs to rise unchecked.

Yet, managers within organizations still do not apply enough diligence to behind-the-scenes functions such as SG&A, R&D, legal, and basic infrastructure investments. SG&A is a huge category in and of itself. Many times an organization will incur costs that no one knows how to categorize. Where does it go? It gets expensed as SG&A. These cumulative support or overhead areas tend to be viewed as a cost of doing business. That is true in a way. Nonetheless, management should remember that they also constitute inputs that will be expected to produce a defined output.

Current management practice in medium-sized and larger organization often consists of mere budget adjustments up or down. Often, these decisions too depend on available cash flow or profits. Hidden losses from a lack of innovation or the nonresponsiveness of internal monopolies can escape measurement. These agency costs pull significant resources away from productive use.[26]

The transition of industrialized countries to service economies brings about some unexpected effects. The intensive human capital component of the new environment changes the old capital-intensive rules. Recent recessions in the last decade or so now exhibit different characteristics. Let us look at why.

The usual pattern of recession demonstrates a fall off of economic activity. Demand decreases. The capital on hand cannot be put to productive use in a manufacturing dominated economy. Plants operate at less than optimum or full capacity. They may even be idle. The equipment sits on a balance sheet depreciating every day, hitting the income statement.

Overall productivity in the mechanized economy tends to fall off fast because the capital cost structure is fixed. All that money has been invested even as the market has gone flat.

New rules apply in a service economy. Many productivity gains hide in the human capital component when times are flush. In other words, not all the gains that result from new tools knowledge techniques transfer from the individual to the organization. At least not at first.

In good times, agency costs increase as companies churn out profits. There is less pressure to manage expenses. You have seen the effects. Organizations throw lavish parties. Managers charge more lunches or dinners on expense accounts. Departments stock up on supplies. Organizations pick up additional staffing, not all of whom get tapped to their full potential. Utilization lags. Employees may even perform personal business on company time.

Service organizations in particular use a lot of labor. The service industry itself now comprises the largest labor component in modern economies. This in turn exacerbates the impact of agency costs. What happens when a recession hits?

Employees suddenly begin to get very creative as forced cutbacks occur, resulting in job reductions. The service workers quickly learn to do things with greater efficiency. They find new uses for the vast array of flexible tools at their disposal. They shoulder more responsibility to avoid a layoff. They extract more productivity from the PCs, the laptops, the networks, the software applications, and the other tools in their midst.

Once again, nothing focuses the mind like live ammunition. Recession, with its attendant layoffs can have a significant impact on worker behavior. The surge in productivity continues into the recovery. It lifts the economy upward for months or years. Perhaps even a decade.

Still, slack creeps into the system over time one way or the other. New technologies are introduced. Additional headcount is added. As usual, managers and employees fail to make full use of them. The stage is set for the next recession-driven productivity gains in the service economy.

Recent economic statistics now support this very scenario. The typical pattern of sharp productivity decrease for an extended period did not occur in the 2001–2002 U.S. recession. In fact, according to widely cited New York Federal Reserve report, productivity increased immediately after that recession began.[27] This change in the nature of the economy suggests why the aftermath of the 2001–2002 recession got labeled a jobless recovery. Improved competition-led productivity enabled firms to hold off hiring even after economic activity picked up again.

The new economy is challenging some old assumptions that come to us from revered economists. One aspect of the elimination of slack in organizations is now possible because economic upheaval makes managers and employees more flexible. In Keynes most famous work, *The General Theory of Employment, Interest and Money*, he discusses the concept known as wage rigidity. Keynes noted that wage rigidity was the psychological resistance that workers have about pay cuts.[28] Union contracts and minimum wage laws represent institutional manifestations of wage rigidity.

It is true that no one likes to take a salary cut. In order to assuage the effects of wage rigidity, governments inject moderate doses of inflation into the economy that make some adjustments unnecessary. This kind of gradual approach tended to work pretty well until the 1980s. Steady, incremental inflation reduced real earnings but left nominal wages intact for a long time. In other words, the amount on people's weekly or monthly paychecks never went down though the cost of living went up. Prices go up a little; wages do not change. This reflects an invisible pay cut.

Researchers Richard Vedder and Lowell Galloway studied the effects of Keynes' wage rigidity. Their analysis provided a number of valuable insights. The two researchers determined that with enough wage flexibility in an economy (as opposed to rigidity), unemployment levels fall much faster. Wage flexibility also shortens the durations of unemployment.[29] Of course there is a catch. It means that laid off workers must agree to accept lower wages than their last job, which remains an unpopular option for workers.

Resistance of workers to take pay cuts is starting to change as a result of increased global competition. For example, workers of all types in the United States appear more willing to adjust expectations in the new world we live in, there being no other choice.

People have begun to see things in a new light: that in order to remain competitive with their counterparts in other countries that possess similar skills, they must reevaluate their situation. Overpaid managers, relative to world market standards will work for less money as opposed to no work at all.

France and Germany, which maintain higher mandated wage levels by global standards, still really have not embraced this new reality. Their generous social programs imposed at the corporate level do not help either. These governments eschew a more efficient approach that would make use of tax credits for lower-income individuals as William Lewis, Founding Director of the McKinsey Institute suggests. Their governments instead, choose to burden industry directly with onerous taxes and regulations. These added costs distort market signals and has resulted in two decades of double-digit unemployment for France and Germany. The levels remain twice that of the United States.[30]

Such a problematic scenario does not suggest an optimal use of human capital. It also does not position organizations in those countries well, for more vigorous global competition. Better to allow the market to produce outputs in an efficient manner and then implement social policy on the back end of the governmental transaction.

More worker-output and corrected wage levels, when taken together, combine to produce a real impact on the productivity of economies in recession. Further, because of ongoing global competitiveness, layoffs occur now in the United States during periods of economic growth as well as recession. Companies reduce their labor force when faced with pressure from competitors. The overall shape of the economy serves to discipline organizations as well as the competitive response of other companies. Such stark new realities break down the traditional resistance to wage flexibility.

Clearly these developments can be disconcerting. Yet they can also be uplifting in an odd sort of way if they prompt us to get better. Market signals provide us with more direct feedback on performance. The new reality is that a service economy can react faster to changes in the economic climate than a manufacturing economy. The ability to be nimble offers us the promise of getting to the next generation of productivity that much sooner.

Complacent Principals

We have discussed agents at some length. What about principals? Principals consist of shareholders, group members, or electorates. They all exert influence on organizations. You might be surprised to learn that these principals remain a pretty complacent lot. How can that be, one might ask.

The agents comprise our cast of characters from previous sections. You know them as professional managers, employees, and politicians among others. Agents run the day-to-day operations and in many cases they get left to their own devices. If management still tends to micromanage, then principals remain too detached even in the Sarbanes-Oxley, post-WorldCom, post-Enron, post-Tyco environment. Agents continue to protect their interests at the expense of the greater organizational or societal good (i.e., the interests of the principals).

Even so, it is not hard to see why principals are detached. Shared ownership means shared responsibility. A collection of thousands of shareholders (principals) exemplifies public companies. Principals keep their day jobs. They devote limited time to the oversight of agents. Even board members of organizations often appear to fall prey to diffused responsibility. Principals do not always act right away when their interests get compromised. Agency costs can climb above transaction costs for quite a while, before principals will do anything. However, eventually this sets in motion, the potential for other corrective forces that will kick in one way or the other.

Principals do look for opportunities for reward in a competitive economic system, which can serve as a disciplinary tool. Shareholders may not always vote their proxy, but they will find reasons to invest in successful companies. Customers will take action as well. They will buy a different brand if they find one overpriced, if they determine that a company's service is lethargic, or if its products do not meet their needs.

Sometimes these corrective mechanisms prove insufficient. When that happens, the market will impose more pointed measures.

Pressure will build slowly at first. The cause for substandard performance could be any number of factors mentioned earlier. For a while, management may be able to withstand market forces because the accumulated pool of resources built up over previous successful years acts as a buffer. Market-based environments will limit how long this can go on. Below-market performance cannot be sustained, even if the principals do not put pressure on the agents. The organization, perhaps along with its very structure, will then be forced to change through one or more of the following means:

1. *Capital Markets*: Investors and investor groups (mutual funds, venture capitalists) insist on competitive rates of return. These groups put pressure on firms to outperform less risky investment vehicles such as government or corporate bonds.

2. *Management Labor Markets*: Managers who demonstrate sustained performance results, can reap significant rewards. Management efforts can be channeled toward organizational goals that drive more market-oriented behavior. It encourages them to act more as principals than as agents.

3. *New Entrants*: These can take the form of direct competitors who enter a market enticed by the above-market returns of incumbent firms. Sometimes other organizations offer substitutes, often abetted by lower cost models and newer technology. These factors keep pressure on the incumbent firms or other organizations to maintain competitive cost structures.

4. *Outsourcing Proposals*: They can arrive solicited or unsolicited. Senior management may be forced to use outsourcing proposals as a tool to implement faster organizational change. Prudent implementation of outsourcing solutions improves performance. Outsourcing can generate cash. It can also reduce costs. Sometimes the above factors drive the use of outsourcing as means to remain competitive.[31]

The market exerts pressure in these cases because principals inside the organization have failed.

The debate no longer revolves around whether outsourcing and other market-based mechanisms will become inevitable. The writing is on the wall. Organizations cannot ignore the many choices available to them. External pressures will just increase. Whatever it takes to induce operational effectiveness will be considered.

CHAPTER 5

EXTERNAL GOVERNANCE

From Manufacturing to Services

Service industries now make up almost 70 percent of economic activity in the United States, which includes over 85 million jobs. It took a while, but the U.S. Census Department has finally begun to track many services that were not part of the old Standard Industry Classification (SIC) codes developed in the 1930s. The Census Department last updated SICs in 1987. In its place, is a new system called the North American Industry Classification System (NAICS). NAICS officially replaced SICs in 1997 and was updated again in 2002. Completely new categories of services in NAICS, not explicitly recognized in the SIC system, include:

- Information Services
- Professional, Scientific, and Technical Services
- Administrative and Support, Waste Management, and Remediation Services
- Education Services
- Health Care and Social Assistance
- Arts, Entertainment and Recreation
- Other Services (except Public Administration)
- (See Appendix A for more a complete list of the new service industry classifications tracked by the U.S. Census Department.)

The new NAICS classifications also broke out hotels and restaurants from retail trade. All of the new categories encompass far more than the service industry mainstays that had been tracked by the Census Bureau in the manufacturing dominated economy. The older sectors that will ring familiar if you know the outdated SICs include retail trade, wholesale trade, finance/insurance, real estate, and public administration. The more traditional service classifications consistent with SICs were more of a sideshow to manufacturing. They have been a familiar part of the economy for at least a century.

However, targets for services outsourcing that include growing job categories in the future will now tend to be found in the updated NAICS sectors. The new classifications far better reflect the realities of the new economy than the old SIC system did.

IT and the bulk of services outsourcing (which includes the fast-growing BPO or business process outsourcing category) trace its origins at least as far back as the 1960s. ADP processed payroll for many organizations even in the 1950s. The first instance of IT outsourcing involved the tabulation of the data collected during the 1890 U.S. census. Herman Hollerith used his card punch/reader system on behalf of the government to accomplish this task.[1] Some suggest that Matthew Boulton first introduced outsourcing into the manufacturing realm. Boulton sourced standardized parts from vendors that he used in the production of the Watt steam engine way back in the 1770s.[2]

Clearly, outsourcing in manufacturing finds itself much farther along in comparison to services because of its hundred year head start. Longer, if you side with most people who say that the current wave of information technology-related outsourcing only began with Ross Perot in the early 1960s.

As one of the company's top salesmen, Perot tried to convince IBM to create an internal computer services division. He proposed to IBM that it should manage the data processing facilities for other companies. IBM declined. So Perot left IBM to form Electronic Data Systems (EDS) in 1962. Perot attempted to convince executives of other companies that he could manage their large data processing facilities at less cost. Things got off to a slow start until Perot signed his first customer after 78 sales calls. EDS built up a solid base of clients after that.[3] Years later, IBM entered the services market to compete head-on with EDS. The rest, as they say, is history.[4]

The outsourcing of services can take many forms beyond IT. According to estimates from the Outsourcing Institute (www.outsourcing.com), IT constituted just 40 percent of all service outsourcing activity, as the twentieth century came to an end. Distribution, logistics, real estate, and facilities management made up 30 percent of the total. Other service functions such as administration, customer service, human resources, marketing, finance, and transportation functions rounded out the remaining 30 percent. IT constituted simply the early emphasis for services outsourcing.

In part, it was managerial ineffectiveness that drove organizations to outsource services and information technology in the 1960s. Noncore areas like data processing posed significant challenges because at the time, management still remained unfamiliar with the IT function. Outsourcing solved many of the complex mainframe as well as work process issues.

The ability to free up cash flow provided another motivation to outsource. Organizations could monetize previous capital investments through the sale of IT assets. These IT assets provided an attractive one-time boost to earnings in many cases. The data processing centers tended to operate at less than optimum effectiveness anyway.

It must be emphasized that most organizations considered the entire concept of outsourcing as an experiment at first. Management often viewed the practice as a tactic of desperation by distressed organizations. Then in 1989, a watershed event occurred when Kodak outsourced large portions of its IT function to IBM. The Kodak deal effectively legitimized outsourcing because it marked the first time that a well-regarded company had signed such a comprehensive multi-year contract. The "Kodak Effect" changed operational strategy, along with the rules of organizational governance for good. Now executive management considers outsourcing an acceptable way to run service operations.[5]

Of course, the picture is not uniformly positive. Many studies report mixed results from the use of outsourcing by organizations for a variety of reasons. Not least among them, are the contractual difficulties. More complex functions make deal structure more problematic. Management often fails to install adequate provisions that protect the organization. Successes tend to get publicized. Failures get hushed up. Paul Strassmann, author and former CIO of several large organizations, notes that anecdotes about outsourcing problems remain hard to uncover. Everyone wants to avoid unfavorable publicity.[6] Even so, service and IT outsourcing over the past 30 years has become so pervasive that somebody must benefit from the practice. Outsourcing can indeed be a beneficial supplement to operations as will be discussed later in this chapter. Certain steps have to be taken of course. Management must ensure the proper establishment of terms and conditions as well as service levels in order for the tactic to work.

Successful purchasers of outsourcing services rely on a crisp definition of the service they receive. This definition takes the form of service level agreements (SLAs). Yet, too many functional managers still ask, "What is an SLA?" It is the bread and butter of the outsourcing world and as discussed earlier, it will be the basis on which in-house operations are increasingly managed.

No one should enter into an outsourcing deal without a solid set of SLAs, preferably woven into the contract structure. Problems arise when management does not do a good job, specifying the services it wishes to purchase. Incredibly, sometimes no SLAs get written at all. In other cases, SLAs that do get written down, may be vague or one dimensional.

Manufacturing precision in the mechanized age took time to develop. Techniques for services outsourcing will be no different.

It is interesting to observe how outsourcing often comes under fire because jobs may get relocated overseas. Yet the outsourcing formula has always contained an element of job loss or transference. Recent overseas outsourcing that garners a lot of press attention seems somewhat incongruous if you look back at the history of domestic outsourcing starting in the 1950s and 1960s.

Most outsourcing arrangements involved the transfer of employees from one organization. The difference back then was that, affected employees were usually within the same country. While little or no net in-country job loss occurred as a result, other factors caused upheaval. Employees still grumbled about the impact on job security or compensation.[7]

Here is what happens when a function gets outsourced to another company: The bulk of employees in an outsourcing deal will have to transfer employment to the outsourcer as part of the contract in most cases. The transferred workers are subject to pay cuts if their salaries are above market or outside the guidelines of the outsourcer. Needless to say, things do not always work out for everyone with the new arrangement. Many times transitioned employees do not find a fit with the outsourcer's culture, so their only other choice is to move on.

Outsourcing shines the harsh light of the market onto departmental functions performed in an uneconomical fashion. Management and staff feel the effects right away. While the protective features of the internal monopoly furnish shelter prior to the outsourcing agreement, afterward, it is the market benchmark that holds sway.

Forrester Research provided estimates and projections for this trend for service occupations in the United States. While in the United States in 2003, only about 300,000 jobs had been outsourced overseas, in 2005, that number had risen to over 800,000 jobs. Projections indicate that by 2010, as many as 1.7 million jobs in the United States could be outsourced overseas. By 2015, this number is projected to rise to over 3.3 million. It is worth noting that the United States still employed 135 million workers overall in 2006, but clearly the numbers of outsourced jobs are growing significantly nonetheless.[8] The ability to outsource almost anything means that this scenario will be repeated over and over for years to come. We have only begun to scratch the surface.

Services Outsourcing Basics

The nature of the contract continues to be the fundamental difference between functions performed within an organization and outside. Employment contracts tend to be implicit. Organizations hire workers at will and management can terminate these same employees at its discretion. From an organizational governance standpoint, outsourcing is not like that. It involves an explicit agreement that contains consequences for performance. There are terms for dissolution that cannot be skirted. This means that the importance of good contract techniques cannot be overemphasized because you can expect to see a lot more contractual relationships as organizations become more permeable.

Contracts can help organizations as well as governments achieve their objectives. Good contracts allow an organization to benefit from the services provided by an outside company. This stands to reason, because of an outsourcer's ability to deliver expertise that other organizations just cannot replicate. External procurement of services can enable a quick ramp-up of some key capability.

Problems arise when there is a lack of a formal and documented alignment prior to the execution of a contract. This divergent set of expectations between parties almost never surfaces in advance. An agreement that overlooks important specific details may get signed anyway, to the detriment of all involved—the customer in particular. The terms, conditions, and written assumptions need to serve as the elemental components of a successful relationship. This will be a crucial point for any organization. Yet, many managers still allow an outsourcer to drive the terms of the relationship.

Why is that a bad idea? There are lots of reasons for this.

The outsourcer accumulates extensive experience in negotiation with customers. Outsourcers write contracts all the time. Chief Information Officers (CIOs) or other purchasers of outsourcing services may oversee only a handful of outsourcing contracts in an entire career, at best.

As prime examples of agents, outsourcers will be far more familiar with the nature of the task to be performed. And that is just the beginning.

Outsourcers can extract above market prices from organizations if a limited number of competitors supply a given market. Something called asset specificity suggests one example of how this can become as issue. Let us discuss what asset specificity is. Few competitors make a substantial investment into a limited market unless it gives them leverage over the buyer. They will want to be able to protect their investment. Opportunism, on the part of the outsourcer, becomes a potential threat in these circumstances.[9]

Another type of contract related problem occurs during the innovation stage for new products or services. External relationships may not be appropriate at this phase of development. The nurture of new ideas often requires the cohesion found only inside the organization setting, more than it requires market efficiency.

So let us be clear about a few things. Outsourcing does not always represent the optimal solution. Certain aspects of an outsourcing relationship cannot be specified in advance in all cases. If the contract cannot be written in such a way to protect the buyer, you have no choice but to keep or bring an activity in-house.

What if management decides that it does make sense to go to the market and engage an outsourcer? What sorts of mistakes get made?

Management too often fails to understand that any right not identified in contractual relationship will benefit the outsourcer. You need to dissect the contract vehicle a bit to see why this is true. A contract consists of two types of rights: specific and residual. Contract theory suggests that one party or another should purchase the residual rights.[10] This might work if one of the contractual entities wants to pay for those rights. Maybe one day. In the meantime, you can figure that any rights not specified remain residual. In other words, all nonexplicit rights will become the property of the outsourcer.

This dynamic has significant implications for organizations that employ an external governance option (like outsourcing). Organizations in general will not be able to purchase the residual rights because that is just not the way contracts get written. The only alternative is to make sure you document all of the critical items. Then they become specific rights.

What else do organizations need to do to protect themselves in external contractual arrangements? Let us look at what happens if it turns out that for some reason you want to get out of an outsourcing deal.

Termination clauses in outsourcing contracts provide important, often underutilized, leverage points. These types of clauses can furnish a lot of flexibility that formal service arrangements often lack. The utility of termination clauses can extend well beyond deals between companies. Governments and municipalities can also benefit from good termination clauses in the case of so-called natural monopolies. Cable-franchise agreements provide a good example.[11] Municipalities often seemed powerless to rein in renegade cable suppliers who provided poor service or charged exorbitant rates.[12] Yet, such situations could have been avoided with specific termination-for-cause provisions in municipal contracts.

A good outsourcing contract will always contain language that gives the buyer the opportunity to get out of the contract under certain circumstances. Outsourcing leading practice allows customers to terminate agreements either for convenience or cause.

Failure of the outsourcer to perform as promised can invoke termination for cause. A series of corrective actions gets invoked when an outsourcer fails to deliver on the terms of a contract. The customer stipulates penalties in advance. These result in a series of consequences that leads to breach, if warranted. The next step would be actual termination.

Customers can also install termination for convenience provisions in their contracts. These clauses can be invoked at the buyer's discretion. It will be typical for the customer to pay a fee to the outsourcer in order to exercise the convenience option.

Customers will find themselves over a barrel if they do not include termination provisions in their agreements. Contracts too often rely on the outsourcer's contract language. Outsourcers will want to be compensated for the remainder of the unearned revenue on any given contract. Customers of all types become locked into unsatisfactory contractual arrangements in such a manner. A municipality that wants to dissolve a cable franchise contract, cannot do so, because of such onerous contract terms. Termination may cost the municipality as much as the decision to stay with the current cable franchiser. Too much taken on faith, prior to signing a contract can be fatal afterward.

The terms ought to be more equitable for the buyer in either termination for cause or termination for convenience. The appropriate contract terms should compensate the outsourcer for the unamortized portion of their investment in the case of termination for cause due to poor service. Nothing more. In the case of termination for convenience, the municipality might also pay a prearranged fee. Under no circumstances would the outsourcer receive additional compensation for lost revenue.

Cable assets deployed, could be valued based on a fixed depreciation schedule. Negotiation of terms would occur prior to the execution of the agreement. Termination of any kind would release the cable company (outsourcer) from further obligation. This leaves the outsourcer whole, but not in a position to collect windfall profits. Rebid of the cable properties then becomes an option. The municipality would sell the assets to a more responsive cable service provider under the same terms as before.

Contractual clauses for termination make contract dissolutions more amicable because they get spelled out in advance. The contractual process becomes more palatable. Where customers fail to do this, you can bet that outsourcers will adhere to the contractual terms favorable to them. Outsourcers often stipulate contract minimums that customers must pay under any circumstances. An organization would find itself vulnerable if unexpected events occur. The unplanned sale of a sister division could cause a steep drop in demand for outsourcing services and yet have no impact on the monthly invoices from the outsourcer. Ouch!

In what other ways can agreements with outsourcers go south?

Organizations often tend to manage outsourcers in too loose a fashion. Service outsourcing remains a new governance mechanism, so this should not come as too big a surprise. Some organizations on the other hand, also manage outsourcers with too tight a grip.

A large insurer once developed 6000 metrics to manage its internal IT functions. It planned to use all of the metrics as the basis for any outsourcing arrangement as well. This type of micromanagement hampers the use of an external governance vehicle. Outsourcers just do not perform well under such circumstances. The existence of so many priorities will prove unmanageable.

Outsourcers will be effective if they can focus on the key items that will be measured. Organizational management should worry about outputs or results. Process only matters at the interface points. The customer must rely on consequences when outsourcers miss targets of performance. The outsourcer has got to be allowed to manage the process itself. Who cares *how* they get it done? The work could be done by a monkey in the back room with an abacus. It just does not matter to the customer. If management insists on getting anal about the fine details of process, then the function might as well be managed in-house.

The point bears emphasis even though somewhat counterintuitive. Control must be transferred from the organization to the outsourcer. It will be the only way to maximize the effectiveness of this governance tool. Control gives the outsourcer, the latitude to find the best process to complete a set of tasks.[13] Ownership of a process also gives the supplier an incentive to continue to invest in their assets.[14]

The case of the insurer proves once again instructive. An attempt to use 6000 metrics suggests that management spends more time on the development of them than follow-up to ensure the targets get met. When so many things are priorities, nothing gets real priority.

External governance should also shift fixed costs to the outsourcer. Scale economies place the outsourcer in the best position to benefit. This also enables the buyer to operate on a variable cost basis so that it reduces short-term risk. A variable cost operational model can also make it easier for small organizations to compete with larger ones. Capital outlays can be reduced. Organizations can scale up or down faster.

Well-managed relationships with outsourcers have to be firm yet fair. They must be documented in a clear manner. Responsibility for proactive management of the relationship belongs to the senior managers of the organization—always.[15] A mismanaged relationship can be the cause of inefficiency just as with the internal monopoly, so managers must be thoughtful if they want to navigate the issues.

Executives make two kinds of mistakes on a consistent basis. The first one is to treat external governance too much like internal governance.

Implicit arrangements, so common with internal governance, just do not work well with outsourcing contracts. A lot of deals do not come off as planned because so much room gets left for interpretation. The customer always assumes that the outsourcer will do everything that was discussed during contract negotiations. The outsourcer, on the other hand, wants to adhere to the terms documented in the contract, which is invariably a shorter list of obligations. That can leave a huge gap in expectations between the two parties.

The other kind of mistake that managers still make is the failure to give the outsourcer an open evaluation. Let us look at each factor.

Service Level Components

When the topic of outsourcing and services levels comes up at conferences or in meetings, managers consistently ask to see examples. In most cases, what they are really asking for is how to write service levels. More specifically, what format should they take and how can they be measured?

All good questions.

Service levels are a way of defining what you need to run your business. You do not have to figure out how the outsourcer will develop the outputs an organization needs—you only have to figure out what *you* need.

In general, the measurement of service levels makes use of the following six basic tools:

1. Checklists
2. Responsibility Matrices
3. Service Descriptions
4. Service Levels
5. Action/Consequence Matrices
6. Measurement Mechanisms

Let us take each one in order.

Checklists

The first step is to determine the key areas that the organization needs to address. Checklists are used in the early stages of the outsourcing process to ensure all of the needed services will be identified. Think of checklists as a collection of noncore areas that the organization wishes to outsource to a qualified supplier. A very short list of examples includes such functions as network operations centers, human resource department functions, help desks, and tier-1 X-ray analysis.

Managers should examine what key duties are performed in a particular area. As should be clear by now from the use of the market benchmark, the process used to gather and document this information has to be collaborative. Input should be solicited from all prospective stakeholders, with a competent facilitator overseeing the process. Strong personalities cannot be allowed to hijack the information-gathering sessions.

Information can be collected through conference calls or even email, if the impacted parties are forthcoming with their requirements. However, it may be necessary to get everyone in the same room in order to ensure participation. Checklists establish the framework for the subsequent management and tracking of the outsourced functions.

Responsibility Matrices

When a function is outsourced, some very basic questions will arise. "Who will do what?" figures prominently among them. This is where faulty assumptions must be corrected. Otherwise they can sabotage the use of outsourcing as an external governance mechanism before things even get started.

Management must decide which of the activities identified in the checklists the outsourcer will perform, and which ones in-house staff will take on. Responsibility can be further broken down within the organization by department or individual, since the different areas of the organization are likely to be affected. A simple table will do the trick. Responsibility matrices are also useful in clarifying the interface points between the organization and the outsourcer, which are critical to a good working relationship.

Service Descriptions

What is the nature of the activity or area that will be outsourced? What is the purpose of the activity? How does it benefit the organization?

Service descriptions provide context for the activity, including information about why it is important. The descriptions should focus on outputs, not process. Remember, the process belongs to the outsourcer. Service descriptions need to provide enough detail to be meaningful, but at the same time not be overly long—no more than a few paragraphs for each activity.

Service Levels

Here is where the measurements for the services to be provided by the outsourcer get defined. The organization should specify targets, as well as minimally acceptable standards. This will establish a range in which the outsourcer can operate.

Any performance below the minimally acceptable level will trigger consequences that are defined in the action matrices. The relative importance of the service should be indicated here also, as that will determined what type of action will be taken if the outsourcer performs below acceptable standards.

The service level documents associated with a process or related set of activities also address what corrective actions will be taken if the outsourcer fails to perform adequately. In some cases, the missed targets may be minor and sporadic, in which case they need only be reported on a daily, weekly, or monthly basis, depending on the needs of the organization. More serious cases will warrant a forensic review to analyze the nature of the problem and diagnose it. The most critical lapses in performance may require immediate notification from the outsourcer so that emergency action can be taken.

Action / Consequence Matrices

All outsourcing arrangements should result in consequences for failure to perform adequately. Otherwise, management has no real recourse against the outsourcer.

There should be an escalation process for repeated failure to perform adequately. Penalties should be invoked at well-defined stages up to some maximum, typically no more than 30 percent of the monthly invoice. The reality is that if the situation gets to that point, the outsourcer is likely in breach of the contract. In such circumstances, termination for cause may be invoked if there is no reason to believe that the situation has a reasonable chance of improving.

Measurements

Of course, without good measurements, there is no way to objectively track the quality of service received from an outsourcer. This is where the rubber meets the road in outsourcing arrangements.

In an ideal world, all measurements would be automated. Of course, that is not the case, so manual tracking of metrics is an acceptable place to start.

The methodology for tracking outsourcer performance should be agreed upon by both parties. The organization receiving the service should also retain the right to audit any tracking mechanisms that the outsourcer has implemented.

Management would be wise to specify reporting formats and frequency, prior to signing any agreement with the outsourcer. In fact, all of the six items listed in this section should be defined, documented, and included in the Request For Proposal (RFP) that goes to prospective bidders. That way, everyone is clear upfront about what will be expected from the outsourcer.

Bear in mind that these same tools and techniques are indicative of the approaches that managers will use inside the organization. As the internal hierarchy is redefined and reshaped, micromanagement will be replaced by a focus on discrete, measurable outputs. Employees, contractors and managers will be managed in much the same way as outsourcers.

The Bias Against Outsourcing

Operational managers believed for a long time that some complex technologies remained too critical to outsource. This ignores the fact that EDS started by outsourcing functions that many organizations considered at the time to be fairly complex.

Suffice it to say that no hard and fast standard exists in order to determine what to outsource. That much should be clear by now. The best rule of thumb for the organization is to start with an honest assessment of internal abilities. In our age of increasing specialization, many times the ability of external firms will exceed that of internal organization. The market should always be the *first* to be consulted before the decision gets made to perform a function in-house. This is a minimum requirement.

Another issue the organization needs to address, centers on relative cost between performing a set of activities in-house or outsourcing. Having said that, most managers take only a superficial look at the situation.

Prices from a credible supplier can seem expensive by comparison to in-house costs. This often proves illusory because in-house departments will simply go through the motions of a cost analysis. We saw this issue surface with the internal monopoly. Not that managers do not put on a good show. An in-house group ostensibly takes a good hard look at external governance, but the analysis shows very often that an outside supplier will be more expensive. Why is this so? There are several reasons for this.

The bias of the department preserves internal jobs if they keep a function within the organization (at least for a while). More functions in-house mean more people on staff. It expands internal empires. Agency theory points this out neatly.

Even within the same organization, bias can creep in across departments or divisions, thwarting an objective analysis. In the late 1980s and early 1990s, AMR (the parent company of American Airlines), maintained at least two distinct IT groups. One was housed within the Sabre group, the successful airlines system that dominated the CRS (Computerized Reservation System) market for years. Another was known as AMR Information Services (AMRIS), which was a collection of smaller units engaged in outsourcing to external clients. One of the AMRIS companies, AMR Travel Services, entered into a partnership with Marriott, Hilton, and Budget Rent-A-Car to design and build a reservations system for hotels and cars. The effort was intended to replace the partners' older systems, as well as replicate the success that Sabre had previously with airline reservation systems.

At the earlier stages of the requirements gathering process, but before the coding had begun, AMRIS had to make a decision about who would undertake the development of the large-scale reservation system. Making use of the Sabre division's well-earned expertise in developing such systems would have seemed like a no-brainer. In fact, the option of outsourcing much of the development to Sabre, the sister company of AMRIS was considered but ultimately rejected. Based on their own internal analysis, AMRIS determined that use of Sabre developer resources would be too expensive. Instead, management of AMRIS chose to build its own development organization organically—and very quickly. The targeted timeframe for development of the new system was about two years.

In addition, management of the project opted to make use of a computer aided software engineering (CASE) tool that would automate development of the software code. Unfortunately, this case tool had never been employed before on a project of similar scale.

The development strategy was fraught with risk from several perspectives. AMRIS application coders, worked for the most part, in isolated groups, many of whom had only recently been hired to the organization. Most of the development staff had never worked together prior to the project. Unlike the approach Microsoft used when developing the NT operating system, which consisted of testing the interfaces between the individual system components daily, the AMRIS system component interfaces were cobbled together for testing only very late in the game.

It probably comes as no surprise that the project was a colossal failure. AMRIS and its partners spent US $175 million on a system that never went into production. In retrospect, the seemingly expensive in-house Sabre expertise that was shunned could have made a huge difference. In fact, it was the Sabre developers and management who were called in to audit and sort through the fiasco. Turf wars across organizations are bad enough. Turf wars inside organizations are inexcusable.

Even professionals can make mistakes. Take the case of the Big 4 consultancy that built a human resource system using in-house IT resources rather than its own externally focused consultants, in an effort to save money. The first phase of the project was so problematic that the firm finally did relent and use the same consultants that it provided to its clients, in effect outsourcing to itself.

There is always a tendency by department heads or even executives to believe that outsourcing will be too expensive. Sometimes this belief stems from a perception that an outsourcer will try to provide expensive features that may be unnecessary. Let us take the up or down decision about commercial off-the-shelf (COTS) packaged software as an example. In-house management will examine the solutions available in the marketplace and conclude that they are too pricey. Instead, managers or developers often suggest that they can develop a scaled-down version of the COTS software at a lower cost. This fiction suits most internal budget processes well because most of the expenses show up in the out years anyway. Consultants see these kinds of scenarios pop up time and again. Unfortunately, no amount of good advice will deter determined clients from this course of action. A competent advisor can show clients the right door to take, but they are the ones who have to walk through it.

Why are in-house departments so often allowed, even encouraged, to reinvent the wheel? It happens because management can employ an incremental approach that makes obtaining approvals to go forward, much easier. Outsourcers must lay out their pricing before they can walk in the door. Executives, who may not be well-versed in IT, see the sizable expense of the outside vendor on the one hand versus more modest cost estimates from in-house developers. The use of on-staff "free" resources becomes the magic bullet to pull off the development effort. Sometimes the accounting and finance departments follow in the wake to supply the remainder of any lack of credibility. All involved parties hope to stretch out the internal costs over a long period of time. The ultimate success depends on an odd combination of extreme optimism piled on top of unrealistic expectations.

Even so, all of this constitutes secondary considerations for many in-house groups. The real triumph rests on the fact that the dreaded outsourcer got vanquished along the way.

Only later does the unpleasant reality set in when management discovers that the extra features offered by the COTS provider did exhibit real value and have to be developed anyway. Unnecessary bells and whistles start to look more like solid functionality. The in-house system, assuming it works in the first place, takes on a life of its own because of the need for ongoing system enhancements. An annuity for in-house development staff has been created in the process.

Then there is the notion of cost-free or unused resources. This remains one of the great organizational myths of all time. Management should rid itself of internal resources that sit idle because they represent excess overhead to the organization. Such resources should be redeployed or released. It will become imperative that managers recognize the opportunity costs in such situations. No resource is free. If in-house staffs are engaged on other projects, management will put those efforts behind, if they tap developers for a pet project.

Pricing issues with prospective outsourcers represents a very common theme. In-house managers often miss many applicable items when they undertake an internal cost analysis. The casual observer often overlooks real costs like overheads incurred by other departments that provide support.

Tools such as Activity Based Costing (ABC) remain far too underutilized. ABC identifies the direct costs of specific services very well. Sure, it can take time. It may appear tedious to managers of the mechanized age. However, the alternative is to continue to operate without reliable information. Mechanized management gets left with estimates or best guesses in the absence of an ABC discipline.

Even today, for example, services remain the bastard stepchild of formal management research. By contrast, management theory loves the manufacturing process. Academics write endless books on the manufacture of goods.

Why not? The manufacturing process allows for more straightforward measurement. It dominated the economy for a century when overhead comprised a small percentage of the overall costs. The soft costs associated with a business operation did not need a rigorous allocation.

All of that has changed.

The transition to a service economy means that these fungible activities will constitute the bulk of organizational expense. More and more of manufacturing operations consist of service costs. These include human resources, management, accounting, and other administrative functions. These soft costs must be allocated against the value they add, in order to provide effective management to an organization.

Use of the market benchmark functions as a time saver. It avoids wasted effort. Many business processes or software solutions start to look like commodities under close examination and provide little core value.[16] Why would management believe that it could develop something better than several external suppliers who offer the same service or product? In order to succeed, suppliers must be able to provide services for less cost than competitors, which includes any organization's in-house development group. Many times an outside supplier's offering furnishes higher performance than is available elsewhere. Perhaps both.

To add insult to injury, the initial development of in-house software will be the lesser half of the burden to carry. Assuming the software works in the first place, the costs of ongoing maintenance provides the real sticker shock in terms of overall cost. Users will typically want frequent enhancements that add up over time. How can management spread the costs over multiple users, customers, or markets? The COTS supplier can answer this question. Internal management may be at a loss. No organization would attempt to recreate the operating system for its desktop or laptop computers. Yet organizations still try to build complex, industry-specific software systems. In most cases, the in-house development efforts could not be materially different from COTS packages. A replication of generic functionality guarantees that in-house systems will be inferior for a long time. Yet these boondoggles get funded anyway.

The COTS provider spreads development costs over a broad number of customers. Most organizations do not realize that three-quarters of software costs incur after system implementation. This means the majority of software life cycle costs become applicable in the post-implementation phase. Few organizations outside the COTS industry (and even some within) understand this very real expense. The costs tend to get hidden or forgotten over multiple accounting periods as well.[17] So what is the bottom line? Any activity an organization carries out must undergo critical examination against available external choices.

Proper cost analysis will be vital as technology becomes more complex, more specialized. Organizations will have to be very selective about what activities to undertake. Management will be required to subject each internal activity to an evaluation against external options.

Steering the External Organization

EDS and IBM struck long-term agreements with clients for as long as 10 years in the early days of outsourcing. Sabre even established a 25-year outsourcing deal with U.S. Airways. Such lengthy, soup-to-nuts outsourcing arrangements are becoming increasingly rare. Outsourcing advisors now recommend short-term deals that span a term of three years at most. Long-term outsourcing contracts just do not serve organizations well because of changing market conditions.

Added to the fact that transaction costs come down all the time, contractual relationships get more affordable. As the outsourcing process matures, agreements can be better defined. Technology continues its rapid change. The sophistication of organizations in the use of outsourcing will increase as methodologies are further refined.

Part of that sophistication manifests itself in better overall process. The use of shorter-term agreements constitutes just one example. Changes in technology over the past 50 years provide insight as to why.

If we go back to the introduction of the mainframe computer in 1950s and 1960s, we can note that there were fairly incremental improvements for at least two decades afterward. Data processing costs for large organizations declined in a predictable manner. Outsourcers could take advantage of steady decreases in cost curves back then. Long-term deals could be priced in an aggressive manner because outsourcers could afford to lose money in the first year or two. The useful life of IT assets was stretched out over many years to make up the difference.

The advent of minicomputers and other new technologies in the 1980s altered some of the rules. Costs for telecommunications equipment can drop like a rock in the span of a single year. When that happens, a customer stuck in a long-term telecom deal will get saddled with higher relative expenses in the contract's out years. The outsourcer still wins. We can assume that all technology learning curves benefit the outsourcer because they will generally be more familiar with the impacts. Shorter-term contracts can help assuage those advantages in favor of the customer organization.

Many types of outsourcing contract vehicles can be arranged. Several types of outsourcing of services now fall into the category of a commodity. This means that not all outsourcing contract vehicles look alike. In fact, organizations may choose from among several options. Common methods for classification of outsourcing include the following:

- Commodity
- Continuous Improvement
- Shared Risk

Cost and basic reliability characterize commodity or utility outsourcing arrangements. The old mainframe-based deals that got services outsourcing, started to fall into this classification. Penalties may be established for nonperformance. Incentive clauses that might encourage the outsourcer to exceed standards, serve no useful purpose. Why would they be needed?

A provider of commodity mainframe processing services will be required to hit a pretty high uptime target of around 99.999 percent Say the outsourcer hits 99.9999 percent. What extra value does the organization receive?

Of course, sometimes it does make sense to pay more for those kinds of numbers. Consider the mission-critical airline reservation systems. Or online retail systems. The extra 0.0009 percent should be specified in these cases because the additional charges on the invoice will be worth the expense. For most organizations, it will not.

Commodity outsourcing constitutes the most common types of contract vehicles. However, sometimes the organization requires more. When this is the case, organizations should expect to incur higher costs for these enhanced levels of service.

An organization may enlist an outsourcing firm to provide continuous improvement for certain processes in addition to a fixed set of other

services. The outsourcer establishes baseline metrics. The customer identifies defined targets. Progress then gets charted to keep track of outsourcer
performance toward the targets, with key performance indicators to
measure the value added. Incentives often prove worthwhile for these
types of outsourcing arrangements. Appropriate incentives better align the
outsourcer with the organizations own goals.

A third general type of outsourcing arrangement remains far less common. It looks as much like a business partnership as an outsourcing deal.
The organization wishes to create value through the use of an outsourcing
company in these instances. Management of a given organization makes
the decision that organic development of a particular service may not be
feasible. So it seeks help from the outside. Why?

Perhaps critical skill sets do not exist within the organization. There
may be few such resources on the market to be hired. Perhaps the organization requires the implementation of complex processes that would otherwise require years to establish. Such expertise may constitute a form of
intellectual property that will be more expensive to procure in comparison.
Either way, the organization looks to alternative governance options to
mitigate financial risk.

These often time-sensitive outsourcing arrangements represent high
organizational priorities. Significant revenues could be at stake. Sometimes
strategic or regulatory directives drive such mandates. The Sarbanes-
Oxley Act of 2002 (also known as the Public Company Accounting
Reform and Investor Protection Act of 2002) provides an example of
a mandate that requires all sorts of outside expertise to implement by
specific dates.

The outsourcer often commands a premium or a share in the revenue
stream in such deals. This scenario may still be most cost-effective though
is also expensive. You have to know the rules to pull it off.

Potential goal conflict with the outsourcer always exists. Divergent goals
will cause complex deals to go off the tracks every time. Knowledge of
intrinsic motivations remains key. What does the outsourcer consider most
important? An outsourcer holds the following priorities, in order:

1. Profit maximization
2. Revenue growth
3. Customer satisfaction.

Of course, outsourcers will never tell clients this. Further, smart outsourcers
know that achieving customer satisfaction is a necessary prerequisite to get
to priorities 1 and 2. Nonetheless, be assured that these motivations
represent good ballpark indicators just the same. They do indeed drive

behavior. The ability to leverage these consistent motivations to better direct outsourcers, can be a powerful tool.

Take the case of a communications company that needed to develop a backbone network. The company determined that it could not complete the network on its own quickly enough. The telecommunications industry was evolving so fast at the time that the company could not hire the right people or develop talent inside.

The network had to be completed in a year or less because of competitive pressures. The communications company would collect revenues that much sooner, every month the project came in ahead of schedule. So management sought to develop an outsourcing arrangement. The telecommunications company enlisted consultants specialized in the management of outsourcing vehicles. The team crafted a contract together. The terms stipulated that the outsourcer qualified for a bonus under certain conditions such as, completion of the network on time in accordance with well-defined specifications. This was simple enough. The telecommunications company decided to include an additional bonus. The outsourcer would receive the extra incentives as a direct function of the early revenue streams. The more revenue the communications company collected, the more incentives the outsourcer received. The outsourcer received a bonus in direct proportion to how soon the project came in ahead of schedule. There was a downside too. The client assessed a penalty to the outsourcer in the same contract if the completion date slipped past the plan. The degree of organizational motivation by the outsourcer was palpable.[18] Well designed agreements can focus external providers on the organization's goals like nothing else. These arrangement can make the outsourcer look almost indistinguishable to internal departments or product groups if done right. Outsourcers will put their best people on a given project if they see a clear upside (or downside). They will pay more attention to these types of projects. The case of the communications company above, demonstrates how well such an approach can work. The outsourcer in our example finished the network in accordance with the specifications and over two months ahead of schedule.

Faux Pas and Fairness

Another way to slice services outsourcing arrangements centers on payment terms. These also fall into three categories:

- Fixed Price
- Time and Materials
- Milestones or Transactions

Fixed price contracts can benefit the buyer because the service provider often takes some hits. Why? Such arrangements will tempt the customer to pack as much into the project as possible. Functional requirements just seem to grow *ad infinitum*. Outsourcers know this expansion of deliverables as scope-creep.

Well-defined product or service commodities present no problem for fixed price deals. More complicated transactions must be handled with more care. The contract has to be well defined in order for such deals to be profitable for the outsourcer. Any deviation from the scope should result in additional charges.

Time-and-Materials arrangements will tend to favor the outsourcer because late deliverables result in little or no penalty except for a perturbed client. A good song-and-dance routine will fix that. Many times the client carries some of the blame anyway. Clients very often fail to provide documentation, resources, or personnel as promised in the original schedule. Whatever the reason, Time-and-Materials agreements mean that the organization (not the outsourcer) will pay more if the project takes longer than planned.

The best types of outsourcing structures will be those that use milestones or transactions as payment markers. Such approaches resemble a series of well-scoped fixed price contracts. Defined targets establish clear, measurable outputs. The outsourcer receives payment only after delivery.

Simply specifying the components of the transaction, however, may be inadequate. Take the case of an outsourcer that performed central reservation services for hotel companies using two types of transaction-oriented pricing options. One option was based on the number of telephone calls placed to the outsourcer's central reservation center. The other choice was a function of the number of reservations actually booked by the outsourcer. Since not all calls in the center resulted in a sale, the second pricing option (charging on a per reservation basis) was more expensive on a transaction basis, although clearly more value was delivered. It also provided the outsourcer with a stronger incentive to make the sale.

A medium-sized upscale hotel chain opted for the per reservation pricing on a net basis. In other words, the hotel chain paid the outsourcer for total reservations booked, less any cancellations. Reservations were taken at the outsourcer's central reservation site and then transmitted to the applicable hotel for entry into their local property management system. The corporate headquarters for the hotel chain would then charge each property a service fee that varied with the number of net reservations booked.

This outsourcer performed central reservations services for many different clients and, over time, it became clear that upscale hotel chain was producing an inordinate number of cancellations. Further investigation revealed that the individual hotel properties were communicating cancellations to the outsourcer in order to avoid the reservation fees that their corporate headquarters was assessing them. The outsourcer was forced to change its transaction pricing from net reservations booked to gross reservations booked in order to curb the practice by the individual hotel property managers. The nature of the transaction from all perspectives must be considered when determining how an outsourcing relationship gets defined.

The price of outsourcing services should be based on comparable attributes just like any other purchase. No one would expect a new top-end Lexus to cost the same as a basic economy car. Yet, organizations fail to define such distinctions before they go to the marketplace for services. The discussion of price begins almost as soon as discussions gets underway. Outsourcers prefer this approach because they can start to zero in on the deal's revenue potential.

It must be emphasized that there can be no substantive discussion about price until you define the services to be purchased. There must be a clear consensus about service descriptions before a discussion of price can have any meaning. The organization must take careful account of its needs that includes a thorough documentation of requirements. Successful procurement from external providers for service functions means you have to understand what you want to buy first.

A major airline once solicited bids from outsourcers to take over its call center operation. The airline sold travel packages that included air, hotel, sightseeing tours, and ground transportation. The executive in charge of the travel unit identified an outsourcer who could take on the operation. The outsourcer proposed to work from different facilities to provide equivalent services. The numbers indicated that the outsourcer's solution would indeed be much more economical than the airline's own operation. The move appeared to make sense. The agents in the airline's facility hailed from the union ranks, which meant that these older employees were expensive call center resources. The call center operations transitioned to a different facility operated by the outsourcer, once an agreement had been struck. The outsourcer staffed the separate facility with lower cost, non-airline employees, as planned. The airline transitioned the well-paid call center employees to new roles within the company where they could. Otherwise the airline laid them off. The travel unit found itself, in for an unpleasant surprise. Management did not understand the full value that it offered to customers before the operation was outsourced. Sales of the travel unit dropped by double-digit percentages not long after the transition.

A detailed analysis attempted to determine what caused the new call center staff to perform below expectations. Management suspected a training issue. They were on the right track, though the problem turned out to be a bit more complicated.

The airline's travel service call center staffed itself with former airline employees before the transition to the outsourcer. Most of the employees boasted extensive travel experience. They had flown all over the world. They had taken advantage of the company's flight benefits over their years with the company. This meant they had visited many of the destinations listed in the travel unit's vacation packages. Imagine that you have to describe Nice over the telephone if you have never been there. Sure, the agent can look at pictures of the south of France (where Nice is situated) in the brochure. So can the prospective traveler. A typical response by the new agents would be along the lines of, "I hear it is lovely." The airline employees on the other hand, demonstrated superb confidence in their explanation of the destination packages. This poise came as a direct result of their extensive real-world travel experience and had sold a lot of these travel packages in prior years, as a result. This great insight became apparent only after the entire operation had been transitioned to the outsourcer.

The outsourcer was in no way prepared to offer a comparable service. It paid the much more junior call center employees, something in the vicinity of minimum wage. The younger staff possessed limited travel experience. The agents could do little more than offer a regurgitation of the unit's travel brochures. To add insult to injury, the airline's travel unit had sold packages to more than just end customers. It provided wholesale support to travel agents as well as on the retail side with travelers. Together, these two channels represented the bulk of the unit's revenues. The travel agents who had depended on the expert airline resources to help them sell travel packages were now confronted with almost useless call center agents. The travel agents knew more than the airline's outsourced travel operation did about the product.

The airline's attempt to lower costs resulted in an inadequate specification of the service levels in the contract. Management did not understand the true nature of the value of the service it wished to outsource. These factors resulted in lower revenues as well as decreased market share.

The market benchmark can be an effective tool if employed in a thoughtful manner. It can be a stern taskmaster too. External governance mechanisms like outsourcing require a comprehensive definition of the value proposition of all services. Organizations that engage in outsourcing must be crystal clear about all facets of the services contracted.

It should also be noted that fairness remains as essential as clarity in a good outsourcing arrangement. While management of the purchasing organization will want to press for good deals when they craft a relationship, they should not be overzealous in attempting to do so.

An analogy from an old line service institution may be useful. Restaurant industry profitability relies quite a bit on portion control. This comes into play from two opposite perspectives. Portions served up too large increase food costs. They cut into profit margins causing the restaurant to lose money. This is bad for business. You can go too far in the other direction as well. Undersized portions may cause customers to take their business elsewhere. So the key is to provide not too much, not too little. Precision can mean the difference between success or failure.

Outsourcing of services works much the same way. An outsourcer may indeed win a deal on an aggressive bid. Bad news can come later, when it learns the actual costs of delivery. While an outsourcer should know better, faulty assumptions sometimes creep into very large and complex RFP responses. Imagine the ugly realization to learn that costs will far exceed the revenues associated with a contract that has already been signed. The potential downside can run to hundreds of millions of dollars on a big enough project.

EDS's mammoth multi-billion dollar outsourcing deal with the U.S. Navy Marine Corps Intranet (NMCI) demonstrates a case in point. The project contains all the earmarks of a situation where the outsourcer underestimated the costs of delivery. EDS incurred significant losses on the NMCI project in 2004, despite much fanfare after the initial win in 2000.[19] According to several sources, EDS substantially underbid the contract. Press reports have indicated that they will make no money on the agreement.[20]

Customers might be tempted to enforce such very unfavorable terms. This kind of mindset will cause things to come to a bad end for all. The outsourcer will not provide good service or else it will try to cut corners. The organization that receives the service will suffer as a result. Invariably, the relationship will be damaged. It would then be better to terminate the contract in such cases. Sometimes, terms can be adjusted in order to make the transaction more equitable if the parties are amenable. This in fact, appears where the EDS-NMCI deal is headed.

Componentization and Cultural Innovation

Plug and play portends important implications for the information or new economy. The long overdue maturation of information technology will finally fulfill its early promise. We are not there yet, but it is coming.

For a long time, the use of IT constituted a period of experimentation. Other new technologies throughout history have followed a similar pattern. In the case of IT, few enough formal industry standards existed for decades. Instead, vendors established proprietary de facto standards.

IBM provides a classic case in point. Many of its operating systems, as well as much of its hardware, served as the IT industry standard for years. This kind of scenario, while common for a time, will become much more rare, even for companies like Microsoft.

Use of a proprietary standard to extract above market profits from customers will be a tougher sell to make as time goes on. Companies will simply not let themselves get locked into one-source deals the way they once did. Going into new business arrangements, they now more or less, refuse to be put in a position where they can be held hostage by an outsourcer, hardware vendor, or software supplier.

Not that suppliers can be blamed. Introductory Marketing courses encourage firms to find a way to increase switching costs. If it is hard to switch suppliers, fewer customers will do so. Supplier attempts to create this sort of client dependency are nothing new.[21] You can often lock in customers for years, if you can impose proprietary standards on them. This makes perfect sense from the perspective of a lone supplier for variety of reasons. In-house development provides an environment that encourages tight control. Proprietary standards make it more difficult for customers to move to a different vendor. Besides, industry-wide consortiums soak up valuable time and require lots of compromise.

Proprietary standards may be good for one particular organization, but they do not benefit entire industries or society as a whole. The problem is that standards do not constitute a priority for anyone early in industrial phases. Standard interfaces for embryonic product development efforts sometimes do not even make sense because the process or product remains in development. The market is not large enough or may even be nonexistent. Interfaces have not come into play yet.

Standardization starts to take hold only as more organizations travel up the learning curve. Repetition leads people to work smarter over time. Developers remove inefficiencies. Engineers improve processes. Managers realign systems. The larger market presses for the removal of nonstandard interfaces as the number of external buyers increases. Competitors start to gain a foothold. Proprietary organizational knowledge spreads because people leave one firm to work for another. They take knowledge with them when they go. These hot skill sets will find their way into the mainstream sooner or later.

Sometimes organizations watch others to learn also. Market demands for efficiency increase as this knowledge spreads. Market size continues to grow. More people get into the game. Standardization often becomes the price of admission for a given market with many suppliers in competition. Organizational dynamics will change as industry-wide standardization increases. The more focused organizations that specialize start to benefit as interchangeable interfaces drive more transactions. More specialization means more market niches, more opportunities. Industry associations, governmental bodies, or a cabal of customers impose standards to displace nonutilitarian differentiation. Vertical integration starts to disintegrate or divest along the supply chain as this process evolves. What used to be a distinct collection of activities within a particular enterprise now becomes commoditized here and there by outside organizations.[22] These trends toward standardization and commoditization hold true for both, products and services.

The old arguments for building larger organizations no longer apply. Management recognizes that the scope of an enterprise's core activities needs to shrink. Generic capabilities have become distributed throughout a given industry. They are available from a wide number of suppliers. These principles have applied to manufacturing industries for some time. They will come soon to service industry worker outputs including IT.[23]

The IT industry houses a key source of organizational inefficiency because it continues to struggle with standard interfaces one would expect of mature industries. Not for much longer. The Internet got things started with standard network protocols. The need for end-to-end process-based solutions will displace the current silo product-based mentality. Market forces will continue to intercede to enable interconnectivity across platforms.

Pieces of information technology were well on the way to increased standardization as the twentieth century drew to a close. Creative management will continue that effort in the following key IT areas:

- Hardware configurations
- Component interfaces
- Processes standardization
- Application reuse[24]

This offers some good news for higher skilled workers in industrialized countries for what, in many other ways, seems like a dismal story. We need to remember that offshore outsourcing of basic organizational functions cannot add value in isolation. To pull all the pieces together will require the strong management expertise found in abundance in the G7 economies. This holds true for coordination of all the related parts of service outputs or the ability to link specialized components. Management of external organizations will be an important job category in the years ahead. Experts will have to bring different pieces of technology together in terms of people, tools, techniques, and environment.

Superior know-how will still command higher salaries as always. So will the ability to coordinate or assemble the different pieces produced all over the world. The advanced economies remain well-positioned to provide these services.

Tasks that can be performed anywhere will move anywhere. For now, that means they will migrate to producers in low-cost countries. Comparative advantages for basic application coding will reside in India or China. The United States or Germany will have to add value elsewhere.

Leading edge coordination will go to the process innovators who seize the opportunity. It does not matter what country they live in. The outcome of that particular competition remains up for grabs.

The reality of all of this may sound harsh. Global competition will relegate much of the old well-paid IT functions to commodity status. This includes simple application development or troubleshooting basic hardware issues. Why should we expect these kinds of jobs to command a premium in the marketplace? Yet, this hard reality has not sunk in with many programmers in the G7 countries who earned hefty salaries to do routine work for years. That the gravy train lasted for as long as it did remains the real surprise.

All learning curves are dynamic. Most intellectual properties find their way into the marketplace over time, unless protected by copyright or patent. Innovative new knowledge sets become undifferentiated. Yesterdays skills are commonplace. The challenge for management as well as workers will be to build ever-newer competencies. Many potential opportunities exist. The development of well-oiled interfaces between systems provides one example. Organizations will have to be interfaced too. These types of projects constitute some of the engines of job creation in the next decade.

Work groups across the globe will mix, match, and coordinate efforts on a project-oriented basis. Product interfaces between information technology components will follow the same rules. Mix and match. Plug and play. The free market rules remain very consistent. The foundation of exchange economies rests on innovative specialization powered by the ability to conduct market exchanges in the form of trade and transactions. The flexibility inherent in markets can enable producers to refine and combine factors of production to create positive sum games. In the process, each participant in the transaction ends up better off. Market forces will continue to pressure IT component makers into action that will benefit entire industries and society at-large. Both, customers as well as competitors will insist. The IT industry will adopt standards that increase flexibility.

The number of transactions will increase along with overall value. Savvy managers who understand this dynamic will prosper.

Outsourcing drives the componentization of enterprises, now underway. This process traces its roots back to two hundred years ago, as a logical extension of the works by Adam Smith in *Wealth of Nations* and David Ricardo in *Principles of Political Economy*. Componentization encourages specialization and trade. Componentization also leverages enterprise capabilities beyond those of a single organization or a single country.

It is unfortunate that outsourcing carries so much baggage. Crossborder job relocation makes it a political hot potato. Why this unsettles constituencies in the high wage economies needs little explanation. How governments respond does warrant some consideration. Crude or blunt measures of the type suggested by Lou Dobbs, anchor and managing editor of his CNN show that regularly criticizes outsourcing, will be futile. The creation of an artificial environment will not solve the problem because it does not address the problem. Nor will it be sustainable.

You can pay people above market salaries. That will drive up the price of stuff they buy later as consumers. They must use their higher salary to buy higher priced things. No free lunch there. In other words, you can require organizations to pay people a "living" wage but that will just push up the cost of living overall. It will be the start of an unproductive cycle. People will be paid more, sure. They will not be any better off.

Job losses will accelerate in the other scenario. Lou Dobbs may think they can be protected. They cannot. Artificially high salaries will raise the cost of employee services and make them too expensive on a worldwide basis. It will push undifferentiated work to lower cost offshore economies even faster. The impact of geography-independent information technologies is going to be felt one way or another.

Firms do not have a choice. They take their option to shift work to other regions or countries to stay competitive. The enterprise will cease operations altogether rather than operate at a loss, if regulation forecloses that option. This is basic economics.

The issue should turn on the ability to find new ways to compete. The keys to success in the new economy will reside in organizational capability. Low cost wages for commodity work will offer fleeting advantages anyway. Competitive use of management is different. The use of employee talent to drive innovation can be sustained. The effective use of people and organization offer the benefit of imbedded cultural advantages, which provide greater durability.[25] Culture speaks to issues such as work ethic, desire for objective knowledge based upon the classical ideal, and the sanctity of the individual. All of these things must be learned and passed on to others. For a society or nation, culture takes at least a generation to change. At the same time, culture can remain stable (or stagnant) for centuries.

For a large organization, culture takes at least a year to transform. Often longer. This means competitors cannot replicate it very fast. Culture can confer advantages for sustained periods to the innovator. It remains far too underrated as a competitive tool.

CHAPTER 6

THE GLOBAL PERSPECTIVE

The Government Construct

Markets cannot substitute for government. Each has a role to play. Tension often exists between them because we again find that it is often tough to draw the boundaries. The strain between the two remains a function of the rules of the game. Some rules are inviolable. Some can be bent. Some are merely conventions that often get broken. The efficient use of contracts that can provide predictable enforcement mechanisms require more than a market. It requires a legal environment conducive to contracting and fair play. In short, it requires a system based on rules.

The role of government continues to be a subject of debate. It has responsibility for the establishment of the legal framework in which organizations operate. Some argue that government should also be a benefactor. They say that government should distribute the fruits of industry in a fair manner. Others postulate that government should promote certain industries in support of national champions.

These views of a proactive government mask several problems. In consultant-speak it masks several *issues*. The ability to be objective gets compromised when a nation takes sides or distorts market signals. A government that picks favorites unknowingly abrogates its duty to manage for the overall good of society.

The government attempts to foster organizational success. Few would dispute that. How best to go about that mission? The answer is that the government operates best as a referee. Any other role promotes a lack of genuine competition. It encourages organizational inefficiency. Society suffers as well. Government officials would like to collect taxes from organizations that flourish. It may instead be forced to pay out to support laggard home firms.

Unhappy consequences will result if the state acts as a distribution point for the spoils of the tax system. The payouts subsidize slackers, and penalize successful enterprises, which will spur unproductive activity. Business firms will focus their energies on winning favor with the government.

That is not where companies should focus their energy. Firms should instead work to develop innovative offerings. They should strive to lower costs. Organizations lose their ability to compete on a global basis in a cushy environment. Enterprises become disadvantaged without the rigorous discipline of the market. Politicians struggle to understand that organizations need tough love to thrive.

Governments can foster commerce through the establishment of a strong institutional framework that encourages predictable transactions. They do not have to tilt the game field to do that. In fact, a rigged match just debilitates home organizations in a misguided attempt to assist them.

Governments exercise a monopoly on the use of force. The nature of business competition implies conflict. Somehow these issues must be resolved. Government acts as the final arbiter on matters that cannot be resolved elsewhere. Political power can translate into the ability to prosecute, or the threat of incarceration. Sometimes such measures will be required to bring an open issue to conclusion.

Governments learned one stark lesson in the aftermath of so many post-conflict situations after the fall of the Berlin Wall and the end of the Soviet bloc. The state in the modern world sustains itself through the use of some type of Hobbes' Leviathan. Policymakers should consider well, the scope of governmental endeavors. Such power should not be wielded in a frivolous manner. The first duty of governments must be security. The ability to provide a framework for efficient commerce must follow on fast. Markets are the mechanism that provides the ability to conduct commerce. They are the golden goose that funds fiscal policy, including safety nets as well as security. The ability to conduct commerce relies on predictable enforcement of contracts as a prerequisite. This economic framework takes the form of both macroeconomic reform as well as the establishment of a competitive microeconomic environment that does not discriminate among firms.[1]

The government fulfils a unique role in the modern state. All other interested parties—individuals, companies, lobbies, interest groups, associations, labor unions, clubs—have an axe to grind. Each entity proffers particular points of view, the merits of which invariably compete. To sort them out even under the best conditions remains a challenge. When the government takes sides between organizations on market-related issues, it must do so on the basis of the economic merits. Any other criterion diminishes its credibility and places a greater drag on society as a whole.

Protection of specific industries invokes a series of negative effects: Government can be blamed for handing out corporate subsidies. The organizations in protected industries that receive subsidies will get lazy only to become uncompetitive in the global market. All governments will be forced to come to terms with this fact, unless they wish to tax us all to prop up laggard firms. Such short-sighted policies place a small hidden tax on every member of society. Each of those little taxes adds up over time. They become a permanent part of the overhead of a government trying to balance way too many disparate demands. All of the stakeholders will ask for more subsidies. They will cajole for additional protections. Such policy is irrational as well as wasteful. It passes muster only because it provides political cover. The real tragedy is that many of the benefits will accrue to the toll takers such as lawyers and lobbyists. These groups provide yet another example of increased transaction costs.

Governments must choose the appropriate interaction with the teams on the field. They cannot lead the cheers while trying to referee the game.

The Developing World Comes of Age

The United States, Western Europe, and Japan served as the premier locations for higher skilled occupations over the last half of the twentieth century. As Bob Dylan sings, things have changed.[2]

Educational systems in India and China improve all the time. Exchange students from countries all over the world take advantage of higher education opportunities in developed nations. Continued pressure will come from economies with lower cost structures as they move up the value chain. Developing country workers will perform higher skilled job functions. Management in all countries seeks to take advantage of these developments by modifying governance structures to operate globally. Organizations will fill jobs with workers across a wide spectrum of occupational skills wherever the economics make sense as we go forward. Whatever city, whatever country.

Even formerly insulated industries will be subject to componentization. Outsourcing will become viable if costs for a function or service get too far out of line with the worldwide market. In the healthcare industry, for example, the remote transmission and analysis of X-rays, chips away at costs that rise faster than the rate of inflation.[3] These types of developments suggest profound implications for advanced countries such as the United States, Japan, and the EU. The cost structures in the G7 countries, for the same work performed in many areas, sit out of balance with the rest of the world. These discrepancies will be forced to find greater equilibrium.

A favorable institutional climate of a given country will attract investment capital that creates new jobs. This factor benefits the more mature economies for now.

A stable economy lowers risk for investors. The costs of operations go down as well. Some countries will offer lower wages or property costs. These advantages may not be enough to offset other institutional or infrastructure deficits. Too much risk associated with a given economic landscape will ensure that no one will invest. It does not matter how inexpensive the labor or land.

That said, infrastructures in many developing countries do change for the better on a regular basis. It remains more than a little ironic how global competitiveness that promotes economic self-sufficiency for developing nations used to be very fashionable in the abstract. Academics, politicians, corporate PR departments, the press, international aid organizations, concerned citizens, and movie stars all welcomed the proposition. Who could argue with the idea that the developing countries should get a leg up? We now see that happening throughout the world to greater and lesser degrees. Why is it that not everybody seems pleased about these developments? Instead we often hear calls for legislation to protect us from cheap foreign labor.

Globalization sounds good if you expect to come out ahead. The industrialized nations tended to do well in the game of global competition in the mechanized age after World War II. Multinational corporations established global facilities. The large companies supplied exports to the rest of the world for years. The United States encouraged other countries to join in the fun. Many did. The same side does not always win all the time. There is no rule that says the competitive edge cannot shift in the process of globalization.

Exports of Japanese automobiles to the United States in 1970s, signaled just an early example of the democratization of trade and globalization. The golden age of the mechanized, old school manager had begun its decline even then. The outsourcing of IT programmers or call center functions to India, China, and the Philippines just mark more recent developments. Global competition does not constitute a zero-sum game. All the same, some developing economies will gain more in the decades ahead than the industrialized ones.

One U.S. dollar buys more stuff in India than in the United States. That same dollar buys even more in less developed places. So for the present, workers in these countries can compete as low cost labor suppliers, which they do.

As recently as the late 1960s, insular world markets provided much comfort for many years for industrialized countries. Higher productivity and higher wage jobs could be maintained for a time. All this changed in the 1980s and 1990s.

Financial markets deregulated. Corporate takeovers put bloated, unproductive managements on guard. Executives who acted too much like agents, began to be persuaded to act more like principals or owners. Mutual funds and pension plans increased their relative share of company stock positions. They demanded that corporate management pay more attention to the bottom line. Distributive information and communication technologies like the Internet also came into general use. Borders between nations became more porous. Employees with talent or investment capital could move across geographies with ease. The transition of many countries to market economies after the fall of the Berlin wall increased the size of global labor pools.

These developments benefited consumers in the form of lower prices and higher quality goods. Competition among firms increased in the process. Organizations always look for opportunities to decrease costs. They invest in more automation, implement process improvements, or perhaps even improve work processes even without additional investment in automation. Significant downward pressure on worldwide wage rates became more prevalent. New technologies gave workers everywhere, access to jobs in the industrialized countries.

Wages in emerging economies will one day rise to take some of the pressure off. One day. Wage levels for many jobs in the industrialized world will go down in the meantime. Either way, the long-term net result will be the same. High value differentiated work will collect a premium. Low-skilled commodity functions that large numbers of people can perform will not. When output becomes commoditized, the jobs associated with those skills will migrate to lower cost producers. No politician in the industrialized world will admit to this reality. And certainly the transition will be difficult from a political standpoint, with those most directly affected creating the most political upheaval.

People take time to readjust to structural changes in the economy. Their frustration is fodder for political campaigns. How the United States, Japan, and the higher-wage EU economies respond to the challenge of new organization structures will determine success, mediocrity, or outright failure in the decades ahead.

This push and pull on wage levels between nations will continue. While wages will never be in perfect equilibrium, they will find greater alignment, which highlights the effects of something called wage arbitrage.

Arbitragers in financial markets seek to find situations out of balance and profit from them. An overvalued currency here, an undervalued equity there. Overseas outsourcing represents a variation on that theme. Significant current wage incongruities across the planet cannot be sustained because new technologies shorten physical distances and make international borders more porous. New technologies will continue to decrease transaction costs, but the number of transactions will go up, thus increasing trade, componentization, and transparency.

Protection of markets will not be effective. In fact, all that protection will do, is to cause the eventual correction to be even more painful. Global competition will force organizations to restructure one way or the other. Traditional organizational hierarchies will be doomed in the process. Policy efforts to create a level playing field across nations will only succeed in being a ham-handed attempt at a political quick-hit. Such grand schemes sound good in theory, but can only be accomplished at a very broad level or over a very long period of time. Global associations might be able to establish limited environmental guidelines or enact basic regulatory reform, but any attempt to get large number of governments across the planet to agree to comprehensive programs will prove problematic at best. You cannot micromanage labor market reform through policy or legislation on global basis. Why? Simple really, when you look at the situation from a game theoretic standpoint. If you get inside the shoes of the other participant, a lot of things become clear.

The operative comparison for most workers in developing economies is not the United States, Germany, or France. Much of the rest of the world, views workers in industrialized economies as pampered, complacent, and overpaid. The operative comparison for a developing country worker will be relative to their personal option of life on a subsistence farm or in a sweatshop factory. A higher paid clean job in the service sector in their own country represents a much more attractive opportunity.

Lou Dobbs can rant all he wants. Simple-minded panaceas will fail. The eventual result for the advanced economies will depend on how well organizations adapt. This means the managers and employees inside those organizations must be prepared to be nimble.

The reality of other countries with lower cost structures will not disappear overnight. Governments can try to close borders or cling to outdated governance mechanisms, but such solutions will backfire. Governments will debilitate companies on an international competitive basis if they impose oppressive regulation or protectionism. Regulators cannot stop the cross-border diffusion of knowledge without sinking their economic ship in the process.[4] Any attempt to protect jobs may offer short-term political benefits, but it will also have the unfortunate drawback of preventing the formation of new jobs in the future.

A landscape conducive to competition keeps organizations on their toes. It keeps them competitive in a global economy.[5]

Organizations will create jobs if they take a proactive approach to the new competitive landscape. The countries they reside in, will prosper as well. Globalization will result in benefits to many nations that have been in the backwaters for decades, perhaps centuries. This may mean that recent winners in the industrialized countries will not be able to take primacy for granted.[6] Unlike governments, the market benchmark does not pick favorites.

Specialize or Stagnate

Job creation as well as loss occurs every day in the course of economic growth. New niches get discovered and populated as an economy evolves. Workers specialize to ever-greater degrees. The increased use of specialization derives from David Ricardo's theorem of comparative advantage based on his book *On the Principles of Political Economy and Taxation*, first published in 1817.[7]

Comparative advantage goes something like this: No one person, no one company can produce everything with a whole lot of efficiency. An individual or group might be self-sufficient in a primitive economy. The downside remains that this primitive economy must be more or less stagnant. Quality of life will stay in a relatively primitive Amish-like or radical Islamic sort of steady-state equilibrium. Very incremental progress occurs, whether technological, social, or economic.

Trade becomes necessary in order to accelerate productivity and it improves living standards as well. Nations, companies, and individuals opt to trade for what they cannot produce with any sort of efficiency. Or at all. There must be a surplus or excess of some other good or service in order to trade. This surplus commodity whether corn, wheat, labor, or intellectual capital serves as the basis for direct trade (or indirect trade, with the use of money). Individuals buy what they need in this fashion. Comparative advantage always leaves both parties better off.

Trade still makes sense even if a nation's exchange partners can produce everything faster or better or cheaper. Other nations can be smarter. They can possess more natural resources. They can be better off than you in every way. It does not matter from the standpoint of trade. You do not get anywhere if you try to subsist in isolation. Refusal to participate in exchange economies because of an insistence on self-sufficiency leaves everyone poorer. It is true that lower efficiency will not result in economic supremacy. That is not the point. People will be better off in a materials sense through open commerce than if they seal off the borders. Period.

The answer to the riddle lies in relative specialization. In Afghanistan, for example, the populace may not produce nuts and raisins, or even carpets in the most efficient manner on a worldwide basis. Even so, their relative advantage in those product categories looms large compared with their other choices. (We leave the issue of poppy farming for another day.) Take the country's ability to produce laptop computers as an example. Literacy rates remain among the lowest in the world. On top of that, the country has no near-term prospects for high tech production facilities. For now they should produce nuts, raisins, and carpets. The surplus they generate can be used to acquire computer equipment.

Specialization increases the ability to produce a *finite* set of goods or services in surplus. This excess can be used to trade. Specialization does not guarantee an absolute competitive advantage to a nation or society. The benefits to be gleaned from trade just require a *comparative* advantage.

This path leads us to ever more specialization as societies. Think of it this way. No one person or organization could produce all of the products available today. Complexity presents one constraint. The sheer scope offers another. Improved standards of living depend on increased specialization. More specialization will continue to impact organizational structure. The need for greater focus killed the undiversified multinational conglomerate. Madcap enterprise diversification seems to come into fashion every few years even though the approach cannot be justified on any rational basis.

Specialization drives the formation of more firms. More job functions too. That means more jobs period. Sounds good so far. We should remember that the process works both ways. It also means some jobs will be lost too. Some will be transformed.[8] Specialization might seem like a double-edged sword. You will feel that way if technology makes your plush job obsolete. The reality is that most of us plebes get more from specialization than we give up. The effectiveness of specialization will become ever more crucial in the days ahead. The ability of an economy to carry it off must be an imperative. So, society at large should better understand the dynamics at play. They can then use them to advantage to achieve shared goals.

We digress when we philosophize about whether specialization is good or bad as Adam Smith muses in the *Wealth of Nations*. It now comprises an integral part of the economic engine that serves society. Sure, specialization can cause people to become narrower in focus in some ways as a by-product. By the same token, the access to resources made possible by the surplus can round out the individual in other ways. The potential richness of life experience in terms of widespread access to education, art, entertainment, and intellectual pursuit remains unmatched today, than in any other time in human history. Whether and how people choose to take advantage of that potential—well that is another matter altogether.

Old Economists and Old Jobs

Financial panics in the late 1800s wreaked havoc on global markets. Our society used to experience wild swings in the economy on a regular basis in the first half of the twentieth century. This caused economists to spend a lot of time thinking about the prevention of another depression. John Maynard Keynes (1883–1946) owes much of his fame to the solution he proffered to governments across the world. Keynes supplied the prescription that, deficits in a recession could provide a stimulus to the economy in the short run. The flipside to the tonic held that governments should pay down the deficit once the economy began to grow again. Our worldwide modern political economy does not always appreciate this discipline. His macroeconomic theory seeks to provide a means to smooth out economic cycles. The use of government intervention to avoid prolonged periods of unemployment constitutes the key component of Keynes' theories.

Keynes' work in economics overshadowed that of a contemporary of his, Joseph Schumpeter (1883–1950). Nowadays that seems odd. Schumpeter's theories suggest that radical innovation should foster economic growth in the private sector. He coined this term *creative destruction* in 1942 in his seminal work *Capitalism, Socialism and Democracy*.[9] Schumpeter postulated that the tired lethargy of old businesses would lead to obsolescence. The old firms would be replaced by new pioneers. Good stuff as far as it goes. The story gets even better if we drill down a little more.

Schumpeter attained far less celebrity than Keynes at the time but his theories have grown in popularity since the 1980s. The upheaval caused by job creation and destruction in a healthy economy seems counterintuitive. The necessary dynamic does not appear well understood by the public, or politicians for that matter. The press reports macroeconomic statistics that focus on net gain or loss of jobs on a regular basis. These aggregate numbers mask the dynamic beneath the surface. Politicians live to bask in the glow of steady job gains in the course of an administration. The activity under the surface could be better described as very messy indeed.

It may be useful to think of the economy as an ecosystem. Continual birth and death describe the process in a more accurate fashion. Policymakers serve us well when they remind us that small business provides the key engine for long-term economic growth. Large organizations do not start out that way. Those exposed to any kind of market pressure must somehow earn the privilege to stay in operation. Some players succeed. Others do not. A healthy economy ensures the loss or destruction of many jobs and many businesses. The upshot will be that an economy creates far more jobs and firms than those lost. Overall growth increases.

A dynamic economy challenges current business models day in and day out. A lot of them just do not make the cut.

Economic reporters who announce Labor Department statistics about job growth or job losses, intend to refer to the *net* job gain/loss for a given period. The terms they use on the air or in print reflect a need for simplicity as well as the high-level nature of the survey data. Journalists who report economic numbers in this fashion leave out a huge part of the story. In fairness, the government labor departments do not track or provide the full scoop either. Regardless, such oversimplification of reported employment statistics fails to acknowledge the continual need for both job creation and destruction.

Old skills become obsolete. New types of skills become necessary in the process. The demand for blacksmiths decreased significantly after the introduction of the automobile. About 238,000 people made their living as blacksmiths in the United States in 1910. Today, just a few thousand do.[10] Secretaries who take dictation do not find much work these days either. If secretaries do still exist, you better call them assistants. Oh yeah, they will not take dictation either.

The theory of creative destruction implies that many skill sets confer minimal market value. The length of time spent in school may be irrelevant. Train all you want. It is still possible that there will not be much market value in a particular skill that you may nonetheless find endlessly fascinating. A cartoon by Roz Chast in the January-February 1998 edition of *Harvard Business Review*, highlights this issue. The title caption of the illustration reads "All-But-Completely Unskilled Labor." It includes three examples. The first panel depicts a man who is "Expert in Mayan pottery; can play a little slide trombone, if necessary." The second panel gives equal time to the opposite gender: a woman who "Has published two books of poetry and one of short stories; knows how to drive." The third panel shows another man, who in this last instance "Reads and writes Latin fluently."[11] The displacement of workers invokes substantive corrective mechanisms that ripple across the economic landscape. Job loss prompts people to seek training. They find incentive to realign their skill sets with a changed marketplace. This epitomizes the salient characteristic of a vibrant economic engine.

Donald Hicks, professor of political economy at the University of Texas at Dallas, studied sales tax returns for businesses in the state of Texas to better understand this issue. The state granted him unprecedented access to its archives that spanned a period of 22 years to analyze the birth and death process of businesses. The goal was to figure out what it would take for the state to create 3 million new jobs by 2020. Hicks learned that the areas with the most vibrant job growth and highest wages also turned over the most in terms of both creation *and* destruction of jobs. A really, healthy metropolitan economy turned over jobs like crazy. The evidence indicated that in order for Texas to add 3 million *net* new jobs, the economy would actually need to produce 15 million new jobs by 2020. You can look at the results another way. It also meant that 12 million obsolete jobs would go away in the same time period. Not an attractive prospect to sell to voters. No one seems to want to hear this kind of story. So the State of Texas decided not to release the report.[12]

Net job growth may look like a deliberate process. It is not. An awful lot of churn roils under the surface. Any attempt to preserve particular jobs or particular industries imposes a big drag on an economy. Opportunity costs increase. Fewer jobs get created overall. What most people do not know is that the jobs-not-created remain invisible. The counterfactual scenario gets almost no notice by the general public. Even ardent researchers seem oblivious. The jobs-that-never-were and the workers-that-would-have-held-them represent no entrenched political constituency. It is like the Frank Capra movie "It is a Wonderful Life" where the character of Jimmy Stewart gets a look at the hole that his absence creates for the people in his hometown. In an economy, the impact of flawed policy shows up in the form of higher unemployment rates and an acceleration of the transfer of jobs to more competitive economies.

Demand for skills changes all the time. Worker competencies have to find a way to move with that demand. Organizations must be given the latitude to eliminate certain functions. They must be able to transition jobs into more productive ones. Market signals in the form of incentives do indeed matter.

Yes, buffers such as job training programs or unemployment assistance serve as necessary tools to ease the transitions. By the same token, they should be temporary. It helps if the government funds them in an explicit fashion. Politicians who hide these crucial services in convoluted government budgets dampen productive capability. The funding mechanisms mask market signals. They distort tax structures. It does not make sense to fund educational programs from cigarette taxes. That kind of funding source dries up once all the smokers have died. Then what? Or do we want to encourage people to smoke so our kids can go to good schools?

Large companies should not receive undue favor either. It seems plausible that societal goals consist of the maximization of job creation. Part of that entails the maintenance of a vibrant economy. Industry protections should be eliminated altogether if we can assume that a somewhat dispassionate economy is best. Competitive enterprises on a global stage depend on this kind of rigor. Artificial support of noncompetitive industries or jobs will never result in improved efficiency or better innovation. It just gives people a feather bed to lie on while the rest of us slog out a harder living.

Discarded skill sets litter the job landscape. They provide marginal utility to society as far as functional value goes. We can debate the importance of bodies of knowledge all we like. The fact remains that the market will support some finite number of skills. The intrinsic value of other bodies of knowledge can provide fodder for hours of philosophical discussion in our free time. Thousands of unproductive or unnecessary positions linger for every poet laureate that society deems worthy of preservation. Any such luxuries must be funded by taxes on productive efforts so society has got to be judicious about what to support. We can do what we love in a free market economy, but we have do understand that we may not get paid for it either. The market benchmark provides the best guide to deploy resources to their most productive use.

Information and the Matrix

Many of the old rules will change as society transitions from a manufacturing economy to an information economy. Capital was a difficult resource to obtain years ago. Now it can be acquired with a good business plan.[13] Information is different. It does not lend itself to quick acquisition. Measurement can be problematic. Valuation sometimes seems impossible. We need to dissect the nature of information to get our arms around the issues.

Information can be explicit or tacit. Let us start with explicit information. It is not too hard to store and communicate *explicit* information. This includes traditional measures like market shares or sales volumes that come to us from the manufacturing era. *Tacit* information is not like that. It constitutes a much more formidable challenge for management. It defies bullet-point PowerPoint presentations. Sound bites do not capture the rich detail of such fungible information. Tacit information often remains part of the ether. It hides in that fuzzy area between what we can articulate and what we just sort of know. It may consist of strong suppositions or real world experience not quite yet codified. All the stuff that only you know about how the office really works, for example. Tribal knowledge or expert knowledge.

Tacit information relies on interlinked sets or structures of information that cannot be exploited or understood in isolation. These strains of insight will serve as currency in the new economy similar to the way that raw materials drive manufacturing.

The market cannot readily make use of such ethereal knowledge, so it often falls to the organization to put this asset to work. It also explains why subject matter expertise remains quite valuable in the new economy. Such squishy knowledge must be transformed into a marketable form in order to be useful. This highlights another reason why organizations often do some things better than the market. Organizations are created to take advantage of information that defies easy definition.

Tacit information can cost a lot to manage. The inseparability of people, information, services, and transaction costs implies that the price tag to make use of each piece will be high. It requires skilled knowledge workers to extract value from tacit information.[14]

Of all the transaction costs that an organization must deal with—search, information, bargaining, decision, policing, enforcement—the most important is information costs. Why? Other transaction costs go down when information costs decrease.

The ability of the Internet to provide certain types of information reduces search costs for many products and services. Identification of more choices gives buyers a better ability to bargain, and so on.

The associated costs of information explain why enterprises still add value in an economy. Hierarchies serve to define formal relationships. Functional departments create a structure that enables faster coordination. The organizational hierarchy can promote clarity of information exchange for specialized knowledge. It can facilitate the establishment of a shared language. Organizational culture often develops common values that provides for better cohesion or sense of purpose. Employee satisfaction increases too.

The appropriate organizational structure in a service economy will have to avoid excessive rigidity or dysfunctional behavior. These characteristics could pass muster in the mechanized age. They will not get by in the information age. Information flows across departmental boundaries will be one of the main sources of value provided by an organization. This includes informal flows as much, or more than formal ones. Part of the problem that organizations still face is that the old school managers too often obstruct these information transfers. The discipline that will be brought about by markets and outsourcing has not taken hold fully.

The shared information should initiate action often. Sometimes the action results in a continuation of vigorous debate. That is okay. Regular interchange leads managers to better understand important issues. These frequent interactions inside organization will clarify goals. Regarding opportunities, management will develop plans to pursue these opportunities. Options and contingencies should be part of the mix. This sort of diligence will clarify the appropriate courses of action as managers map these items out.

The ability to deal with information costs continues to present a challenge to management. Information changes every day. So does its value. Context remains a real key. Something important in one setting becomes useless in another. Flow of information too changes as technology makes all sorts of interactions possible now. Managers often exercised control through restriction. This is not the case any more. The Internet now enables the bypass of traditional gatekeepers with minimal effort. The role of the old school boys will change. They might even become superfluous (if they have not already). Collaborative technologies will require collaborative management styles. It is just that simple.

Easier transmission of information produces more matrixed, less hierarchical organizations (figure 6.1). Matrixed organizations do offer more flexibility. The matrix can help increase efficiency as well as improve the quality of decisions up to a point. People in a matrixed organization are often more accessible. Less emphasis gets placed on the chain of command because process tends to be more important.

The ability to make full use of information that will take us to increased productivity remains in the early stages. Agents (managers, employees) within organizations continue to hoard information. The fact that organizations do not create a systematic transfer of information exacerbates this. Yet, shared information is essential to decision-making. How else can you produce sound strategies for action? The inevitable redesign of organization combined with a shift in culture will usher in the change.

The new culture should put everyone on notice that certain behaviors will not be tolerated. People who ask questions deserve answers, not reprisals. Executives or managers who browbeat or patronize others do not steward the greater good of the organization. They serve their own egos perhaps. Maybe they attempt to hide a lack of competence.

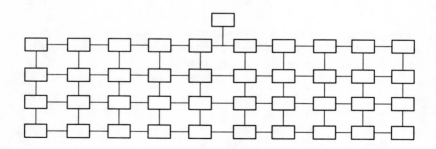

Figure 6.1   Matrixed Organization

Organizational design, or redesign, provides the necessary framework for action. Assembly lines inside traditional hierarchies translated into mechanized management structures. In the information age, these old-style arrangements will be insufficient. Organizational vehicles will have to ramp-up for a project and then disband to re-form somewhere else for the next one. Far more emphasis will be placed on processes that cross over traditional functional boundaries.

Tools such as war rooms or project-specific command centers that bring resources across the organization together in-person for a finite period of time can be very useful for information organizations as well. Microsoft maintains two of them. The company uses both at once in crisis situations, as when a nasty virus surfaces that infects their operating systems. War rooms facilitate real-time transfer of relevant information for a finite period or on a project basis. They are purposeful and project-oriented.

We need to think of the new economy as an information system. The market serves as a channel for information flow through the many communication vehicles available. The value of tools like the Internet comes from the ability to match up disparate players in the right context and at quick speed. People with questions meet people with answers. Buyers find sellers. Prices become more transparent. Unfocused thoughts get blogged into clarity.

Constant interaction among market participants increases, as more people find their way onto Internet every day. This interaction creates a series of two-way messages that cause reactions across organizations. New messages get generated as the cycle continues back and forth. All of this information jostles around at various levels in the economy just like synapses in the brain. It is true that messages do not always get received. Hierarchies as well as markets can distort the information. Yet, all the players generate countless messages nonstop. Useful information, or what we call knowledge develops in this fashion. It accumulates and then gets disseminated. Tacit information becomes explicit information. Pure research is still important, but it is not the only way to generate knowledge.

As communication technologies permeate society, management will challenge itself to identify and exploit new knowledge. To better tap the flow, organizations will become more transparent. Boundaries will change in response to competitive pressure to increased economic efficiency.[15]

Changes in information costs will alter the structure of organizations and the market. Organizations maintained an edge in the olden days when it came to regular coordination. Feedback was better inside the closed structure of the organization, so it was pretty easy to synch up. Shorter communication paths complemented cleaner messages. People spoke a common language. To a large extent, this is in the process of changing. Componentization will drive organizations to acquire more stuff from external sources. The need for an insular organization has come and gone.

To facilitate and process tacit information, organizational hierarchies will continue to have advantages over the market. Many development activities that involve specialists will be better harnessed within organization as well. What we cannot do, is take for granted (the way we usually do) that building an organization is always the best way to go. We must challenge our old assumptions. It is a new day. The market stands ready to intercede when some aspect of internal organization falls short. Welcome to the real world.

CHAPTER 7

MANAGEMENT STYLE

What is next?

The Internet represents a pervasive medium because it is versatile. It consists of a decentralized or loose-knit network of computers that use open standards for communication. New technologies drove new forms of organization in the past—the current environment will be no different. Organizational realignment will model the loose, networked structures. In effect, enterprises will reshape themselves to better take full advantage of new technologies.

As highlighted in the first chapter, rigid hierarchy began to be replaced by the divisional organization just after the turn of the twentieth century. Organization charts retained many consistent characteristics, even if they did vary by organization. Executives and strategists designed divisional organizations around the needs of the large-scale manufacturing enterprise. Such an old school structure could serve the service organization for a while because competition was still in its formative stages.

The transformation of service enterprises will proceed in the same way that the simple line and staff organizations, used by the railroads, gave way to the divisional structure. We do not use the optimal service organization model because it has not been designed yet. Most executives still do not even recognize the fundamental transformation underway, nor have they embraced the new styles required.

The recent introduction of matrixed organizations characterizes an early attempt by some to address the needs of the new economy. The problem is that matrixed organizations prove unwieldy. Too often, strong personalities resolve internal conflict as a function of multiple bosses or dotted-line reporting structures. A matrixed organization operates more like a one-off decision-based system without clear rules of engagement. A workable system for the long-term will have to be rule-based. Otherwise it reverts back in function—if not form—to a divisional hierarchy.

The optimal structure for an organization in the new economy will vary just as organization charts from divisional enterprises do. There will still be a CEO. There will still be worker bees. Reporting dynamics and communication flows—well, that is another story. Formal departmental lines of authority will be crossed on demand. This may sound a lot like a matrixed organization on the surface, however, the similarities pretty much end there. The use of project-oriented approaches will increase, for example. That is contrary to the matrix. Organizational boundaries become more porous, more fluid. A matrixed organization will prove inadequate because it aligns too much with the organizational logic of manufacturing. Many of the subunits in the new economy organization of the future will not be internal departments or divisions. They will instead be external organizations that take the form of outsourcing of one sort or another. Coordination across other organizational boundaries is now just too easy. Successful management in the new economy will institutionalize organization charts that can do this. Figure 7.1 shows what the organizational chart of the future might look like.

Modularity will increase so that outsourcers can perform just like internal departments. Figure 7.2 takes a cut at what this potential interchangeability might look like.

Organizations in the new economy will demand more flexible communication flows. Why is that so crucial? The answer lies in the number of choices available at any given time. Communication across large organizations used to be limited to in-person meetings, telephone conversations, or written documents. Now communication paths across organizations look a lot like the ones inside. Organizations used to exist so that people could meet in person often or participate in the manufacturing process. We can now substitute face-to-face meetings with a whole array of alternative communication mechanisms. The manufacturing process sheds workers every day. This means that for organizations to provide value, they will have to do different things. You can bet that the new rules and routines will take a lot of people outside their comfort zones. The demarks for organizational boundaries just do not depend on in-person communication anymore. Some guidelines for factors that should now determine what activities organizations conduct are highlighted in figure 7.3.

Organizations should start to move activities outside when transaction costs become lower than internal agency costs. This might seem like a wash since both agency as well as transaction costs decrease over time. At first glance the choices in figure 7.3 look either equivalent or static. That is not the case. We have seen how evidence suggests that transaction costs have gone down much faster since the 1960s. This explains why use of the

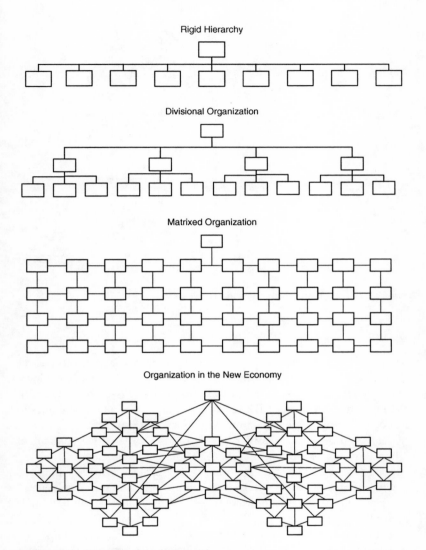

Figure 7.1   Organizational Transition

market (e.g., outsourcing) often appears attractive when in the past it did not.[1]

Managers will go to the market for their commodity needs, a category that gets broader all the time. Management will define in-house expertise much tighter.[2] The use of outsourcing continues to increase as management

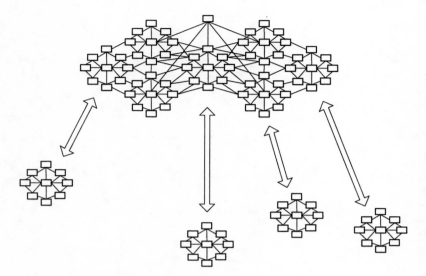

Figure 7.2   Organizational Modularity

downsizes across the board. Other changes will be enabled by collaborative technologies. Industry-wide standards will be imposed. Contract techniques will improve. Crossorganizational coordination overall will become easier. What is actually happening is that management is using all of these tools to restructure organizational design to do business in a new way.

As should be clear by now, there remain no hard and fast rules about where organizational boundaries should be drawn. Just guidelines. Each situation must be evaluated on the merits. This includes analysis of both the specific details as well as the larger environment. The moment you are ready to pull out the cookbook recipe for strategy, a new twist will make it obsolete.

Let us look at one of our generalizations from earlier discussions. The presence of asset specificity will tend to make outsourcing look unattractive. Yet, a market that has a limited number of suppliers does not always rule out that option. Sometimes cultural factors intervene to preclude opportunism by the outsourcer. The establishment of supplier networks in Japan provides a strong disincentive for outsourcers to use asset specificity to take advantage. Japanese firms tend to operate in close coordination.

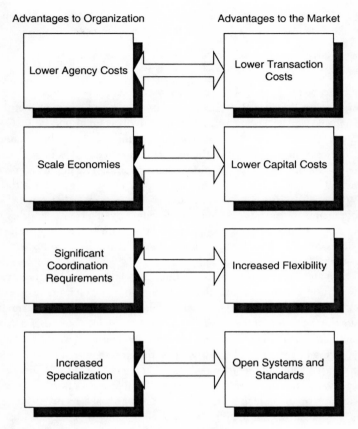

Advantages to Organization   Advantages to the Market

Lower Agency Costs — Lower Transaction Costs

Scale Economies — Lower Capital Costs

Significant Coordination Requirements — Increased Flexibility

Increased Specialization — Open Systems and Standards

Figure 7.3   Advantages to Organization and Market

Further, both parties view the arrangements as long-term relationships and refuse to jeopardize them in any way.[3] Such cultural features make the placement of activities outside an organization feasible despite the usual admonitions. Considerable trust increases the likelihood that contracts will be honored in Japan.

Sometimes, vertical integration does make sense up to a point. The flip-side remains that organizations cannot increase their scope into infinity. Sooner or later the market will do a better job because a single organization cannot keep up. Vertical integration gets dicier as an organization gets larger.[4] Organizations can almost always find a sufficient number of suppliers to make outsourcing tenable once a market reaches a critical mass.

Winner–Take–All Revisited

The concept of a winner–take–all society has made the rounds with some economists and received a fair degree of notoriety.[5] Like all seemingly unstoppable trends, this one too will correct. Robert Frank and Philip Cook, who wrote *The Winner-Take-All Society*, make the point that this phenomenon that was once confined to the entertainment industry is now invading other professions such as law, business, and academia. The implication is that there will be a huge mass of losers who support a few winners at the top.

Winner-Take-All is one of those scary propositions that can be very demoralizing. It can also be very misleading. Even now, it appears that superstar individuals in professional team sports can be counterproductive to success. High-salaried players drain resources from franchises and earn resentment from other players.

There are some truisms about the new economy that do not hold water under scrutiny. While it is true that the ability to make unlimited copies and globally distribute the best art or entertainment is at hand, one could certainly debate the definition of the word "best." Like the market for other products and services, the market for entertainment is becoming more diverse all the time, giving buyers more choices. Witness the growth of online music that is written, arranged, and recorded by bands that are not signed with any record company. Or the increasing number of self-published authors using print-on-demand or ebook technologies. Look at how digital camcorders and editing software allows aspiring directors to make movies or short clips that can garner some fleeting fame. Notice how cable channels and the Internet have humbled the once dominant television network news broadcasts.

Perhaps equally salient is the fact that many familiar artists or examples of popular art would have to be classified as mediocre at best. Marginal actors, unremarkable talk show hosts, prosaic writers of prose, and hack artists can all be seen making millions of dollars.

The same technologies that prop up take-all winners also enable enterprising individuals. For example, the flipside of the ability to make an infinite number of copies of a work of art contrasts with the Internet's ability to provide infinite shelf space.

The market is ultimately a highly democratizing force. And while lots of mass market goods and services rightly become commoditized, people are always looking for something new. Society can only support so many take-all winners. There is a lot of basic blocking and tackling at the middle levels of any profession that will keep people productively engaged and adding value. In many cases, such work will even make us comfortable, as long as we keep our eyes open and our minds receptive to new opportunities. From a practical standpoint, this clearly requires looking at the world in a different way. These changes in the works will mean that the hierarchies in the new economy, along with the people who manage them, will be so different in the decades ahead as to be unrecognizable by today's standards.

Copycat Management

The professional manager as a widespread occupation has been with us for a little over a hundred years. In spite of the lengthy tenure, it is still surprising how often senior management will use a single case study—in effect, a sample size of one—to generalize issues to a wide variety of other situations that are not necessarily applicable. Most typically, high-level executives see some success story at another company, perhaps in another industry that looks attractive. They either admire the business model or fear it, but either way, they decide to emulate it.

Good strategies are crafted by gaining a shared understanding across the organization. They also make the strategy difficult for other organizations to duplicate. Ultimately, copycat managers will be able to borrow only bits and pieces from competitors. These pretenders still retain their own organization's existing culture and strategies. All of the residual baggage will trump any attempt by management to graft another organization's strategy onto theirs. If managers and executives want to copy something, they should move a couple of levels down from grand strategy and use tools such as strong organizational facilitation, robust forecasting, scenario planning, and three dimensional measure of progress.

There is nothing as vapid and useless as high-level vision statements by senior leaders that lack so much specificity as to be almost meaningless. Two examples include United Airlines'(UAL) vision under Stephen Wolf's first term with UAL to be "The World's Best Airline," and Enron's vision under Jeff Skilling to be "The World's Leading Company." It would appear that neither of them succeeded. Although the two slogans sound great, they mean a lot of things to a lot of different people, including the employee base. It is hard to get people on the same page when you are speaking in such extreme generalities.

Vincent Barker III, a research professor at the University of Kansas School of Business, has uncovered some problems in the technique that executives use to diagnose organizational failure. There is a tendency to rely on too much data that has been filtered by the old organizational hierarchy.

Executives pay too much attention to obvious or fashionable ideas that masquerade as pertinent information. In some cases, they employ selective perception that precludes a full appreciation of the problem at hand or prematurely forecloses potential solutions.

To combat these biases, Barker developed a short prescriptive list to serve as guidelines for determining the sources for organizational decline:

1. Top managers should directly engage the environment. An overreliance on traditional accounting data to diagnose problems instead of engaging customers or front line employees can badly flaw the analysis.
2. Top managers need to be self-confident but avoid hubris. Good management must have the ability to make tough decisions. At the same time, overconfidence can lead to hubris, which makes managers reluctant to change their views even in the face of contrarian evidence, or for managers to admit mistakes.
3. Have a diversified management team that shares individual viewpoints. In order to get a more systematic view of the issues facing the organization, sharing of all relevant information combined with honest debate serves to unlock the best ideas from top management.
4. Get outside advice on major problems and issues. A fresh perspective can sometimes uncover solutions that the senior management team did not identify.[6]

Drawing from as many resources as possible for problem solving or strategy development is crucial. Superficial analysis will result in superficial solutions that have a poor chance of succeeding.

The Problem of Succession

Organizations exist to fulfill the needs of client community, whether they be customers, donors, investors, employees, or regulators. Organizations come in all sorts of different forms. Yet, they have a couple of things in common. They all require leadership, and they often have rules.

Bureaucracy might otherwise be termed an organizational rule set. Bureaucracy possesses distinct advantages over other alternatives. Most of us do not have much good to say about bureaucratic rules; however, it may help to consider the alternatives first. German sociologist Max Weber (1864–1920) reasoned that few choices exist for organizational leadership. Bureaucracy is one option. Patriarchal or charismatic leadership models are really the only other two choices. Let us have a look at each.

Patriarchies derive from family units. They often extended to the concept of business until the late 1800s. Patriarchies resemble bureaucracies in some ways because they tend to provide a stable form of leadership. Families have used such systems to pass businesses on to their offspring for generations and created formidable enterprises in the process. They almost always have some rules. Problems still come up anyway. Heirs have a tendency to grow in number over time. All of these part owners may not agree on how to run the business. Perhaps the heirs want to cash out.

How do families tend to deal with these issues? They may feud for a while, but the end result often consists of the sale of the businesses to the public. This takes us right back to a bureaucratic model of governance that publicly-held companies employ.

So what other options do we have? We can search for the mythical superman (or woman). How does that scenario play out?

A charismatic leadership structure maintains even fewer rules. Such a system may recognize no set procedure for appointment or dismissal. The bearer of charisma undergoes no formal training. If formal rule sets exist at all, they tend to become irrelevant because they get subordinated to the dictates of the charismatic leader.

It is true that both patriarchal and charismatic systems can provide effective leadership over a finite period. There is no denying that. Yet sooner or later, problems arise because both systems hinge on the issue of succession. An organization dependent on a patriarch or charismatic leader may run fine until the leader dies. What then? The next leader could be the idiot son or incompetent protégé. Does Kim Jong-il from North Korea ring any bells?

Problems with charismatic leaders also include the fact that good leaders do not come along every day. An organization might wait years or decades until the next competent charismatic leader arrives. Once again we find ourselves looking back fondly on the bureaucratic model's sustainability. Bureaucracy democratizes the leadership selection process through a rule-based system.[7]

Bureaucratic forms of governance may not select the best candidate in all situations. That is not their function. It is just that the presence of a rational structure helps to limit the downside. A systematic transition can save organizations or nations from disaster.

This analysis is not meant to imply that bureaucracy contains no potential pitfalls. Lethargy can combine with excess bureaucracy to sap innovation or draw down scarce resources from any organization. Bureaucratic rules often discourage a focus on high quality service. But of course, we know this already. What inferences can we draw from the history of large organizations over the last hundred years?

The founders of successful large businesses or philanthropic institutions understand the concept of service better than many of their professional management successors do today. These rare founder-leaders nurture the organization as a start-up. They continue to run it spot-on into maturity. Sometimes the founders put their name on the door like Sam Walton at Wal-Mart (sort of) for example. Or Ford. Sometimes they do not, as Bill Gates and Paul Allen did with Microsoft. Either way, the great founder-leaders understood that their first duty was to the organization.

This timeless principle too often gets lost for professional managers, which includes CEOs as well as the boards of directors tasked with over-sight. Executives should be judged on their contribution to the continued future viability of the institution. Profitability ranks as a key criterion for firms, but with a caveat. Shareholders do not invest for next quarter's earn-ings at the expense of the organization's overall survival. Investors purchase a stock (whether they understand this or not) valued at the best guess of the entire future profits of the firm, discounted to present value. That is why when stock prices go to la-la land, it makes sense to get out of the market until they return to valuations based on fundamentals.

So it means that not only are next quarter's profits important, so are the profits for the next year and the next decade. This requires a management team tasked with stewardship for the long haul. Large enterprises should not be treated as vehicles for executive ego, regardless of how promising the out-look of immediate earnings looks. Yet, even as we have started to better appreciate timeless leadership tenets, celebrity and ego-driven CEOs remain.

Some management theorists back in the 1980s, even went so far as to argue that executive fame was a prerequisite for success in a media driven age.[8] This myth is steadily being exposed.[9] Celebrity-CEOs live to serve themselves at least as much as the organization they shepherd. No doubt, their personal currency of fame benefits from appearances on talk shows, morning news programs, or "Saturday Night Live." The organizations in their charge, however, often gain little from such exposure.

Of course, some occupations require celebrity or fame. Movie stars, television personalities, and even politicians use celebrity as part of their stock and trade. But in these cases, the individual *is* the product in the enter-tainment industry. Star popularity goes hand-in-hand with their success.

In the business world, celebrity serves as a distraction for organizational leaders. Boards of directors should recognize that all parties would benefit from new leadership once CEOs achieve such notoriety. Some CEOs gar-ner so much attention that they can in fact usurp their organization's own brand identity. Famous CEOs should move on to the lecture circuit or academia in such cases. Perhaps they can fill a public service role. A new leader will be better able to focus on the organization's mission along with its long-term success.

These are critical issues. An organization's reputation depends on its brand that encompasses far more than a CEO's image. The market measures performance by the quality of service provided to the targeted constituencies. A CEO's popularity does not contribute to this mission.

A well-functioning organization does not need celebrity. However, it does require sound leadership plus seasoned judgment. The professional manager is a hired hand. Executive success does not revolve around any one individual. His or her contribution relates back to the overall success of the organization. That is how they add value.

Competent professional managers constitute one of the main reasons the divisional corporation supplanted so many other types of governance. The corporate form of governance now extends well beyond the business enterprise. Successful nonprofit and professional organizations all follow a model little more than a century old.

Weber reminds us that the problem with charismatic, celebrity leaders continues to be that they often leave a void when they depart. Sure, they might even be great leaders during their tenure. However, at some point they die or retire. When that happens an heir must be selected.

Lee Iacoca at Chrysler and Michael Eisner at Disney, both resisted repeated attempts to identify or groom successors. Many qualified candidates became tired of waiting for their turn to lead. Others were simply forced out. At Disney, Jeff Katzenberg was widely regarded as the driving force behind the success of a string of animated hits culminating with "The Lion King." His style was inclusive and collaborative, which enabled him to work successfully with high-powered, often ego-driven Hollywood talent. Despite his success, Michael Eisner remained ambivalent at best about Katzenberg's talents and referred to him unflatteringly as "the little midget." Katzenberg left Disney and soon after co-founded Dreamworks Studios along with entertainment industry heavyweights Steven Spielberg and David Geffen.

More recently, Sumner Redstone, Chairman of Viacom, appears to be guilty of the same reluctance to relinquish power. Between 2000 and 2006, five senior executives left the company, including the well-regarded Mel Karmazin, costing it approximately $US484M. All this, after removing Tom Cruise from the Paramount roster—arguably the most bankable star in Hollywood—without consultation from senior staff.[10]

New management styles will succeed because they will not be so capricious. Large organizations succeed when they attract strong managerial talent and keep it—not drive it away.

The Toleration of Bad Management

The military turns out many former officers who do well in a business environment. There should be no mystery as to why. The military benefits from clarity of purpose. A very strong *espirit de corp* within the ranks confers significant advantages as well. What are the implications for other types of organizations? For one, it means a focus on core competency. Another key factor is the maintenance of high employee morale. The members of the organization must be motivated above all.

In some ways the military possesses inherent advantages over commercial pursuits. The organization's leadership insists on well-scoped charters. Many businesses and other organizations, by contrast, still struggle with that. True, once in a while military leaders display a fair amount of charisma. One has to look no farther than the exploits of General George S. Patton during World War II to see that. However, the rigorous, rule-based system of the military also restrains and channels the actions of its leaders.

Measurements of success in the military revolve around a limited number of unambiguous items. The key focus constitutes a short list—maintenance of strategic capability, for example. Basic logistical support is another. However, the most important feature of a strong military organization results in the form of battlefield victories. Achievement of mission objectives captures everything in a nutshell. As such, success or failure rests on well-defined criteria.

Likewise, organizational success depends on rigorous discipline as a necessary foundation. Individuals in their private lives can follow intuition or take chances. They can chase moving targets with minimal deadweight loss imposed on society. Market-based, democratic economies in fact revel in such an atmosphere of individual autonomy. The picture changes as resources get aggregated, directed by ever-larger hierarchies, controlled by ever-smaller numbers of managers and executives. The deadweight loss that society has the potential to bear goes up in a disproportionate manner. Large organizations as well as governments carry an enormous responsibility for prudent stewardship of these massive pools of resources. A renegade or Bozo CEO can wreak havoc on thousands of shareholders, stakeholders, and taxpayers.

It seems odd then that the mechanism to choose CEOs remains a clubby affair. The CEO's ability to single-handedly shape the character of its board of directors exacerbates the issue of effective governance. The recent corporate debacles of Enron and WorldCom, among others, exposed some of the flaws in corporate governance. These failures accrue in part to cozy relationships at senior management levels. Yet, the titles of CEO and Chairman of the Board continue to be combined with great frequency. This informal board of director network remains inadequate given the massive resources over which corporations hold sway. The generous golden parachutes awarded to marginal managers make no sense either. Jean-Marie Messier at Vivendi jettisoned with a huge severance deal after a very questionable run at the helm. His case serves as one of the many, many examples. Messier proved to be an egocentric, brash, and ineffective administrator, by all accounts. Yet a court upheld his 20+ million dollar exit package. The decision centered more on legal considerations than any assessment of the quality of management on his watch. It still points out the tendency of boards to be too generous in CEO contract negotiations. Directors continue to fail to place enough emphasis on the expectation of results. Executives do not experience consequences for the failure to map a prudent strategy that leads to sustained success.

Disgraced military leaders must suffer ignominy in exile as Napoleon did on Elba. Sometimes they endure worse fates. Displaced CEOs on the other hand, vacation in the south of France. Perhaps they seclude themselves in the Hamptons to enjoy luxurious anonymity.

Sometimes organizational boards of directors look for leaders in the wrong, often obvious places. They hire headhunters, which can push up the cost of an already overpriced market for CEO talent. They rely on the recommendation of the previous CEO even though the track record for selecting one's own successor is, mixed at best.

Competent leadership often shows up where you least expect it. Some great leaders wait in the wings, perhaps a bit farther down on the management hierarchy because they could not get into the old boys club. They may not possess a singular desire to lead. In order to be a good leader, an individual needs much more than the simple desire to run things.

Consider this old story about a job interview. The hiring manager asks, "Are you a team player?"

The candidate responds, "Yes! Team Captain."

Many qualified people will lead, if called to do so. They will lead when a vacuum exists.

Not everyone should be a leader either. Nor does everybody want to be or have the ability or temperament. Yet, organizations often make this mistake over and over again when they attempt to create a "culture of leadership."

Some people perform well as technicians. They do not aspire to run the company. The Peter Principle describes this issue quite well: people tend to rise to their level of incompetence.[11] The promotion of managers on the basis of technical expertise can lead to very unhappy outcomes.

Some people prefer to be followers. Some people just *should* be followers. The organization will suffer if the wrong people get promoted in either case.

A good leader-manager must be focused on the organizational mission. He or she should exude discipline as well as expect it. Leaders must be ever mindful of morale. An effective leader must also challenge myths. They must be skeptical of anything offered at face value. Things "known" to be true, too often turn out to be mistaken assumptions. A department or organization may miscalculate when this happens. Bad assumptions can cause a product launch to fail. An operation might go south. Management must be vigilant with regard to potential pitfalls. They must be determined to confront reality. Material mistakes in judgment at high enough levels in an organization can cause its very demise.

Stream-of-Consciousness Management and Other Dysfunctions

Good management requires a short list of key attributes. It requires consistency, for example. Yet, some managers continue to operate in a world of constant brainstorming. Such managers like to use the telephone. They particularly like cell phones. This device lets them call subordinates night or day, at work or at home to rattle off the latest batch of unfocused thoughts. Presumably, these old school boys dispense the pearls of wisdom to spur some kind of action, yet, the same bosses may press just as hard in another direction altogether, a scant 24 hours later. These are the folks who hold meetings without agendas, rambling endlessly in search of an issue.

We could refer to this as Stream-of-Consciousness management. So named because the thought migrates from the ether to someone's brain, and then rolls off their tongue almost instantaneously. It looks a lot like brainstorming as a management style. It may elicit many potential solutions to problems, but it does little to complete successful implementation. Nor does the approach serve to assess the viability of any of the random thoughts. Brainstorming works well in brainstorming sessions because it can be a useful way to facilitate the identification of ideas. It is not a useful management style. Brainstorming must be considered a first step. The ideas must be examined in more detail. Many will be discarded as unworkable before the process is over.

Constant use of brainstorming or Stream-of-Consciousness leadership as management style confuses others. It often contradicts itself. Good policymakers understand this. A competent executive makes thoughtful policy after lots of input and debate. Then the decision is left alone long enough to implement followed by an evaluation.

Several classes of inept management behavior still flourish in organizations everywhere. People holding positions of responsibility all over the world demonstrate these behaviors despite much improved organizational design over the past century. Clearly we have farther to go.

Some managers, for example, struggle to understand vision. To them, it means some kind of distorted alternate reality. True vision helps management of an organization to marshal resources in order to get from the present state to a more desirable future state. It is possible, though, to get carried away. Managers serve no one if they delude themselves and the organization in the attempt to achieve some unattainable end state. Expectations raised to unrealistic levels will be dashed. Morale will take a big hit in the process. Successful vision must be coupled with rigorous assessments of organizational capabilities. An honest acknowledgment of the landscape has to be made. Only then will the organization appreciate the degree of effort required to reach the goal. Wish lists need much more than naïve optimism to come to fruition.

There are other types of management dysfunctions that are remnants from the old school and also destined for the scrapheap. While it is true that information embodies one of the keys to successful governance in the new economy, as with any powerful tool, it can be misused.

Some managers tend to manipulate the use of information for personal benefit. These managers possess a very good ability to collect bits of information for use later. When issues that require justification surface, they fling out their collected factoids in a haphazard fashion in an attempt to support a course of action they wish to pursue. Like a handful of dirt or other brown substance against a wall, they hope at least some of it will stick. Management, by the use of structured information, will expose this flawed technique of decision-making. It takes time as well as a little help. The remedy will come from more than one direction by managers who do possess a thoughtful grasp of the issues and must press for a systematic alternative approach.

Next comes The Moving-Target-Theory-of-Management. It continues to be popular in many quarters despite the fact that the use of management gurus is becoming increasingly questionable. Management theory remains in relative infancy, as we discussed earlier. New books on the subject come out every day. Some general managers, presidents, and CEOs read such books in an uncritical fashion. Then they set about right away to shape their organizations around the new mantra. At least until the next new management book comes out. It is true that senior management should look for new ideas all the time. Executives should also remember that no magic formulas exist. An attempt to transform an entire organization with a new idea or approach presents a very risky scenario. Management should first experiment with an individual department or small group as a hedge, because sometimes things just do not work out as planned. Steady, informed executive control drives larger organizations to success. Moving targets are really tough to hit.

This last class of manager represents the most dangerous threat to an organization. Part of the reason is that this type of manager is hard to spot. They may have come up through the ranks. They often maintain strong views on certain issues. Their expertise in their own field may be unquestioned. One success in an intractable situation leads to success in other more intractable situations. The messiah complex may take over after enough time. No one knows better than he or she from then on.

The subject matter expertise carries the day for a while. Promotions continue to follow. One day that specialized knowledge taps the law of diminishing returns and a slow downhill slide ensues. Maybe the executive thinks he has learned everything he needs to know. Maybe he or she moved up the organizational ladder too fast and it seemed like everyone else in the office just could not keep up.

Whatever the reason, this is the turning point.

Spirited discussions become less insightful, even mindlessly repetitive. Sometimes there is little or no basis in fact. The soapbox becomes, in essence, a rant. No one notices at first. The moral high ground gained in terms of genuine expertise begins to cover a multitude of ever more egregious sins. Broad generalizations get proffered for pubic consumption and find a receptive audience from eager subordinates. Fortunately, the rants by these executives get called to account in many cases. Perhaps most cases. Senior executives or boards of directors often step in to exert proper diligence by exercising their authority as principals. As is right and proper, the old horses get put out to pasture. Things actually do work that way much of the time. However, once in a while they do not. Sometimes the specious generalizations continue to be accepted across the board. The former subject matter expert, who should be on the downside of an aging career, pulls off something that should never be allowed to happen. They grab the brass ring and become a severe organizational liability in the process. They become a Bozo CEO.

You will not find the term Bozo CEO in any management textbook—yet. Perhaps one day. Management ranks get vetted on a regular basis. Many approvals must be obtained in the course of a career. Even so, sometimes the bozos slip through anyway. They may ascend as the result of political connections. They might be perceived to be superstars. Perhaps they take advantage of fortuitous shifts in management structure. Sometimes they rise to the top spot because they just accumulated enough tenure.

The Bozo CEO runs the company or organization like a personal fiefdom. He or she bullies subordinates. They wreak havoc on an organization because they cannot be questioned. They shut down debate through perceived competency or sheer force of temperament. The curse of the Bozo CEO has plagued large organizations in recent years all too often.

Into this category would fall Al Dunlap. Chainsaw Al got forced out of Sunbeam in 1998 for questionable accounting practices. He slashed employment with reckless abandon and withering condescension. Dunlap did not build organizations as much as he dressed them up for sale.

People in the office thought Bob Fomon, former CEO of E.F. Hutton, had literally lost his mind in his latter days with the firm. Fomon oversaw the sale of Hutton to Shearson in 1987 only after first, almost single-handedly, running the company into the ground.[12]

Roger Smith, who retired from General Motors in 1990, spent US \$40 billion on a failed implementation of robotics and automation.[13] The debacle occurred as a direct function of his hostility to constructive feedback. Smith would become apoplectic if asked too many "impertinent" questions.[14] No wonder that he became a target of Michael Moore in the documentary entitled "Roger and Me."

Jeff Skilling at Enron caused the demise of a multi billion-dollar organization. He countered subordinates who asked too many questions with the comment that they just did not get it. Enron then declared bankruptcy in 2001. Skilling was said to possess a razor sharp intellect until called to testify before Congress. At the hearing, he experienced what can only be described as a phenomenal memory loss about his activities at the company. In May 2006, he was found guilty of making false statements to auditors, securities fraud, insider trading, and conspiracy while at Enron.

In the late 1990s, Jill Barad at Mattel oversaw a mass exodus of the bulk of a qualified senior management team, as well as the disastrous acquisition of The Learning Company. A passive board of directors played a key role as usual.[15]

Ross Johnson at RJR Nabisco squandered multiple millions of dollars of company resources and left with a 50-plus million dollar exit package in 1989. Johnson would dress down other managers with generous condescension by thanking them for a "blinding glimpse of the obvious." This had the neat effect of virtually eliminating internal debate.[16]

Bozo CEOs run off talented managers and decimate organizational competence in the process. Then they bail out of the nosedive with a lavish golden parachute. Sometimes the Bozo CEO does not manage to salvage his or her reputation in the process. No matter. He or she gets set for life as a function of an inattentive or submissive board of directors. In the process, the Bozo leaves the organization in shambles.

Max Weber's call to the benefit of bureaucracy suggests merit in the approach if we resolve to make use of it. Rule-based organizations maintain safeguards. A public corporation does not constitute a kingdom, magic or otherwise. It is built up over a period of decades. No single person should be allowed to take down an institution because of greed, ego, or sheer incompetence. The board of directors cannot be a rubberstamp for the CEO, no matter how many of them he or she appointed.

Perhaps, boards and senior management should also consider the possibility that whip-smart thirty-somethings still possess limited experience. Many young managers take on CFO positions at large companies without sufficient experience and seasoning under pressure. An unrelenting CEO may very well wear down a junior CFO's resistance to issues of basic principle.

Executive management must provide the high-level policy guidelines and feedback mechanisms. Organizational policies should be structured to ensure crossdepartmental communication. The role of senior executives (board members too) should be sound strategy and long-term viability of the organization. These leaders should deal with crises on the basis of exception management, not micromanagement. Above all, executives must remain accountable stewards.

CHAPTER 8

NEW RULES FOR GOVERNANCE

The Discipline of Civility

You will find a lot of smart people in the business world. Many bright folks come out of graduate business programs too. Not that business schools make rocket scientists out of those who matriculate. Just to get into the top colleges means you already have to be pretty smart to begin with. The best schools will not even look at someone with less than a 600 on their Graduate Management Admissions Test (GMAT).

So it makes sense that we should expect to find some mental horse-power in the business world. Why not? The rewards can be great. You might work with some of the most qualified people on the planet in a particular discipline. The job can provide wealth, power, and respectability if you move up high enough in the organization.

People in a business environment also possess some drive. You cannot run a division, department, or a company well, against competitors with a complacent attitude. People who go through the motions will tend not to advance so far in competitive organizational environments. So we should not be surprised to find that a smart bunch of people with drive might demonstrate some of the drawbacks of ego. The problem is that ego does nothing worthwhile in a business environment.

Perhaps some people need to maintain a positive self-esteem that ventures into excessive ego for motivational purposes. If so, these folks should also maintain the good taste and decorum to keep it to themselves. Management theorists or gurus touch on aspects of the discipline of civility in a tangential fashion. Sometimes they refer to it as stewardship of one form or another. Let me define the concept further.

Civility is not difficult to understand. It lets people ask questions with impunity. They do not get patronized or reprimanded. Leaders should demonstrate enough empathy to know how others would like to be treated. Adams Smith says as much in the *Theory of Moral Sentiments*.

Employees are pressured to meet pending deadlines. They put up with angry customers. Irritated stakeholders may weigh in. Senior jerks from other departments offer their two cents. The business environment contains enough stress already, without all these other factors to deal with, as well. To force people to deal with irrational bosses or peers piles on more than anyone should be required to endure.

Seems simple enough. Do not add to the problem with rude or arrogant behavior. It is easy to say, but hard to sustain.

Demonstrating of civil behavior consistently can present a challenge. It may not be so tough when you are feeling good, if you do not have issues with the boss, or if the spouse is not complaining. However, such a sanguine picture cannot last. Stuff happens. We learn what we are truly made of, when the walls start to fall in. Adherence to the discipline of civility every day, as a matter of policy, presents a formidable task for most managers.

To do so, means that managers must divorce themselves from some of the emotion associated with pressure-packed situations. It helps to grow a thicker skin, for one. We tend to react better if we can do that. Circumstances will intervene when you least expect it. Something will always happen that we did not plan for, so managers must be prepared for such unpleasant eventualities.

These are the new rules. Services and information are not manufactured goods. They are the tools of the new economy. People, service, information, and transaction costs remain inseparable. The *things* or physical goods were always easier to manage than people. In the future, it is the people who will have to be reckoned with in a very real sense. We need to wrap our minds around that.

The change will take time. Old school managers still inhabit the executive suites everywhere. They put on such a pretty face when their bosses or clients come around. But otherwise, look out. The term for this behavior is Upward Receptivity. It means that the people above on the hierarchy get lots of attention. Those below receive contempt or indifference. These old school bosses are often masters of Upward Receptivity. They are either perennial grumps under the best of circumstances, or a real terror if things do not go well. There is no reason in the world to run an office or an operation in this fashion. It is because of these antiquated management styles that bosses in the business world often get such a bad rap.

Such behaviors are unpleasant. They dehumanize others. A lack of civility imposes negative effects on the organization. Feedback loops will not loop.

The communications starts to go one-way: straight down. This often enrages old school managers all the more. They cannot understand why frank upward communication ceased. Yet they will bite the head off anyone that comes in with bad news. Sometimes they strike at anyone with any news at all. Who would want to engage these people with the prospect of such a foul outcome? What does this mean for executives who practice this sort of management style?

It means buckle your seatbelt, Dorothy, because Kansas is going bye-bye.

The mechanized manager used to be able to treat people like machinery. Perhaps this could be tolerated in a manufacturing environment. New rules come into play with the importance of people in the new economy. The cost to train new people remains high. Turnover costs can take a real bite out of the already hard-to-define overhead category. Tribal knowledge provides one of the key advantages of the organization over the market. Bad management can cause the people with that knowledge to walk out the door never to return.

The old school boys struggle to understand this. They wonder where all the fun went. They can no longer enfold their ego into the job. They still think that a boss should run roughshod over people once in a while. Imperial CEOs dole out abuse whenever they feel like it. Some of the old boys still think such behavior serves as a good motivator. It does not. People are assets and should be treated as such. Not just because it improves morale and increases productivity. Managers should act in a civil and respectful fashion because it is the right thing to do.

A Mile Wide or a Mile Deep?

One debate that continues to generate questions in the senior management ranks, regards that of two particular aspects of management style. Should managers be big-picture people or micro-detailed oriented. Wickham Skinner provided the answer to this question many years ago in a series of management studies.[1]

Skinner looked at various types of managers and found that both big-picture and micro-detail managers failed in the long run. This does not put the debate to rest in and of itself. Detractors of both styles exist in great abundance. In his attempt to find an answer, Wickham's research yielded valuable insight.

Why do managers on both ends of the spectrum fail? The answer starts with the usual criticisms.

Micromanagers get lost in the details. They display very good technical talent because they are often experts on arcane details. You call these people first if you need a specialist. Such managers who become executives, fail because they cannot shake their myopia to the larger environment. They are masters of the universe within their discipline. They ignore key external events that lead to their downfall perhaps because of that.

On the other side of the continuum, we find big-picture managers. These guys (gals too) receive much derision as well. Managers in this class paint in broad strokes. Often they make deals and leave the details to others. "Just get it done" is their mantra. With such an expansive mandate, sometimes things do not get done so well. Operations spin out of control or go over budget. The big-picture manager cannot react in an effective manner. He/She fails to cope without the ability or willingness to assimilate the details.

Bernie Ebbers at WorldCom and Ken Lay at Enron, appear to be examples of this behavior, at least on the surface. Both almost boasted their lack of knowledge about significant amounts of corporate operations or accounting. At the time, press reports derided these comments as the Sergeant Schultz (of the long syndicated "Hogan's Heroes" television series) defense: "I know nothing!.."

How much Lay and Ebbers knew about the details of their organization's operations may remain a function of who gets to tell the story. The fact that Ebbers received a 25-year prison sentence in 2005 for his role in the downfall of WorldCom may signal that the bar has been raised for the definition of competent management. Lay was convicted of six counts of conspiracy and fraud at Enron before dying of a heart attack in July 2006, prior to sentencing. Executives can no longer claim to be naïve dilettantes.

Effective management requires a combination of a big-picture and detail-oriented style. Managers must do both. But how to know when each style should be employed? The insight of Wickham's research shows that no such hard and fast rule or guideline is necessary. The real key to success requires that managers maintain the capacity to zoom in and out, so to speak.

Managers who focus just on the big picture run into trouble when there are no more deals to make. They cannot dive into the nitty-gritty integration work. The meat-and-potatoes work to bring things to a successful conclusion, eludes them.

Detail-oriented managers lack the scope to administer larger organizations. They flounder when confronted with nonlinear events such as crisis situations.

So, managers must retain the ability and willingness to shift gears between high-level and low-level. Wickham determined that a manager who can do this will improve his or her odds of success. They must see the larger picture on the one hand. They must also dig down into problems on a selective basis.

This means that no hard and fast rule must be applied. The key to the solution lies in the fact that executives do not always need to be right about when to shift gears. They just have to possess the competence to alternate management styles once in a while. They should be able to drill down into the details when legitimate issues arise. Often enough, they will be right, as long as they can do that from time to time.

Bounded rationality assures us that micromanagement will sooner or later hit the wall of diminished returns. When that happens, managers must begin to step back from the specifics as they move up the organizational hierarchy. This will apply even more in the extended organization. Along the way, management requires shorthand indicators and tools, such as dashboards, to enhance the management process. Prudence demands that executives dive into the details in times of crisis. They must get up close to sort out intractable issues as an exception. It cannot be the rule.

These types of timeless rules for effective management remain elusive. The past hundred years provide rare glimpses of insight. Along with the useful gems, comes management by fad. The management *du jour* technique often appears to produce a quick solution. It may fall out of favor not long after.

Good managers will act as competent stewards. Managers should seek to move the ball markers down the field during their tenure. They should run an ethical operation. One day it will be time to go. When that day comes, they should hand everything off to a competent successor. Then get out of the way.

Avoiding a False Sense
of Precision

Ever punch in a couple of rough numbers into a calculator and get a result out to ten decimal places? The calculator analogy would sum up the problem with the methodologies employed by the bulk of forecasters (and by extension, many managers).

Economic predictions often drive the more micro forecasts that organizations use to plan. They also typify how businesses put plans together.

The problem many economic forecasters fail to contend with, centers on their detailed models. Such elaborate equations *might* produce accurate results in periods of relative calm, if even then. How many times do consensus economic forecasts turn out to be well off the mark? You have heard the news reports. The unexpected developments caught forecasters by surprise. Managers should remain wary. Any forecast must be treated with caution.

Even stable environments make simple forecast accuracy treacherous enough. Causal factors that get compounded with additional variables just add to the challenge. Some kind of adjustment becomes inevitable in any system, as pressure builds up over a long enough period of time.

Punctuated equilibrium is a term coined by paleobiologists Niles Eldredge and Stephen Jay Gould in 1972. It provides wide application to a variety of settings that include economic or business environments. The concept suggests that changes do not occur in a gradual evolutionary manner. Rather future events come to us in a series of corrections. A punctuated equilibrium describes one or more significant adjustments after a sustained period of relative calm.[2]

Punctuated equilibria occur more often than we might tend to think. Most forecasting models become useless when they do. In fact static forecasts often prove less than useless in such situations because they imply a degree of precision that can no longer be supported. The system modeled, no longer resembles the uncluttered equations on paper.

The NASDAQ or dotcom equity market collapse demonstrates a recent and famous example. The NASDAQ peaked at 5048.62 on March 10, 2000. At the time, stock analysts charts forecasted continued growth in technology stock valuations into near perpetuity. Investment advisors urged their clients to put their retirement money into high technology stocks as much then as ever before. Funny, how fast things can change. The dotcom forecasts became irrelevant overnight after March 10, 2000. Not that the analysts or stock promoters did not stand by the overvalued shares for a long time. They did. "Buy on the dips" served as a popular mantra back then. The NASDAQ underwent a painful see-saw descent for two-and-a-half years to bottom out at 1114.11 on October 9, 2002. There were lots of dips. Each one turned out to be worse than the last. Each dip produced a sucker-rally. The rubes bought. Lucky traders liquidated their holdings. Not because of forecasts. Some traders just guessed right.

The jury still remains out on whether the NASDAQ is priced at fair value. Who can say if it will fall further still? Forecasters will always have their charts. Can you believe any of them? The NASDAQ hovers somewhat above 2000 as this book goes to press.It remains poised to go either direction. I leave it to you to pick which way.

The future often turns out to be different than we expect for far more reasons that can be documented here. This does not mean to suggest that the lack of ability to obtain extreme precision should cause us to abandon forecasts altogether. It does imply that managers use better methods to plan. Use of meticulous forecasts that demonstrate their flaws only after the fact, provide limited assistance at best.

Scenario plans remains a realistic proactive approach that managers continue to find beneficial. This method to look ahead provides managers with a tool to prepare for several different futures. The idea pops up often in mainstream management literature. Odd that managers still fail to plan for a variety of potential events.

Scenario plans do not need to make use of complex models. The emphasis should instead be on creative thinking. We should look ahead in order to design contingencies for each set of events. The most probable scenario almost always comes to mind first. Map that out. Proceed right away to the worst case. What would happen if Murphy's Law combined with the most pessimistic forecast imaginable. How would that impact the system? Then assign a probability to it. Maybe the probability appears very low—say 1 percent.

Then map the best case scenario. Peg a probability to this one also. The best case should not be the same as the one with the highest probability because it reeks of wishful thinking. Unrealistic optimism clouds judgment. It does not benefit the analysis. Map other scenarios in between. The probability of all identified scenarios should total to 100 percent in order to get a relative proportion (but not an expected value) of the likelihood of each potential outcome.

Remember too, that any scenario can have second order effects. You can plan a product launch where sales turn out to be better than forecast. Sounds good. The better than expected sales may surpass revenue estimates. What is the bad news? They may also outstrip the organization's ability to fulfill demand. This second order effect would result in significant customer dissatisfaction. The organization will suffer a loss of goodwill.

Good news sometimes brings bad news. Management should continue to ask "what if?." Follow the logical responses. Like a series of if-then statements in a computer program. If this, then what? Then what? Then what? And so on. The models should be robust enough to deal with a wide range of possibilities. Then take another scenario and repeat the process.

To model prospective future events like this takes time. It requires thoughtfulness. Organizational resources must be expended. It can indeed be expensive.

The alternative is worse. Compare the above to the cost of inadequate contingencies that lead to dreadful execution. It looks like a real bargain from that vantage. Organizations that are serious about a set of possible events in a particular context will expend this kind of effort. Others will not. This highlights one of the key reasons why organizations with well-conceived strategies maintain a competitive edge. Their approach cannot be copied by superficial observation from the outside.

Even if you do map a scenario, it still requires follow-up. The information must get acted on, to do any good. Scenario planners had predicted outcomes similar to the aftermath of Hurricane Katrina long before it arrived in August 2005. Engineers told policymakers that the New Orleans levees would withstand Category 3 winds or less. So it is not as if no one could foresee the possibility of such devastation.

Scenario plans look at the future. It is a first step. You map out action plans to deal with different potential futures. It also helps us see around the next corner or two. Games and simulations provide a concrete example of how organizations train their members to better deal with a variety of unfamiliar situations. In the United States, spending on such tools is expected to increase from US $6.1 billion in 2005 to nearly US $20 billion in 2010.[3]

What happens after the fact? What measurements should be used then?

Roughly Right constitutes a forensic operational approach that works well. Scenario planning looks ahead (proactive) the way forecasters try to. Roughly Right measures actual results (forensic). Not quite CSI style, because management knows where the crime scene will be, so to speak. Therefore they can plan in advance. Neither technique requires a false sense of precision.

The Roughly Right method enables managers to achieve a degree of accuracy. It avoids the problem of flawed gauges that appear to be exact. It also prevents the opposite problem: the lack of measurements altogether.

Roughly Right, in an operational environment works well for several reasons. First, at a minimum, it forces at least some crude measurements when they might not otherwise exist. It requires little more than critical thinking as a prerequisite. It can be performed as a high level analysis of an operational environment as a first step. The rest of the missing pieces can be filled in over time as the holes become apparent. The thought processes that surround the issue will become clearer.

Roughly Right can be a cost-effective tool to plan for an implementation. It also avoids other drawbacks. Managers acknowledge that the numbers from Roughly Right measurements contain uncertainty. Management will not lock in on a set of unsophisticated metrics because it assumes a greater willingness to revise assumptions. Measures improve over time. More information becomes available. Measures will morph as circumstances change.

The preponderance of effort that goes into way too precise plans do not need to be embodied in a Roughly Right approach. Very exact forensics might suit the majority of manufacturing environments. The service industry remains far too young for such ambitious tools.

The situation may be altogether different by the time most service operations work up to such a high degree of precision. The whole process may need to be revisited because the market moved somewhere else.

Failure to measure emanates from a perceived requirement to achieve extreme exactness. The fact that many service processes often defy ready measurement, might reinforce this belief. The response by management should not be to throw up its hands in resignation. Nor should managers sprint to implement expensive measurement programs in short order with limited knowledge.

Adoption of a methodical, consistent approach will work best. The goal should be to cultivate a deeper knowledge of the processes involved. This can best be done in stages. Establishment of initial approximations, makes the most sense, as a start. This process will identify basic measures to be tracked at the outset. This should lead to more detailed ones later.[4] Many aspects of basic services do get measured consistently. Call center systems can track all sort of things about a service operation: number of incoming calls, abandonment rate (what percentage of callers hung up before the line picked up), how long before the call was answered, duration of the call, time on hold, and so on.

Assessment of the quality or customer satisfaction of a help desk operation in that same operation presents more of a challenge. Call center systems can give you certain metrics. They cannot tell you whether your customers like the way the help desk works.

Help desk operations get broken up into tiers in order to improve efficiency: tier 1, tier 2, and tier 3. All customers start at tier 1. The agents at this level get trained to deal with the most basic questions. The first question for computer hardware might be: "Is the device plugged in?" It is a lot like television sitcom programming that gets geared toward the lowest common denominator.

The caller gets transferred to tier 2 if tier 1 cannot resolve the issue. This should occur as soon as the call center agent recognizes that the nature of the problem goes beyond their area of expertise or responsibility. You must often ask for a supervisor. This is the same thing as a tier 2 escalation. The most intractable issues go to tier 3.

It does not matter how experienced users may be. It will take them some time to get past the tier 1 gatekeeper. All of the questions on the initial checklist must be asked first. A long series of telephone touchtone prompts must often be waded through before customers can reach a live person. Perceived quality would improve for most operations if a fast track were available for higher end users or if the customer service option received the same fast service as callers in search of a sales representative.

The problem with quality measurement of the operation takes us back to chapter 1. It is tough to do research inside the organization. How do most call centers track success? They do it in a couple of ways. Call duration is one of them. It represents the most critical from a cost perspective. Short durations means agents can answer more calls. Fewer call center resources will be needed. Management often presumes that shorter calls also indicate that customer issues will be handled better. Maybe so. Maybe not. A call center system will not answer such questions. This explains why supervisors monitor calls every so often. They want to gauge customer reactions. They need to evaluate the quality of service by an agent. This works reasonably well. Agents who need to be trained can be identified. Early warnings of customer frustration can enable management to head them off in advance.

The other method that determines the quality of service in a call center is the survey. (Once again.) Many of the consistent complaints apply here as well. To get a person to complete a survey was not very difficult years ago. Sometimes respondents even seemed flattered to be asked. Surveyors from everywhere now inundate people. It is fair to say that most people hate to do surveys. This explains the low response rates.

A better method to determine overall satisfaction with the help desk might be to give customers a choice of communication vehicles. Many organizations do provide access via telephone, email, website, bulletin boards, and blogs. Customers should have the option to use any or all them. Some people hate email. Others hate the telephone. And yes, some people still do not have access to the Internet. All avenues for input, unless an organization wants to fire a segment of its customers, should remain open.

It would be nice if customers received the same consistent answer to questions. That would improve perceptions of service. The IRS maintains a toll free number that taxpayers can call to ask questions. Did you know that it is possible to get different answers from different agents for the same tax question? Maybe they should simplify their product offering so that all of its own people know what the rules are.

This book contains a consistent theme. No one answer resides in these pages that will work for all organizations.

When Southwest Airlines sought to benchmark the turnaround time at airport gates, it did not use the large, previously regulated carriers as a point of comparison. What good would that have done? The major carriers typically took an hour or longer to turn around planes at the gates. Southwest did not see the major carriers as its primary competition anyway. Management believed that they were competing with the family car for

200–300 mile trips. So the airline needed to find a way to keep its costs down and its planes up in the air as much as possible. Instead of looking at other airlines for insight into quick airport turnarounds, Southwest benchmarked against Indianapolis 500 pit crews, who can get a car back on the track within two minutes. That is how their organization learned to turn around a plane at the gate in 30 minutes or less.

The main takeaway is that this exercise of refinement for the measurement of services will lead to more meaningful precision. This will constitute a primary focus of management for the service side of the business for decades to come.

Beyond One-Dimensional Measurement

How do we know what we know? Organizational management still fails to ask this question often enough.

Unjustified leaps of faith or strategies undertaken with unrealistic assumptions continue to be the source of many failures. An important step in the right direction will be for organizations to make decisions based on information instead of gut feel. Intuition serves as a fine start. Perhaps even a potential source of inspiration. There should be sound logic to back up the case before millions of dollars of capital get put at risk.

It should be noted that prudence is not the same thing as analysis-paralysis. Some managers remain so risk-averse that they cannot make a decision at all. Safer that way. Few would disagree that this constitutes poor management practice. Still, the inevitable tension between risk and reward must be observed.

Investment advisors often suggest to individual clients, that they set aside a small portion of their portfolios to place wild bets on the market. The bulk of the investor's assets remain sheltered in more traditional vehicles. Individuals can experiment with somewhat risky investments in this manner. They never risk more than they can afford to lose. Investors as well as businesses learned this lesson the hard way in the aftermath of the dotcom meltdown in the early part of the twenty-first century. Organizations should foster the creation of offbeat ideas in the same way. They should nurture them. They must experiment in a judicious fashion. Management should evaluate the viability of new offerings through the use of prototypes and with market trials. Customer feedback needs to be collected in this phase. Only after development of a solid business case, does it make sense for the enterprise to commit significant funds. Experiment like crazy. Evaluate all the time. Go forward with real capital only after a thorough vetting.

The case of Webvan serves as an example of a failure to perform this type of due diligence. Webvan management attempted to use the Internet along with other innovative logistics technologies to offer customers something new. The idea consisted of the development of an alternate channel for home delivery of groceries. It seems that the managers who guided the investors failed to understand the lack of newness of the concept. Nor did they appreciate how many potential competitors they faced in the cutthroat grocery business with its low margins. Yet another strike against the Webvan venture sprang from its attempt to buck a clear trend toward increased customer self-service. Many grocery stores after World War II did in fact deliver groceries. Over time, these smaller stores lost the market to modern day supermarkets. The large, new stores provided cheaper products. Customers preferred the less expensive alternative even though it meant they had to shop for themselves.

Customer preferences can no doubt change over time. Online purchase might prove popular one day. Home delivery could come back into vogue. New technologies that enable workers to pick and pack groceries sounds cool.

The Webvan model relied on some assumptions. Perhaps customers would pay a premium. Maybe Webvan's use of new technology could strip out enough costs from the supply chain in a sustainable fashion to be competitive. This scenario rests on a second order condition that depends on the inability of the now common supermarket to respond. Supermarkets might offer a similar service. They might find ways to lower their prices even more. No doubt, these issues appeared surmountable for Webvan in its formative stages. It seems clear now that the business model was not challenged with sufficient rigor. Unwarranted enthusiasm too, often carried the day in the heyday of the dotcom era.

The point is that you never know. The flashes of brilliant insight that lead to presentations in front of excited venture capitalists, do not always hold water in the real world. A little extra homework often pays off.

Webvan went ahead full bore. They tried to build an entire network as fast as possible. The Webvan approach put at risk, large amounts of investment capital before it underwent sufficient scrutiny. The project failed.

It is difficult to predict what customers will embrace in advance of the fact. Qwest, a major telecommunications carrier, thought it had hit on a hot new product in the Spring of 2000. The idea was to offer broadband data transport of between 3 Mbps up to 100 Mbps over the Internet. Qwest partnered with a wholesale provider that was building out its national footprint. Because the national build-out was in its early stages, it was determined that a market trial would be the best way to gauge which bandwidths and price points, customers would find most attractive.

The fixed Wireless Local Loop (WLL) technology was designed to offer customers substantial bandwidth through the combined network of Qwest and its partner, thus bypassing the incumbent monopoly carrier. This move was expected to reduce provisioning time substantially. It is not unusual, for example, for incumbent local carriers to require 90 days or more to provision the kind of high bandwidth Qwest proposed to offer. Their WLL product could be provisioned inside of 10 days.

The service was based on transmitting point-to-point signals from rooftops of 18 buildings in the San Jose area, that were available for the duration of the trial. Service was limited to the businesses and organizations in the "lit" buildings, all multi-tenant structures.

Operational capabilities were established across departmental groups within Qwest and between its partner. Training materials were developed and rolled out to the Qwest sales force in San Jose. Prior to the trial launch, the sales representatives were queried regarding their perception of the offering. Without exception, the entire sales team was enthusiastic about the product's prospects and was anxious to begin selling it. This perspective meshed well with management's view that Qwest and its partner had a winning technology on its hands.

Immediately after the training, the sales representatives canvassed the tenants in the 18 buildings in which the wireless broadband service was available. After six weeks of intense prospecting, not a single circuit had been sold. Why?

While the initial concept had been attractive (as is often the case with new product concepts), the reality proved otherwise. One of the roadblocks to success had to do with the nature of the customers in the service coverage area. The occupants of the multi-tenant buildings were employees of branch offices of larger corporate entities, or small business owners. Neither group required such large amounts of bandwidth—not even a 3 Mbps connection on the low end of the offering, much less anything approaching 100 Mbps.

Further, pricing of the WLL product was only slightly discounted, relative to the dedicated Internet over fiber offering by other carriers, so WLL was perceived as expensive. Unfortunately, the pricing obtained from Qwest's partner did not enable steep discounts on the service because of their cost to build out the network.

Weather was also a factor, as the signal from building to building could be affected by rain or snow. While this particular issue had been anticipated and could have been addressed by boosting the signal in certain weather conditions, taken together with the other objections, the WLL service was a nonstarter.

One of the assumptions that had been made about the WLL offering was that it could be provisioned to locations where fiber connections were not readily available—across rivers in metro areas, for example. These initial assumptions proved faulty. WLL's reach between buildings was only three miles or less. Further, the reality was that a large corporate site that would utilize such large blocks of bandwidth made for a very attractive customer. One or more telecommunication carriers would invariably dig a trench across almost any obstacle to provide a fiber connection.

So for all the perceived advantages of WLL by Qwest that included short provisioning time, competitive service levels, substantial broadband capacity, there were unanticipated impediments to customer acceptance. New technologies are often viewed from an overly optimistic lens that fails to pan out upon closer inspection. Happily, in Qwest's case, the company chalked up the single-city trial as a learning experience instead of a far more costly failed national rollout.

In addition to an unwavering reliance on hard data as the basis for decisions, organizations must measure the right things. Measurements must change over time. The market is dynamic. Market shifts can take the form of consumer tastes or government-mandated public policy directives. Measurements should be dynamic also. All measurements get stale after a while. A good rule of thumb proposes old measures be discarded once an organization meets them in a consistent fashion. More meaningful gauge of success will be necessary.

Quantification of organizational performance challenges management because it is hard to derive a set of measures that presents a complete picture.[5] The issue stems from the nature of information because it takes different forms. Organizations very often manage through the use of individual data points or statistics. One-dimensional measurements fail to capture a systematic view of things. Managers need to understand performance in terms of structures of information. Multiple points of measurement must be taken for the same item or output. This requires a 3-D view of things, whether for individual service levels or overall business cases.

Excising the Bloat

All useful information we carry in our heads consists of structures. The ability to spout statistics or trivia at the drop of a hat may be impressive. Too often it does not generate sustained value. It does not help you make informed decisions.

Individuals or organizations that provide services of value do so, because they grasp the issues in a multifaceted manner. The nature of their offering will not be as simple as it looks on the outside. The measurement of sophistication of tangible products remains much farther evolved and practiced than that of services. It is not hard to see why.

Products consist of processed materials that lend themselves to definition. They can be seen and touched. The important attributes become clear to customers without much effort. A product can be measured with a ruler. It consists of very specific functions. The output is visible: a piece of furniture, a CD player. Important features for automobiles might include speed, acceleration, size, comfort, or reliability. A product must meet one of its definable specifications. If not, it can be sent back to the manufacturer or perhaps discounted.

Services are not like that. They are more intangible, more difficult to measure. Attributes vary. Even so, certain themes do recur, such as speed of delivery. Cycle time is another such. How long from start to finish? How many errors? Is there a work output such as a report? Measurement of services gets better all the time. What does management do to make that happen?

Organizations improve data collection on everything, from the details on customer defections to share of total customer spend.[6] The impact hits products too. In addition to pure services, organizations combine tangible goods or types of hardware with service components as well.

It is funny how customers often tend to focus on the stuff at the expense of the intangibles. The service component may very well be greater than the cost of the items—sometimes several times greater. We also take a lot for granted when we purchase or specify services. Anyone who ever sealed a bargain on the basis of a handshake can attest to this. Handshake deals create ripe opportunities for a wide assortment of divergent, unspoken assumptions on both sides. Parties anxious to close the deal, often utter those famous last words: "We can work out the details later."

The leverage that the buyer retains in negotiation, disappears after the contract gets signed. The seller finds substantial motivation to provide the minimal acceptable output in order to ensure profitability. The buyer receives no guarantee of performance or delivery without the documented metrics necessary to define a service. The only real opportunity to do this, occurs in advance of a signed contract.

The specification of services to be documented in an agreement requires that you look for multiple measures. The list should also be short and salient. As pointed out earlier, some organizations identify so many metrics—thousands in some cases—that it trivializes the process. A tight list of well-considered metrics for all services consumed by organizations will prove fundamental to managerial success in the years ahead. A discrete process should make use of no more than a dozen attributes. If you come with a hundred, how will you know which ones to focus on?

As the industrialized world continues to transition from a manufacturing dominated economy to a service dominated one, measurement methodologies will improve. These types of thoughtful measures should be used both within the organization and across its boundaries. "Contracts" within organizations lack the rigor of explicit contracts between external parties. This explains why the methodology for outsourcing remains farther along. Managers should tap outsourcing methodologies to induce similar rigor inside their own organizations.

Detailed service descriptions and service levels that characterize good outsourcing agreements also form a very good basis for interorganizational services. Internal monopolies that provide services to the larger organization should be subject to the same discipline that would be expected from an outsourcer. Otherwise internal organizational performance cannot be analyzed in a meaningful fashion.

This principle offers several advantages to management. For one, it provides regular measures of performance for areas not subject to any sort of market rigor. In addition, the way to open up the option for outsourcing relies in large measure on compartmentalization of a given function. All key aspects of service should be spelled out with the same detail expected from an outsourcer for department level coordination. Agreements within organizational boundaries should not look so different from those outside.

Services present challenges in this regard. Direct labor inputs as well as many material costs do not match up to specific service products in the post-industrial age. In order to do so, would mean activities must be tracked and managed. Aggregation of service costs into overhead results in arbitrary allocations back to individual products, departments, or business units. In the course of this exercise, some products or departments get hit with overcharges. Others receive indirect subsidies.[7]

This explains why executives often fail to understand their cost structures in terms of specific resource allocation. Few know the contribution of those resources to the organizational mission. This lack of awareness manifests itself in many ways. The inability to produce an accurate P&L statement by product line or service category suggests one example. Granular P&Ls in large organizations contain black box categories such as SG&A, to the extent that they exist at all. These large overhead items can comprise 20 or 30 percent of the total cost structure for a given division or business unit. They mask a host of inefficiencies.

SG&A costs, too often get allocated in an arcane fashion that can be understood by a few people in the Finance department. If the measures are explicit, then they may be arbitrary. These formulas for overhead allocation can include items like headcount, floor space consumed, or revenues. Such quick and dirty indicators may or may not reflect the actual costs that a company incurs product by product, service by service.[8]

These kinds of superficial measures represent inadequate proxies for overhead. Let us consider headcount. It often correlates well with other questionable proxies anyway, like floor space used. The IT function for a given organization may allocate its costs to other departments as part of the overall SG&A expense. A large department will be hit with much larger overhead costs than smaller groups if you use headcount as a foundation for that allocation. The large department may contain basic computers with basic applications that use minimal network or mainframe resources. Compare this with a small group of engineers who drive heavy horsepower desktops that pull substantial network or mainframe resources from the IT infrastructure. This group of power users will pay a much smaller overhead tax on a departmental basis.

Such an approach does not describe an equitable arrangement. Nor does it paint an accurate picture for senior management of the resources consumed, relative to their value added. Yet, such blunt methods, to pass along the SG&A burden across an organization, remain very common in medium or large organizations.

Specific service or information (e.g. SG&A) costs for bundled products also get harder to identify. This occurs because the proportion of service inputs for physical goods overall, increases all the time.

It is often difficult to cut through the SG&A fog to see what value is actually added in any given area. These include information technology, human resources, procurement, and finance/accounting. Potential savings or efficiencies cannot be identified. Here again, the thoughtful search for appropriate, meaningful measurements must become an ongoing effort. Prospective benchmarks must be vetted and debated, prototyped and tested. Establishing a solid baseline—an accurate "before" picture of the function targeted for improvement (including costs)—will be essential. Refinement will then come over time. It is not magic, but it is still a process too often neglected by senior management.

It bears repetition. A service economy is *not* a manufacturing economy. This means that the next frontier for management will be the dissection of the internal service monopoly found in manufacturing as well as service organizations. Estimates suggest that just US $1.4 trillion of the US $19 trillion spent by companies worldwide on SG&A, or about 8 percent, is outsourced.[9] The amount of SG&A functions outsourced will be certain to grow in the years ahead. Research demonstrates that high

SG&A overhead is a reliable predictor of information services outsourcing. This is a direct response by management efforts to reign in excessive cost structures.[10]

Governance mechanisms like outsourcing serve as a tool. The utility of outsourcing frees organizations of the need to become expert in too many areas. Outsourcing should not be used to relieve management from its responsibility. Yet that happens. The prospect of outsourcing often gets invoked as a last resort by management to attempt to rectify its own failure to impose discipline on the organization from within.

A case in point can be illustrated with the case of a privately held industrial company in the Southern and Midwestern United States. The company comprises several semi-autonomous facilities. They nonetheless shared many common needs that included IT functions. The facility general managers accumulated significant IT resources on-site that consisted of hardware, software, and personnel. The general managers refuse to give up these resources. This, despite the clear gains in organizational efficiency that could be derived. The company's top management entertains the idea of outsourcing, every few years to try to address these issues.

The headquarters executives know an outsourcer would consolidate the six or seven geographically separated data centers into one or two right away. A no-brainer. Executive management should have pushed this idea through long ago. Yet they lack the resolve to do so. The general managers have dug their heels in the ground, which leaves headquarters management stumped. If the data centers ever do get consolidated, it will take an out-sourcer to push the change through. The SG&A for the company in the meantime, will remain much higher than necessary. It will be masked by inaccurate overhead allocations.

Good management also means good measurement. Such analysis would help managers identify areas in need of an operational shakeup. Executives can use outsourcing to implement unpleasant change but disciplined and innovative management would achieve the same ends. So, the question that organizations in the industrialized economies face, focuses less on outsourcing per se than one might imagine. The issue revolves around the discipline that outsourcing might impose on the internal monopoly.

The fact that organizations often do not understand their cost structures at a rational, actionable level continues to be big problem. It leads executives to some pretty dysfunctional behaviors.

Executives still invoke across-the-board cuts of say 10 percent. A nice round number that is also a very blunt tool. Such tidy organizational directives demonstrate a clear admission by management that while inefficiencies exist, no one knows where they are. So the solution consists of shared pain all around. This may seem attractive from a political standpoint. It requires minimal analysis. It sure makes things simpler. In other words, it is a quick fix.

Departments or product groups that operate with comparative efficiency or that nurture new service offerings in the early stages of growth get punished. Bloated departments benefit from their ability to pad or game the budget process. The mature product groups that should be harvested to fund new areas of growth, instead emerge from the process more or less intact.

Across-the-board cuts should be another red flag to board members and investors (our often complacent principals). Management signals its inability to manage the enterprise in a systematic manner when it goes this route. Executives that shoot from the hip in such fashion, chart a course for failure. More thoughtful competitors who base their decisions on facts will displace the one-dimensional old school boys.

Intuition, underpinned by superficial surveys of the landscape too often proves incorrect. Sometimes you have to know what you do not know. It can be just as important as what you do know. In the final analysis, executives should be cautious about any attempt to draw too straight a line from problem to solution based on "common sense."

The Value of Information

George Bush, the senior, once said that we should be careful how far we rely on a nonmanufacturing-centered economy. He commented that we could only deliver so many pizzas to each other. This view of the new economy far oversimplifies the notion of service in an economy no longer dominated by manufacturing and agriculture. It fails to acknowledge the positive changes that will be driven by the digitization and portability of information. Voice recognition technologies drive improved productivity in communications, finance, and travel industries. Shape recognition technologies can be used to catalog irises or facial features for identification purposes. Individuals are empowered through better information and more control, if perhaps the new technologies also include an element of self-service.[11] The transition from a product-oriented economy to a service-oriented economy portends many implications that are not well understood in the main. Yet, we have been through this kind of transition before. Agriculture constituted the bulk of the output of the U.S. economy prior to the industrial revolution. Now it makes up about 2 percent of employment. In fact, the industrialized countries must impose tariffs or quotas in order to preserve what little agricultural work still exists there. Manufacturing jobs often receive similar artificial protection. One wonders what the steady state portion of the workforce will turn out to be for manufacturing. Higher than the 2 percent for agriculture probably. Perhaps 4 percent? 10 percent or 15 percent? Who can say? Where will new jobs come from if this is true?

Services, in all of its manifestations, will continue to comprise more and more of the economy's employment. Services will be an integral part of the overall value proposition of manufactured products in many cases. Either way, manufacturing will make up an ever-smaller relative share of the economy in terms of jobs. We got very efficient at production of food over the past hundred years. We get more efficient at the production of goods every day.

The service component of everything we buy or consume changes often as well. It must be emphasized that services should not be defined as a luxury or overhead. They form an integral part of society's ability to increase standards of living. Managers continue to develop new techniques for the service economy. By and large, this will be done on a trial and error basis, just as was the case with the rise of the divisional organization in the manufacturing era.

Managers now realize that organizations possess organizational or information assets in addition to physical capital assets. These provide the potential for definable value although they remain difficult to measure. Much of the value of information interweaves with the capital spent on IT over the past few decades. The manner in which organizations structure themselves to reengineer processes, also derives from the capabilities of information technology.[12]

The changes underway signify a fundamental shift from the manufacturing paradigm. They will define the challenges that dominate leading practice for decades. Firms will transition from an organizational logic based on the industrial era, to one based on the information age. IT resources will become more critical than ever.[13]

Information technology comprises intangible assets housed within organizations. These assets should be engineered to provide durable value to the organization. Strategy needs to reflect all of the assets that an organization maintains, not just the tangible ones. Part of the difficulty lies in the fact that some intangible assets have value. Some do not. Information will become subject to *all* of the following activities to be of use:

- Identification
- Classification
- Documentation

- Reporting
- Evaluation
- Integration
- Leveraging

The ability to do all of these things will be a key challenge in the decades ahead.

A sample measure of success would be how well the intellectual capital of one employee can be transferred or accessed by another one, thousands of miles away. Another would be the degree to which the customer associates the organization's brand with a perception of value that extends beyond any single individual employed by the enterprise. One person in the company does not constitute a brand—not even the CEO—unless he is Colonel Sanders, and he sells fried chicken.

Many measures that appeared to undergo, what one might call a fashionable transformation in the dotcom ramp-up, will revert back to first principles. Market share must, one day translate into profitability. Companies must sooner or later make money for the investors. It does not matter how far-reaching the potential scale economies or network effects.[14]

A key difficulty associated with the new economy revolves around the fact that many of the measures of information assets do not conform well to traditional reporting criteria. An installed customer base represents an asset for a software or web-based firm. Indeed it can be the primary basis on which to base acquisitions. Yet this measure does not merit formal valuation in external financial statements.

Other potential measures of firm value not tracked in a formal way include, relationship-based and intellectual assets. These items show up in aggregate, as a function of the share price or market capitalization of the firm. Worse, they appear in a nebulous entry on the balance sheet as goodwill.[15]

A single fact or measurement cannot define a service. Definition of the important facets of a service can often be problematic. Services must be scoped. A very big process will be unwieldy unless dissected into more granular components. Services should be well defined. They ought to relate back to a business need. Services need to be measurable. The method of measurement must be agreed upon in advance. An often overlooked point is that services must be enforceable. Consequences must be associated with nonperformance. Penalties for failure to meet minimum thresholds remain essential. The use of rewards to shape behavior can be appropriate as well.

Services become subject to sporadic or nonexistent measurement without such a structure. This introduces an unwarranted lack of objectivity into the equation. It means that the value provided will be dependent on interpretation.

Contrast the above potential subjectivity of a service with that of a physical product. It must meet some combination of weight, physical dimensions, and performance characteristics in order to be accepted. A box of rubber bands, half of which are broken and the other half inflexible, would be rejected by the buyer. No manager or peer could remark that the box of rubber bands performs well or has desirable characteristics. Yet cursory impressions often carry the day, with service contracts or outsourcing arrangements. Significant disagreements often surface about the value provided as a result of the transaction. This should not be the case.

New and Improved Organization

Organizations undergo a transformation of sorts as they grow. A small shop that used to be a flexible, turn-on-a-dime operation becomes more stable. It develops into a more rule-based entity if only because many more people need to know the rules. Social cohesion and organizational consistency depend upon it.

The large organization can be more difficult to direct. This explains why CEOs successful at smaller organizations often fail to make the transition to larger ones (and sometimes vice versa). Large organizations retain the power to allocate greater chunks of societal resources and management must accept an implicit responsibility to manage them.

The mix of responsibilities of the CEO changes as organizations grow. Managers of small organizations can make intuitive, hip shot decisions with minimal ill effect. This truism applies because often those decisions can be reversed almost as fast. Poor decision-making will be much more expensive or even fatal for larger organizations.

A large organization consists of a bundle of capabilities. It develops a combination of skills over its lifetime. Effective deployment of assets does not happen overnight. Processes are unique. Capabilities remain static at any point in time, similar to a balance sheet.

Strategy must align with those organization's capabilities in order for it to be successful. A gap occurs when strategy changes because of market or regulatory changes. Part of effective management involves the recognition of the gap. Then management must be realistic about how to close it. Bigger gaps between the targets versus capabilities means longer lead times to redirect the organization. More resources will be required to bridge the divide.

This demonstrates why sweeping strategy changes implemented by a mercurial CEO's vision can be so problematic. The apt analogy would be to try to operate a supertanker like a speedboat. A supertanker will not win a short sprint. On the other hand it can accomplish large-scale operations quite well. It can weather storms like no speedboat.

Large and medium-sized organizations maintain a certain leverage that is still not well understood. Very basic decisions at high levels can drive action that propagates across many divisions. Departments will be affected across the board. Product groups will be forced to take time to sift through the implications. Prudence must always be in order.

The impacts of decisions have much far-reaching effects as economies transition from physical labor to services. Larger organizations make the issue even more salient because executives hold sway over so many more resources. A laborer who misapplies a technique in production can do just so much damage. Perhaps a few hundred or thousand dollars. A mistake at a more strategic levels by an aloof, autonomous, high-level executive can cost millions, even billions of dollars. The organization may even fail to survive at all.

Challenges continue to persist in the search for competent governance to manage growth. Executives will always struggle to maintain focus. They should evaluate the activities taken on, in every instance. This will become an ever greater priority ahead. Management often picks up activities not related to the core mission as organizations grow over decades. Though growth often gets touted as a key goal of most organizations, sometimes it can be less than optimal.

Internal firm governance tends to become less efficient than the market as organizations grow. More data on usage patterns and features becomes available once a product or service gains acceptance. More firms enter the market. More firms or suppliers mean buyers have more choice. Standard interfaces also increase the number of competitors. Organizations develop more specialized enhancements in the process. Management harvests business units. Outsourcing increases. Start-ups emerge. A new cycle of growth begins.

Again, no absolute rule exists about what type of control structure works best for an organization. As with economics, the dynamics of organization contain elements of individual choice, group behavior, and history. All organizations must operate within environments whose rules get set by a larger constituency.

Organizations must also decide what to control from headquarters or delegate to the field. The dominant communication patterns of the business will dictate the appropriate amount of control in some cases. It will make more sense for senior management to coordinate at a high level where significant network synergies exist. Airlines fall into this category because of their high degree of interactive connectivity. Network effects for hospitals and retail stores figures in less than customer service issues. A more distributed or decentralized hierarchy will apply in these cases.[16]

Organizational form will continue to change based on the increased availability of distributed technologies. They will depend on the innovative managers who take advantage of them. New types of organization will emerge. Old ones will continue to die off.

No doubt, an organization can take on too much. The availability of so many services offered by so many companies means that the burden of proof should fall on the management. The leaders of these organizations (and governments) must demonstrate why any particular function ought to be performed on the inside. The market now provides too many alternatives to ignore.

The Challenges and the Trends

Why are the old school boys headed for obsolescence? The reasons go beyond personalities or temporary trends. The factors beneath the surface derive from structural elements.

Today's old school boy lasted so long because the outputs of the manufacturing era could be measured. Technical skills counted at least as much as people skills for mechanized manager. When the machines do most of the work, less emphasis gets put on interaction with people. So the system tolerated old school. They functioned well enough in an environment that made limited demands. That was then. Things have changed.

Most managers on the service side of the economy, for the bulk of the twentieth century, got by one way or the other. Fat profit margins cover a multitude of sins. Bankers, brokers, attorneys, CPAs, insurance agents, consultants, and many others in the service industry lived a charmed life for years. Now they too are under siege by competition from many quarters just like everybody else, as services are forced to become more productive.[17] Government, a huge service industry in and of itself, will be subject to similar pressure from taxpayers who will be able to see individual transactional efficiency (or lack thereof) with much greater ease. As the world changes and puts strain on existing systems, our heretofore complacent principles (stockholders, taxpayers) will not be so complacent.

Alfred Sloan of General Motors provided a glimpse into the style of the prototype executive in the new economy. He understood the value of information. One tool he used consisted of anonymous visits to automobile dealer showrooms throughout the country. Sloan did this to get first hand knowledge of the system. He wanted to know what worked well and what did not. He asked what customers liked and what they did not like. He nosed around until he got a three-dimensional view of life on the ground for the dealers, his customers.

This sounds a lot like the theme Tom Peters harps on, called MBWA or management-by-walking-around, and will continue to be important. First-hand information of a specific situation informs like nothing else. It can make otherwise complicated issues blaze with clarity.

Such an approach has limits though. The scope of organizations will continue to grow. You cannot walk around to everywhere. You cannot put your eyes on the entire planet. This gets back to outputs and process interfaces as opposed to the process itself. These must be the focus of management in the new economy. Shorthand indicators will be vital. Management must be able to synthesize larger bodies of information.

This kind of approach requires a blend of Occam's Razor and insight from Albert Einstein. The rule of Occam's Razor states that you do not posit more than necessary when you look for answers. If, something can be explained in an equivalent fashion in more than one way, the simplest explanation will always be preferable. Einstein said that everything should be made as simple as possible—but not simpler. We get something like this if we combine the two axioms: Avoid unnecessary complexity. Do not oversimplify either.

Let us look at some examples. It got easier to think one step ahead with the introduction of new management applications after the advent of the computer. Spreadsheets in the 1980s, provided the widespread ability to map out unlimited amounts of numerical analyses. Management employed them for budgets or to chart linear trends. Robust forecasting techniques improved as well, when better applications came along.

Forecasting must be considered one of the key tools of good management despite previous cautions. It provides the ability to think ahead. Otherwise competitors will see the future first to claim it for themselves. The problem is that accurate forecasting constitutes a difficult art. Competent organizational management requires that you think multiple steps ahead. Then you must consider multiple scenarios. The most probable scenario should be laid out. Then another one, and so on and so forth until management identifies many potential futures. Competitive responses along with second-order effects must also be considered. This facet of scenario planning is a variant of game theory. The reactions of others figures into the analysis. Such an approach offers dual advantages. It appears opaque to competitors. It also does not require a great deal of complexity.

No one can say for sure what will happen in the future. Forecasts do not need to suggest that kind of certainty. The forecasting exercise serves to enable the organization to be prepared for a number of possible futures.

This helps management allow for unexpected situations that might not otherwise receive serious consideration.

Robust forecasting as well as scenario planning should include sufficient use of if-then analysis. You might be surprised to learn how much complexity can be generated from multiple iterations that start with simple programs.[18] We should try to understand the nature of these simple rules first, because they can weave very intricate fabrics. We can always look for more complex explanations later.

Lengthy iteration remains far too underutilized as a management tool. The technique requires that you run extended scenarios over and over again. Each time you run it with somewhat different assumptions. While unremarkable at the outset, the final output can provide unexpected insight when run at length.

Instead, managers tend to rely too much on deduction or fundamental insight. These wicked brainstorms might *perhaps* result in the dramatic transformation of business models or entire industries. Often they disintegrate under scrutiny. Still, adherents abound. The mainstay of solid management technique lies elsewhere.

The best organizational strategies do not rely on staggering complexity. They do depend on well-thought out, well-executed strategies. This basic fact alone gives other organizations trouble when they try to compete head-on.

Most people fall into a rut when they try to look ahead into the future. The average manager does not make use of more than a few years worth of history. It is easier to remember. While secular (long-term) trends may be apparent in many ways, the near-term picture gets a whole lot harder to predict. The road to the future cuts and weaves like a bad driver. Figure 8.1 illustrates this effect.

Let us use economic growth as an example. It remains pretty steady over time-on average. Yet the cycles do not confirm to any consistent pattern from day to day or year to year. Even decade to decade.

Investment in dotcom companies created billionaires overnight in the late 1990s. The trend seemed to extend as far as the eye could see. In the year 2000, forecasts of fiber optic shortages and exponential Internet growth harkened back to events that kicked off not much earlier than 1995, with the public offering of Netscape. People can get very optimistic for a while only to then get just as pessimistic. So the route to the future will meander. It will not be a straight line.

Probabilities as well as expected outcomes for individuals or organizations also need to be better understood. Take the risk/regret tradeoff.[19] Were the downsides associated with Bhopal, Chernobyl, Challenger, Exxon Valdez, SARS, Barings, Long Term Capital Management, Enron,

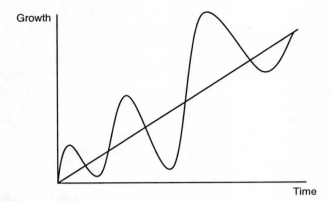

Figure 8.1   The Real Path to the Future

WorldCom, Columbia, and so on considered to an adequate degree? The periodic regularity of such events bears out that organizations (governments as well) do not factor in enough risk to their plans. The risk associated with a strategy or decision cannot be assessed if the worst-case scenario does not get plugged into the analysis. Mr. Wizard cannot wave a wand to get you out if the worst cases become a reality and you do not have an action plan.

Organizations also struggle to truly understand cause and effect. This holds true in particular, for second order effects. A policy change at one end of the organization will cascade down and throughout the system. Senior management sets itself up for failure when it makes command decisions without consultation or consensus. Executives must understand the issues at hand in a multilayered fashion. Otherwise they set themselves up for trouble. The law of unintended consequences often comes up in the context of government activity. It also holds for business organizations and nonprofits. Senior management still too often tends to make broad pronouncements without examining second or third order effects.

Research by Skinner demonstrates that managers must shift their perspectives back and forth, from near-term to long-term, from detail to big-picture all the time. The organization does not operate in isolation. Events that influence success come from many unexpected directions. The emphasis of this book, on views of governance from the inside as well as outside of organizations, derives from the need to shift from micro to macro viewpoints as well. The various perspectives will often provide valuable insight.[20]

Details matter. Executives who can only articulate some fuzzy big picture future will not survive in the new economy. Managers must ask themselves a series of questions all the time when they form strategy: What then? What if this? What if that? We should try to assemble some kind of full-bodied map of the future. This gets us closer to Pasteur's insight about the process of discovery: "Chance favors the prepared mind."

We cannot predict the future with certitude. We cannot even predict every possible scenario. But managers and executives can identify and consider a wide range of future possibilities that help them make smarter, more durable decisions. All of this while still perched in the present. Right now, today, we still have time to act. This presents a more pleasant alternative than being blindsided tomorrow. It is hard to understand why that still happens to so many executives.

The world is messy. It is chaotic. Nonetheless, such realities do not relieve management of its obligation to strive to understand the issues at hand. One can only wonder why executive decisions continue to be made by fiat.

The social, political, and economic landscapes are in the midst of epochal change. Dated management styles that could pass muster for decades in a mechanized age will no longer be sufficient. There also still exists, an entire generation of managers not well acquainted with post-mainframe technologies introduced after 1980. Significant changes in managerial offices and executive suites will occur in the decades ahead as technologies continue to increase process complexity. This transformation mirrors the economic changes at the turn of the twentieth century when large organizations learned to harness unprecedented scale.

The entire principal-agent relationship must be reexamined in order to ensure the adoption of more systematic management approaches. Near term grants of large amounts of stock options (with no appropriate P&L cost considerations) serve as a poor proxy to the true management ownership. The use of stock options appeared to work okay within a horizon of ten years or less. That is not enough. Competent management builds great organizations over a succession of ten-year periods. A CEO-agent who can amass a fortune of tens or hundreds of millions of dollars through the sale of accumulated stock options in four or five years, has to be conflicted. Further, stock options grants can clearly be manipulated to the benefit of senior executives. By October 2006, more than 30 top corporate officials had lost their jobs following option-manipulation investigations that affected at least 100 U.S. companies.[21]

Stewardship of the long-term interests of the organization will rate as an incidental concern with these kinds of outlandish incentives. Governance committees should consider basing senior management compensation on the residual performance of the organization, a year or more after they leave. After all, it will be senior management that designs the systems in place and forms part of the inertia that carries the organization forward for good or ill. Compensation committees should also consider some formula to cap how much corporate stewards receive before policy-makers legislate limits based on public outcry. Exxon's CEO, Lee Raymond retired in 2006 with a lump-sum pension value of US $98.4 million. True, he did spend 43 years with Exxon, but the company also footed the bill for club memberships and private use of corporate jets while he was employed.[22] This highlights just the latest event among many that has soured stakeholders on the current governance practices of large organizations. It is not at all clear that such outsized packages correlate well with performance anyway.[23] The predisposition of board of director executive search committees notwithstanding, it does not necessarily follow that, getting the best organizational talent will cost tens or hundreds of millions of dollars in the form of a single CEO. In fact, as we have seen earlier, extremely poor performing CEOs can earn multimillion dollar compensation packages.

Calpers (California Public Employees' Retirement System) developed a set of recommendations for corporate governance in 1997 that serves as a good start:

- Adopt a more stringent definition of independent director.
- The chairman should be an outside director.
- No director should serve on board than three boards.
- A formal program, in addition to the annual meeting, should be set for shareholders to communicate with directors.

In 2002, after the fall of Enron, *Director's Alert* made the following additional proposals for improved organizational governance:

- The full board of directors should meet in closed session at each board meeting without the CEO or other corporate insiders.
- Likewise, key committees of the board should meet periodically without management present.
- Key committees should be authorized to hire outside advisors and their chairmanships should be held in rotation.
- The assignments to board committees should be made by the board rather than the CEO.
- Outside directors should not do consulting work for the company, nor should their employers provide services to the company.[24]

Sarbanes-Oxley codifies into law, many of the above guidelines, as well as others. Penalties can include not only fines, but prison time also. However, legislation can only go so far. We cannot criminalize bad management, no matter how much we might be tempted to, at times.

Executives must be prudent about where to grow the organization as we go forward. Successive levels of bureaucracy make organizations inefficient because of the subjective diffusion of information.[25] While new technologies can assuage complexity, the scope of the enterprise must be analyzed in a rational manner on a regular basis. Large organizations evolve over extended periods. They never operate at optimal efficiency. They must be considered a work in progress as their operations depend on a complex network of players.[26] It takes time for an executive to gain a meaningful knowledge of any given organization's capabilities. There are no short cuts to sound leadership.

As always, the rigor of the market will serve to continue to improve organizational function in the twenty-first century. The transition to a service economy will be marked by the following realities:

- Componentization of organizations will enable greater collaboration, increased specialization, modularity, and higher efficiency.
- Organizations will develop better service process measurements and crisp points of interface inside their boundaries as well as across them.
- Roughly Right measures of meaningful outputs will be employed— even if early information is imperfect—rather than a dependence on false precision and irrelevant measures.
- Improved, more robust forecasting that incorporates a variety of well-developed scenarios will hedge against the inherent difficulty in predicting the future.
- Greater rigor will be required of executive judgment based on a thoughtful understanding of the issues at hand and an unflinching willingness to acknowledge hard realities.
- Increased accountability of senior managers, executives, and board members for long-term, sustainable performance of the organization will also be required. Greater organizational transparency will help ensure that no more Enrons will be allowed.
- Dysfunctional behaviors at all levels of organization, such as information hoarding and empire building will be exposed for the snake oil they are. Management will be focused on outputs, process interfaces, and clear rules of engagement.
- Management will come to terms with the inseparability of people, services, information/knowledge, and transaction costs.
- Structured, systematic approaches that make full use of information will be the price of admission to the management ranks in medium and large organizations.

- All managers will have to be well-versed with information technology, even those outside of traditional IT departments.
- Markets and outsourcing will impose a steady erosion of regulatory burdens as well as internal monopolies that now cause organizations to operate in an inefficient and uncompetitive manner.

In the end, organizational efficiency will have to compare itself to the market. The charter for all management will be to challenge itself as well as the organization against the discipline of the market at all levels, in all areas, with regard to all functions. The organization cannot afford submarket performance anywhere, if a chain is as strong as its weakest link. Those classified as overhead will come under particular scrutiny. Service functions will be compelled to become more efficient. This will be a growth industry in the new economy.

This means that manufacturing will not be the engine of job growth in the future. It will remain important to society for its outputs just as agriculture has. The next phase of economic development in the leading economies will be focused on people, service, information, and transaction costs. These components will take many forms. They may serve as an input to manufacturing products. They can be products in their own right. They may fuel the growth of nascent industries that have information-laden components like biotechnology. Less obvious, will be the service industries that drive the manufacture of computers, paper, printers, CDs, etc.

The information, service, and intellectual property components provide increased proportions of the value. So it remains essential that managers understand this transition. Effective management of services must ensure that multifaceted plans, combined with consequential measurement mechanisms, remain integral to the refinement of these abstract outputs. The service economy cannot be managed like the manufacturing dominated economy. More sophisticated metrics will be the price of admission.

Management will struggle with these issues. Yet they will be overcome. The apt analogy continues to be the efforts by competent managers in the first half of the twentieth century. They reconciled the implications of unprecedented scale that came with mass industrialization. Service industry managers will reconcile the fungible nature of information.

The process is underway even now. Insightful leaders realize that the disciplined management of service outputs will determine organizational performance.

The 1960s signified the golden age of mechanized management. The next golden age remains decades away. Too much work remains to be done in the meantime. Services constitute the next great challenge to be overcome. Opportunities abound, if perhaps incremental ones. We only just begin to tap the potential of the future that lies before us. We will get there soon enough, but not yet. The winners, whether they be organizations or nations, remains to be seen. The title is up for grabs for the moment.

In short, the service and information economy will necessitate that governance be more systematic than ever before. Organizations will not operate in a closed system that was the hallmark of the divisional organization of the twentieth century. Open, feedback-intensive systems driven by decreased transaction costs, will be the order of the day. Real evidence will be required in order to make decisions. Otherwise, organizations, management, and their stakeholders will be deprived of greater success and better managers.[27] They will be at a competitive disadvantage.

Successful managers will be thoughtful, well informed. They will be open to dissent. No one is so much smarter than anyone else that they cannot demonstrate a little civility. We learn more when we listen than when we pontificate anyway. Executives will also be decisive as well as consistent. Once they make a decision, they will stick with it.

Such a change in approach will be a culture shock for the old school boys. It will be inevitable just the same. Rigor and discipline define the market. The market benchmark is a comparison, a point of reference. It is a reality check to make sure you are not about to drive over a cliff. It is an X-ray machine that will give everyone a good look inside the organizational black box.

The market benchmark should be used on a regular basis. Every aspect of organizational operation will be subject to the market as we go forward. It will be the new standard of performance at all levels of organization.

APPENDIX—NAICS NEW SERVICES SECTORS (2002)

Information (51)

511	Publishing Industries (except Internet)
5111	Newspaper, Periodical, Book, and Directory Publishers
51111	Newspaper Publishers
511110	Newspaper Publishers
51112	Periodical Publishers
511120	Periodical Publishers
51113	Book Publishers
511130	Book Publishers
51114	Directory and Mailing List Publishers
511140	Directory and Mailing List Publishers
51119	Other Publishers
511191	Greeting Card Publishers
511199	All Other Publishers
5112	Software Publishers
51121	Software Publishers
511210	Software Publishers
512	Motion Picture and Sound Recording Industries
5121	Motion Picture and Video Industries
51211	Motion Picture and Video Production
512110	Motion Picture and Video Production
51212	Motion Picture and Video Distribution
512120	Motion Picture and Video Distribution
51213	Motion Picture and Video Exhibition
512131	Motion Picture Theaters (except Drive-Ins)
512132	Drive-In Motion Picture Theaters
51219	Postproduction Services and Other Motion Picture and Video Industries

512191	Teleproduction and Other Postproduction Services
512199	Other Motion Picture and Video Industries
5122	Sound Recording Industries
51221	Record Production
512210	Record Production
51222	Integrated Record Production/Distribution
512220	Integrated Record Production/Distribution
51223	Music Publishers
512230	Music Publishers
51224	Sound Recording Studios
512240	Sound Recording Studios
51229	Other Sound Recording Industries
512290	Other Sound Recording Industries
515	Broadcasting (except Internet)
5151	Radio and Television Broadcasting
51511	Radio Broadcasting
515111	Radio Networks
515112	Radio Stations
51512	Television Broadcasting
515120	Television Broadcasting
5152	Cable and Other Subscription Programming
51521	Cable and Other Subscription Programming
515210	Cable and Other Subscription Programming
516	Internet Publishing and Broadcasting
5161	Internet Publishing and Broadcasting
51611	Internet Publishing and Broadcasting
516110	Internet Publishing and Broadcasting
517	Telecommunications
5171	Wired Telecommunications Carriers
51711	Wired Telecommunications Carriers
517110	Wired Telecommunications Carriers
5172	Wireless Telecommunications Carriers (except Satellite)
51721	Wireless Telecommunications Carriers (except Satellite)
517211	Paging
517212	Cellular and Other Wireless Telecommunications
5173	Telecommunications Resellers
51731	Telecommunications Resellers
517310	Telecommunications Resellers
5174	Satellite Telecommunications
51741	Satellite Telecommunications
517410	Satellite Telecommunications

5175	Cable and Other Program Distribution
51751	Cable and Other Program Distribution
517510	Cable and Other Program Distribution
5179	Other Telecommunications
51791	Other Telecommunications
517910	Other Telecommunications
518	Internet Service Providers, Web Search Portals, and Data Processing Services
5181	Internet Service Providers and Web Search Portals
51811	Internet Service Providers and Web Search Portals
518111	Internet Service Providers
518112	Web Search Portals
5182	Data Processing, Hosting, and Related Services
51821	Data Processing, Hosting, and Related Services
518210	Data Processing, Hosting, and Related Services
519	Other Information Services
5191	Other Information Services
51911	News Syndicates
519110	News Syndicates
51912	Libraries and Archives
519120	Libraries and Archives
51919	All Other Information Services
519190	All Other Information Services

Professional, Scientific, and Technical Services (54)

541	Professional, Scientific, and Technical Services
5411	Legal Services
54111	Offices of Lawyers
541110	Offices of Lawyers
54112	Offices of Notaries
541120	Offices of Notaries
54119	Other Legal Services
541191	Title Abstract and Settlement Offices
541199	All Other Legal Services
5412	Accounting, Tax Preparation, Bookkeeping, and Payroll Services
54121	Accounting, Tax Preparation, Bookkeeping, and Payroll Services
541211	Offices of Certified Public Accountants
541213	Tax Preparation Services

541214	Payroll Services
541219	Other Accounting Services
5413	Architectural, Engineering, and Related Services
54131	Architectural Services
541310	Architectural Services
54132	Landscape Architectural Services
541320	Landscape Architectural Services
54133	Engineering Services
541330	Engineering Services
54134	Drafting Services
541340	Drafting Services
54135	Building Inspection Services
541350	Building Inspection Services
54136	Geophysical Surveying and Mapping Services
541360	Geophysical Surveying and Mapping Services
54137	Surveying and Mapping (except Geophysical) Services
541370	Surveying and Mapping (except Geophysical) Services
54138	Testing Laboratories
541380	Testing Laboratories
5414	Specialized Design Services
54141	Interior Design Services
541410	Interior Design Services
54142	Industrial Design Services
541420	Industrial Design Services
54143	Graphic Design Services
541430	Graphic Design Services
54149	Other Specialized Design Services
541490	Other Specialized Design Services
5415	Computer Systems Design and Related Services
54151	Computer Systems Design and Related Services
541511	Custom Computer Programming Services
541512	Computer Systems Design Services
541513	Computer Facilities Management Services
541519	Other Computer Related Services
5416	Management, Scientific, and Technical Consulting Services
54161	Management Consulting Services
541611	Administrative Management and General Management Consulting Services
541612	Human Resources and Executive Search Consulting Services
541613	Marketing Consulting Services

541614	Process, Physical Distribution, and Logistics Consulting Services
541618	Other Management Consulting Services
54162	Environmental Consulting Services
541620	Environmental Consulting Services
54169	Other Scientific and Technical Consulting Services
541690	Other Scientific and Technical Consulting Services
5417	Scientific Research and Development Services
54171	Research and Development in the Physical, Engineering, and Life Sciences
541710	Research and Development in the Physical, Engineering, and Life Sciences
54172	Research and Development in the Social Sciences and Humanities
541720	Research and Development in the Social Sciences and Humanities
5418	Advertising and Related Services
54181	Advertising Agencies
541810	Advertising Agencies
54182	Public Relations Agencies
541820	Public Relations Agencies
54183	Media Buying Agencies
541830	Media Buying Agencies
54184	Media Representatives
541840	Media Representatives
54185	Display Advertising
541850	Display Advertising
54186	Direct Mail Advertising
541860	Direct Mail Advertising
54187	Advertising Material Distribution Services
541870	Advertising Material Distribution Services
54189	Other Services Related to Advertising
541890	Other Services Related to Advertising
5419	Other Professional, Scientific, and Technical Services
54191	Marketing Research and Public Opinion Polling
541910	Marketing Research and Public Opinion Polling
54192	Photographic Services
541921	Photography Studios, Portrait
541922	Commercial Photography
54193	Translation and Interpretation Services
541930	Translation and Interpretation Services

54194	Veterinary Services
541940	Veterinary Services
54199	All Other Professional, Scientific, and Technical Services
541990	All Other Professional, Scientific, and Technical Services

Management of Companies and Enterprises (55)

551	Management of Companies and Enterprises
5511	Management of Companies and Enterprises
55111	Management of Companies and Enterprises
551111	Offices of Bank Holding Companies
551112	Offices of Other Holding Companies
551114	Corporate, Subsidiary, and Regional Managing Offices

Administrative and Support and Waste Management and Remediation Services (56)

561	Administrative and Support Services
5611	Office Administrative Services
56111	Office Administrative Services
561110	Office Administrative Services
5612	Facilities Support Services
56121	Facilities Support Services
561210	Facilities Support Services
5613	Employment Services
56131	Employment Placement Agencies
561310	Employment Placement Agencies
56132	Temporary Help Services
561320	Temporary Help Services
56133	Professional Employer Organizations
561330	Professional Employer Organizations
5614	Business Support Services
56141	Document Preparation Services
561410	Document Preparation Services
56142	Telephone Call Centers
561421	Telephone Answering Services
561422	Telemarketing Bureaus
56143	Business Service Centers
561431	Private Mail Centers
561439	Other Business Service Centers (including Copy Shops)
56144	Collection Agencies

561440	Collection Agencies
56145	Credit Bureaus
561450	Credit Bureaus
56149	Other Business Support Services
561491	Repossession Services
561492	Court Reporting and Stenotype Services
561499	All Other Business Support Services
5615	Travel Arrangement and Reservation Services
56151	Travel Agencies
561510	Travel Agencies
56152	Tour Operators
561520	Tour Operators
56159	Other Travel Arrangement and Reservation Services
561591	Convention and Visitors Bureaus
561599	All Other Travel Arrangement and Reservation Services
5616	Investigation and Security Services
56161	Investigation, Guard, and Armored Car Services
561611	Investigation Services
561612	Security Guards and Patrol Services
561613	Armored Car Services
56162	Security Systems Services
561621	Security Systems Services (except Locksmiths)
561622	Locksmiths
5617	Services to Buildings and Dwellings
56171	Exterminating and Pest Control Services
561710	Exterminating and Pest Control Services
56172	Janitorial Services
561720	Janitorial Services
56173	Landscaping Services
561730	Landscaping Services
56174	Carpet and Upholstery Cleaning Services
561740	Carpet and Upholstery Cleaning Services
56179	Other Services to Buildings and Dwellings
561790	Other Services to Buildings and Dwellings
5619	Other Support Services
56191	Packaging and Labeling Services
561910	Packaging and Labeling Services
56192	Convention and Trade Show Organizers
561920	Convention and Trade Show Organizers
56199	All Other Support Services
561990	All Other Support Services

562	Waste Management and Remediation Services
5621	Waste Collection
56211	Waste Collection
562111	Solid Waste Collection
562112	Hazardous Waste Collection
562119	Other Waste Collection
5622	Waste Treatment and Disposal
56221	Waste Treatment and Disposal
562211	Hazardous Waste Treatment and Disposal
562212	Solid Waste Landfill
562213	Solid Waste Combustors and Incinerators
562219	Other Nonhazardous Waste Treatment and Disposal
5629	Remediation and Other Waste Management Services
56291	Remediation Services
562910	Remediation Services
56292	Materials Recovery Facilities
562920	Materials Recovery Facilities
56299	All Other Waste Management Services
562991	Septic Tank and Related Services
562998	All Other Miscellaneous Waste Management Services

Educational Services (61)

611	Educational Services
6111	Elementary and Secondary Schools
61111	Elementary and Secondary Schools
611110	Elementary and Secondary Schools
6112	Junior Colleges
61121	Junior Colleges
611210	Junior Colleges
6113	Colleges, Universities, and Professional Schools
61131	Colleges, Universities, and Professional Schools
611310	Colleges, Universities, and Professional Schools
6114	Business Schools and Computer and Management Training
61141	Business and Secretarial Schools
611410	Business and Secretarial Schools
61142	Computer Training
611420	Computer Training
61143	Professional and Management Development Training
611430	Professional and Management Development Training
6115	Technical and Trade Schools
61151	Technical and Trade Schools

611511	Cosmetology and Barber Schools
611512	Flight Training
611513	Apprenticeship Training
611519	Other Technical and Trade Schools
6116	Other Schools and Instruction
61161	Fine Arts Schools
611610	Fine Arts Schools
61162	Sports and Recreation Instruction
611620	Sports and Recreation Instruction
61163	Language Schools
611630	Language Schools
61169	All Other Schools and Instruction
611691	Exam Preparation and Tutoring
611692	Automobile Driving Schools
611699	All Other Miscellaneous Schools and Instruction
6117	Educational Support Services
61171	Educational Support Services
611710	Educational Support Services

Health Care and Social Assistance (62)

621	Ambulatory Health Care Services
6211	Offices of Physicians
62111	Offices of Physicians
621111	Offices of Physicians (except Mental Health Specialists)
621112	Offices of Physicians, Mental Health Specialists
6212	Offices of Dentists
62121	Offices of Dentists
621210	Offices of Dentists
6213	Offices of Other Health Practitioners
62131	Offices of Chiropractors
621310	Offices of Chiropractors
62132	Offices of Optometrists
621320	Offices of Optometrists
62133	Offices of Mental Health Practitioners (except Physicians)
621330	Offices of Mental Health Practitioners (except Physicians)
62134	Offices of Physical, Occupational and Speech Therapists, and Audiologists
621340	Offices of Physical, Occupational and Speech Therapists, and Audiologists
62139	Offices of All Other Health Practitioners
621391	Offices of Podiatrists

621399	Offices of All Other Miscellaneous Health Practitioners
6214	Outpatient Care Centers
62141	Family Planning Centers
621410	Family Planning Centers
62142	Outpatient Mental Health and Substance Abuse Centers
621420	Outpatient Mental Health and Substance Abuse Centers
62149	Other Outpatient Care Centers
621491	HMO Medical Centers
621492	Kidney Dialysis Centers
621493	Freestanding Ambulatory Surgical and Emergency Centers
621498	All Other Outpatient Care Centers
6215	Medical and Diagnostic Laboratories
62151	Medical and Diagnostic Laboratories
621511	Medical Laboratories
621512	Diagnostic Imaging Centers
6216	Home Health Care Services
62161	Home Health Care Services
621610	Home Health Care Services
6219	Other Ambulatory Health Care Services
62191	Ambulance Services
621910	Ambulance Services
62199	All Other Ambulatory Health Care Services
621991	Blood and Organ Banks
621999	All Other Miscellaneous Ambulatory Health Care Services
622	Hospitals
6221	General Medical and Surgical Hospitals
62211	General Medical and Surgical Hospitals
622110	General Medical and Surgical Hospitals
6222	Psychiatric and Substance Abuse Hospitals
62221	Psychiatric and Substance Abuse Hospitals
622210	Psychiatric and Substance Abuse Hospitals
6223	Specialty (except Psychiatric and Substance Abuse) Hospitals
62231	Specialty (except Psychiatric and Substance Abuse) Hospitals
622310	Specialty (except Psychiatric and Substance Abuse) Hospitals
623	Nursing and Residential Care Facilities
6231	Nursing Care Facilities
62311	Nursing Care Facilities
623110	Nursing Care Facilities
6232	Residential Mental Retardation, Mental Health and Substance Abuse Facilities
62321	Residential Mental Retardation Facilities

623210	Residential Mental Retardation Facilities
62322	Residential Mental Health and Substance Abuse Facilities
623220	Residential Mental Health and Substance Abuse Facilities
6233	Community Care Facilities for the Elderly
62331	Community Care Facilities for the Elderly
623311	Continuing Care Retirement Communities
623312	Homes for the Elderly
6239	Other Residential Care Facilities
62399	Other Residential Care Facilities
623990	Other Residential Care Facilities
624	Social Assistance
6241	Individual and Family Services
62411	Child and Youth Services
624110	Child and Youth Services
62412	Services for the Elderly and Persons with Disabilities
624120	Services for the Elderly and Persons with Disabilities
62419	Other Individual and Family Services
624190	Other Individual and Family Services
6242	Community Food and Housing, and Emergency and Other Relief Services
62421	Community Food Services
624210	Community Food Services
62422	Community Housing Services
624221	Temporary Shelters
624229	Other Community Housing Services
62423	Emergency and Other Relief Services
624230	Emergency and Other Relief Services
6243	Vocational Rehabilitation Services
62431	Vocational Rehabilitation Services
624310	Vocational Rehabilitation Services
6244	Child Day Care Services
62441	Child Day Care Services
624410	Child Day Care Services

Arts, Entertainment, and Recreation (71)

711	Performing Arts, Spectator Sports, and Related Industries
7111	Performing Arts Companies
71111	Theater Companies and Dinner Theaters
711110	Theater Companies and Dinner Theaters
71112	Dance Companies

711120	Dance Companies
71113	Musical Groups and Artists
711130	Musical Groups and Artists
71119	Other Performing Arts Companies
711190	Other Performing Arts Companies
7112	Spectator Sports
71121	Spectator Sports
711211	Sports Teams and Clubs
711212	Racetracks
711219	Other Spectator Sports
7113	Promoters of Performing Arts, Sports, and Similar Events
71131	Promoters of Performing Arts, Sports, and Similar Events with Facilities
711310	Promoters of Performing Arts, Sports, and Similar Events with Facilities
71132	Promoters of Performing Arts, Sports, and Similar Events without Facilities
711320	Promoters of Performing Arts, Sports, and Similar Events without Facilities
7114	Agents and Managers for Artists, Athletes, Entertainers, and Other Public Figures
71141	Agents and Managers for Artists, Athletes, Entertainers, and Other Public Figures
711410	Agents and Managers for Artists, Athletes, Entertainers, and Other Public Figures
7115	Independent Artists, Writers, and Performers
71151	Independent Artists, Writers, and Performers
711510	Independent Artists, Writers, and Performers
712	Museums, Historical Sites, and Similar Institutions
7121	Museums, Historical Sites, and Similar Institutions
71211	Museums
712110	Museums
71212	Historical Sites
712120	Historical Sites
71213	Zoos and Botanical Gardens
712130	Zoos and Botanical Gardens
71219	Nature Parks and Other Similar Institutions
712190	Nature Parks and Other Similar Institutions
713	Amusement, Gambling, and Recreation Industries
7131	Amusement Parks and Arcades
71311	Amusement and Theme Parks

713110	Amusement and Theme Parks
71312	Amusement Arcades
713120	Amusement Arcades
7132	Gambling Industries
71321	Casinos (except Casino Hotels)
713210	Casinos (except Casino Hotels)
71329	Other Gambling Industries
713290	Other Gambling Industries
7139	Other Amusement and Recreation Industries
71391	Golf Courses and Country Clubs
713910	Golf Courses and Country Clubs
71392	Skiing Facilities
713920	Skiing Facilities
71393	Marinas
713930	Marinas
71394	Fitness and Recreational Sports Centers
713940	Fitness and Recreational Sports Centers
71395	Bowling Centers
713950	Bowling Centers
71399	All Other Amusement and Recreation Industries
713990	All Other Amusement and Recreation Industries

Other Services (Except Public Administration) (81)

811	Repair and Maintenance
8111	Automotive Repair and Maintenance
81111	Automotive Mechanical and Electrical Repair and Maintenance
811111	General Automotive Repair
811112	Automotive Exhaust System Repair
811113	Automotive Transmission Repair
811118	Other Automotive Mechanical and Electrical Repair and Maintenance
81112	Automotive Body, Paint, Interior, and Glass Repair
811121	Automotive Body, Paint, and Interior Repair and Maintenance
811122	Automotive Glass Replacement Shops
81119	Other Automotive Repair and Maintenance
811191	Automotive Oil Change and Lubrication Shops
811192	Car Washes
811198	All Other Automotive Repair and Maintenance

8112	Electronic and Precision Equipment Repair and Maintenance
81121	Electronic and Precision Equipment Repair and Maintenance
811211	Consumer Electronics Repair and Maintenance
811212	Computer and Office Machine Repair and Maintenance
811213	Communication Equipment Repair and Maintenance
811219	Other Electronic and Precision Equipment Repair and Maintenance
8113	Commercial and Industrial Machinery and Equipment (except Automotive and Electronic) Repair and Maintenance
81131	Commercial and Industrial Machinery and Equipment (except Automotive and Electronic) Repair and Maintenance
811310	Commercial and Industrial Machinery and Equipment (except Automotive and Electronic) Repair and Maintenance
8114	Personal and Household Goods Repair and Maintenance
81141	Home and Garden Equipment and Appliance Repair and Maintenance
811411	Home and Garden Equipment Repair and Maintenance
811412	Appliance Repair and Maintenance
81142	Reupholstery and Furniture Repair
811420	Reupholstery and Furniture Repair
81143	Footwear and Leather Goods Repair
811430	Footwear and Leather Goods Repair
81149	Other Personal and Household Goods Repair and Maintenance
811490	Other Personal and Household Goods Repair and Maintenance
812	Personal and Laundry Services
8121	Personal Care Services
81211	Hair, Nail, and Skin Care Services
812111	Barber Shops
812112	Beauty Salons
812113	Nail Salons
81219	Other Personal Care Services
812191	Diet and Weight Reducing Centers
812199	Other Personal Care Services

8122	Death Care Services
81221	Funeral Homes and Funeral Services
812210	Funeral Homes and Funeral Services
81222	Cemeteries and Crematories
812220	Cemeteries and Crematories
8123	Drycleaning and Laundry Services
81231	Coin-Operated Laundries and Drycleaners
812310	Coin-Operated Laundries and Drycleaners
81232	Drycleaning and Laundry Services (except Coin-Operated)
812320	Drycleaning and Laundry Services (except Coin-Operated)
81233	Linen and Uniform Supply
812331	Linen Supply
812332	Industrial Launderers
8129	Other Personal Services
81291	Pet Care (except Veterinary) Services
812910	Pet Care (except Veterinary) Services
81292	Photofinishing
812921	Photofinishing Laboratories (except One-Hour)
812922	One-Hour Photofinishing
81293	Parking Lots and Garages
812930	Parking Lots and Garages
81299	All Other Personal Services
812990	All Other Personal Services
813	Religious, Grantmaking, Civic, Professional, and Similar Organizations
8131	Religious Organizations
81311	Religious Organizations
813110	Religious Organizations
8132	Grantmaking and Giving Services
81321	Grantmaking and Giving Services
813211	Grantmaking Foundations
813212	Voluntary Health Organizations
813219	Other Grantmaking and Giving Services
8133	Social Advocacy Organizations
81331	Social Advocacy Organizations
813311	Human Rights Organizations
813312	Environment, Conservation and Wildlife Organizations
813319	Other Social Advocacy Organizations
8134	Civic and Social Organizations
81341	Civic and Social Organizations
813410	Civic and Social Organizations

8139	Business, Professional, Labor, Political, and Similar Organizations
81391	Business Associations
813910	Business Associations
81392	Professional Organizations
813920	Professional Organizations
81393	Labor Unions and Similar Labor Organizations
813930	Labor Unions and Similar Labor Organizations
81394	Political Organizations
813940	Political Organizations
81399	Other Similar Organizations (except Business, Professional, Labor, and Political Organizations)
813990	Other Similar Organizations (except Business, Professional, Labor, and Political Organizations)
814	Private Households
8141	Private Households
81411	Private Households
814110	Private Households

NOTES

Chapter 1 The High Level Framework

1. Whyte, William H. *The Organization Man*, New York: Doubleday (1956).
2. Peters, Tom and Robert Waterman. *In Search of Excellence*, New York: Harper and Row (1982).
3. Maccoby, Michael, *The Gamesman*, New York: Simon and Schuster (1977).
4. Peters, Tom. *The Pursuit of WOW!: Every Person's Guide to Topsy-Turvy Times*, New York: Random House (1994).
5. Smith, Adam. *An Inquiry into the Nature and Causes of the Wealth of Nations*, Ann Arbor: Oxford University Press (1776).
6. Smith, Adam. *The Theory of Moral Sentiments*, D.D. Raphael and A.L. MacFie, eds., Oxford: Oxford University Press (1759).
7. Ameriks, Karl and Desmond Clarke. "Introduction: The Nature of Smith's Moral Theory," in *The Theory of Moral Sentiments*, Adam Smith, ed., Cambridge: Cambridge University Press (2002) vii–xxiv.
8. Coase, Ronald. "The Nature of the Firm," *Economica*, 4 (1937) 386–405.
9. Lacity, Mary and Leslie Willcocks. "An Empirical Investigation of Information Technology Sourcing Practices: Lesson From Experience," *MIS Quarterly*, 22:3 (September 1998) 363–408.
10. Roth, A.E. "On the Early History of Experimental Economics," *Journal of the History of Economic Thought*, 15 (Fall 1993) 184–209.
11. Mero, Lazlo. *Moral Calculations: Game Theory, Logic and Human Frailty*, Springer-Verlag: New York (1998).
12. Kim, W. Chan and Renee Mauborgne. "Value Innovation: The Strategic Logic of High Growth," *Harvard Business Review* (January–February 1997) 103–12.
13. Markides, Constantinos. "Strategic Innovation," *Sloan Management Review*, 38:3 (Spring 1997) 9–23.
14. Peters, Tom and Robert Waterman. *In Search of Excellence*, New York: Harper and Row (1982).

15. Collins, Jim. *Good to Great*, New York: Harper Collins (2001).
16. Kopecki, Dawn. "New Fannie Mae Violations Surface," *Wall Street Journal* (September 29, 2005) A1
17. Kaplan, Robert and David Norton. "The Balanced Scorecard: Measures That Drive Performance," *Harvard Business Review*, 70:1 (January–February 1992) 71–9.
18. Tayntor, Christine B. *Six Sigma Software Development*, Boca Raton: CRC Press (2003).
19. McTeer, Robert. "Letter from the President," *Annual Report*, Federal Reserve Bank of Dallas (2003) 1–2.
20. Baily, Martin Neil and Diana Farrell. "Breaking Down Barriers to Growth," *Finance and Development*, 43:1 (March 2006) 23–27.
21. Xu, Jianyi, Matthew Spielelman, Robert H. McGuckin, III, Yaodong Liu and Yuan Jiang. "China's Experience with Productivity and Jobs," *The Conference Board*, Report No. R-1352–04-RR (June 2004).
22. Baily, Martin Neil and Diana Farrell. "Breaking Down Barriers to Growth," *Finance and Development*, 43:1 (March 2006) 23–7.
23. Cox, Michael W. and Richard Alm. "Have a Nice Day," *Annual Report*, Federal Reserve Bank of Dallas (2000) 1–3.
24. Hammer, Michael and James Champy. *Reengineering the Corporation: A Manifesto for Business Revolution*, New York: Harper Collins (1993).
25. Blaug, Mark. *Economic Theory in Retrospect*, 4th edition, New York: Cambridge University Press (1985).
26. Cohen, M.D., J.G. March, and J. Olsen. "A Garbage Can Theory or Organizational Choice," *Administrative Quarterly*, 17 (1972) 1–25.
27. Collins, Jim. *Good to Great*, New York: Harper Collins (2001).
28. Magretta, Joan. *What Management Is*, New York: The Free Press (2002).
29. Rousseau, Denise M. "Is There Such a Thing as 'Evidence-Based Management'?," *Academy of Management Review*, 31:2 (April 2006) 256–69.
30. Pfeffer, Jeffrey and Robert I. Sutton. *Hard Facts, Dangerous Half-Truths and Total Nonsense*, Boston: Harvard Business School Press (2006).
31. Tunstall, Thomas. "Telecommunications Policy Study for the State of Alaska": http://www.state.ak.us/itg/telecommstudy.pdf (accessed November 2002) p. 47.

Chapter 2   Governance Options

1. Poppo, Laura and Todd Zenger. "Testing Alternative Theories of the Firm: Transaction Cost, Knowledge-Based, and Measurement Explanations for Make-or-Buy Decisions in Information Services," *Strategic Management Journal*, 19 (1998) 853–77.
2. Shelanski, Howard A. and Peter G. Klein. "Empirical Research in Transaction Cost Economics," in *Firms, Markets, and Hierarchies*, Glenn R. Carroll and David J. Teece, eds., New York: Oxford University Press (1999) 89–118.

3. Klein, Benjamin, Robert G. Crawford, and Armen A. Alchian. "Vertical Integration, Appropriable Rents, and the Competitive Contracting Process," *Journal of Law and Economics*, 21 (October 1978) 297–326.
4. Oxley, Joanne E. "Appropriability Hazards and Governance in Strategic Alliances: A Transaction Cost Approach," *Journal of Law, Economics, and Organization*, 13:2 (October 1997) 387–409.
5. Malone, Thomas W. *The Future of Work: How the New Order of Business Will Shape Your Organization, Your Management Style and Your Life*, Boston: Harvard Business School Press (2004).
6. Sterngold, James. *Burning Down the House: How Greed, Deceit, and Bitter Revenge Destroyed E.F. Hutton*, New York: Simon and Schuster (1990) 26–34.
7. Malone, Thomas W., JoAnne Yates, and Robert I. Benjamin. "The Logic of Electronic Markets," *Harvard Business Review*, 67:3 (May–June 1989) 166–170.
8. Cheung, Steven N.S. "The Transaction Costs Paradigm: 1998 Presidential Address, Western Economic Association," *Economic Inquiry*, 36 (October 1998) 514–21.
9. Magee, Stephen P. "The Optimum Numbers of Lawyers: A Reply to Epp," *Law and Social Inquiry*, 17 (Fall 1992) 667–93.
10. Klein, Benjamin, Robert G. Crawford, and Armen A. Alchian. "Vertical Integration, Appropriable Rents, and the Competitive Contracting Process," *Journal of Law and Economics*, 21 (October 1978) 297–326.
11. Kraemer, Kenneth and Jason Dedrick. "Strategic Use of the Internet and e-commerce: Cisco Systems," *Strategic Information Systems*, 11 (2002) 5–29.
12. Ricardo, David. *The Principles of Political Economy and Taxation*, London: Guernsey Press (1817).
13. Van der Meer-Kooistra, Jeltje and Ed G.J. Vosselman. "Management Control of Interfirm Transactional Relationships: The Case of Industrial Renovation and Maintenance," *Accounting, Organizations and Society*, 25 (January 2000) 51–77.
14. Niven, Paul. *Balanced Scorecard Step-by-Step: Maximizing Performance and Maintaining Results*, New York: John Wiley and Sons (2002) 145–78.
15. Meyer, Marshall W. *Rethinking Performance Measurement*, New York: Cambridge University Press (2002) 51–80.
16. Bernheim, B. Douglas and Michael D. Whinston. "Incomplete Contracts and Strategic Ambiguity," *American Economic Review*, 88:4 (September 1988) 902–32.

Chapter 3   Organizations Over Time

1. D'Aveni, Richard and David J. Ravenscraft. "Economies of Integration versus Bureaucracy Costs: Does Vertical Integration Improve

Performance?" *Academy of Management Journal*, 37:5 (October 1994) 1167–207.

2. Weill, Peter and Jeanne W. Ross. *IT Governance: How Top Performers Manage IT Decision Rights for Superior Results*, Boston: Harvard Business School Press (2004) 1–24.

3. Ghoshal, Sumantra and Peter Moran. "Bad for Practice: A Critique of the Transaction Cost Theory," *Academy of Management Review*, 21:1 (January 1996) 13–48.

4. Venkatraman, N. and John C. Henderson. "Real Strategies for Virtual Outsourcing," *Sloan Management Review*, 40:1 (Fall 1998) 33–48. See also Keen, Peter and Mark McDonald. *The eProcess Edge: Creating Customer Value and Business Wealth in the Internet Era*, Osborne/McGraw-Hill: New York (2000).

5. Drucker, Peter F. "The American CEO," *Wall Street Journal* (December 30, 2004) A8.

6. Simon, Herbert. *Administrative Behavior*, 3rd edition, New York: The Free Press, Macmillan Publishing (1976).

7. Chandler, Alfred D. *Strategy and Structure: Chapters in the History of American Industrial Enterprise*, Cambridge, MA: M.I.T. Press (1962).

8. Caballero, Ricardo J. "The Macroeconomics of Specificity," *Journal of Political Economy*, 106:4 (1998) 724–67.

9. Cusumano, Michael A. "How Microsoft Makes Large Teams Work Like Small Teams," *Sloan Management Review*, 39:1 (Fall 1997) 9–20.

10. Malone, Thomas W. *The Future of Work: How the New Order of Business Will Shape Your Organization, Your Management Style and Your Life*, Boston: Harvard Business School Press (2004).

11. Drucker, Peter F. "The Age of Social Transformation," *The Atlantic Monthly* (November 1994) 53–80.

12. Greenwood, Jeremy. "The Third Industrial Revolution: Technology, Productivity, and Income Equality," *Economic Review*, Federal Reserve Bank of Cleveland, 35:2 (1999) 2–12.

13. Norton, Seth W. "Information and Competitive Advantage: The Rise of General Motors," *Journal of Law and Economics*, 40 (April 1997) 245–60.

14. Chandler, Alfred D. *Strategy and Structure: Chapters in the History of American Industrial Enterprise*, Cambridge, MA: M.I.T. Press (1962).

15. Araskog, Rand V. *The ITT Wars*, New York: Henry Holt and Company (1989).

16. Maremont, Mark, John Hechinger, and Karen Damato. "Amid Enron's Fallout, and a Sinking Stock, Tyco Plans a Breakup," *Wall Street Journal* (January 23, 2002) A1.

17. Forelle, Charles. "Tyco Looks to Increase Its Value," *Wall Street Journal* (November 17, 2005) A6.

18. Canback, Staffan, Phillip Samouel, and David Price. "Strategy and Structure in Interaction: What Determines the Boundaries of the Firm?,"

Industrial Organization, http://129.3.20.41/eps/io/papers/0303/0303003. pdf (Accessed on March 17, 2003) 1–7.

19. Markowitz, H.M. "Portfolio Selection," *Journal of Finance*, 7 (March 1952) 77–91.
20. Silverman, Rachel Emma, and Ken Brown. "Five Companies: How They Get Their Numbers," *Wall Street Journal* (January 23, 2002) C1.
21. Prahalad, C.K. and Gary Hamel. "The Core Competence of the Corporation," *Harvard Business Review*, 90:3 (1990) 79–91.
22. Quinn, James Brian and Frederick G. Hilmer. "Strategic Outsourcing," *Sloan Management Review*, 35:4 (Summer 1994) 19–31.

Chapter 4　The Black Box Exposed

1. Buckley, Peter J. and Mark Casson. "Economics as an Imperialist Social Science," *Human Relations*, 46:9 (September 1993) 1035–53.
2. Coase, Ronald. "The Nature of the Firm," *Economica*, 4 (November 1937) 386–405.
3. North, Douglass C. "Transaction Costs, Institutions, and Economic Performance," *Occasional Papers*, International Center for Economic Growth: San Francisco, 30 (1992).
4. Madema, Steve G. "Coase, Costs, and Coordination," *Journal of Economic Issues*, 30:2 (June 1996) 571–78.
5. Pratten, Stephen. "The Nature of Transaction Cost Economics," *Journal of Economic Issues*, 31:3 (September 1997) 781–814.
6. Dyer, Jeffrey H. "Effective Interfirm Collaboration: How Firms Minimize Transaction Costs and Maximize Transaction Value," *Strategic Management Journal*, 18:7 (1997) 535–56.
7. Cox, W. Michael, John V. Duca, and Richard Alm. Productivity Gains Showing Up in Services, *Southwest Economy*, Federal Reserve Bank of Dallas, 6 (November–December 2004) 1, 5–8.
8. Downs, Larry and Chunka Mui. *Unleashing the Killer App: Digital Strategies for Market Dominance*, Boston: Harvard Business School Press (1998).
9. Casson, Mark. "The Nature of the Firm Reconsidered: Information Synthesis and Entrepreneurial Organisation," *Management International Review*, 36 (1996) 55–95.
10. Cheung, Steven N.S. "The Transaction Costs Paradigm: 1998 Presidential Address, Western Economic Association," *Economic Inquiry*, 36 (October 1998) 514–21
11. Carroll, Glenn R., Pablo T. Spiller, and David J. Teece. "Transaction Cost Economics: Its Influence on Organizational Theory, Strategic Management, and Political Economy," *Firms, Markets, and Hierarchies*, Glenn R. Carroll and David J. Teece eds., New York: Oxford University Press (1999) 60–88.

12. Guelpa, Fabrizio. "Corporate Governance and Contractual Governance: A Model," *Rivista Internazionale di Scienze Sociali*, 2 (1998) 73–90.
13. Gates, Bill. *The Road Ahead*, London: Penguin (1996).
14. Jensen, Michael C. and William H. Meckling. "Theory of the Firm: Managerial Behavior, Agency Costs and Ownership Structure," *Journal of Financial Economics*, 3 (1976) 305–60.
15. Norton, Seth W. "Information and Competitive Advantage: The Rise of General Motors," *Journal of Law and Economics*, 40 (April 1997) 245–60.
16. Fama, Eugene F. "Agency Problems and the Theory of the Firm," *Journal of Political Economy*, 88:2 (1980) 288–307.
17. Mikesell, John L. *Fiscal Administration*, 5th edition, Belmont, CA: Thompson Wadsworth (1998).
18. This very calculus demonstrates one reason most outsourcers—IT outsourcers in particular—will refuse to reply to an RFP (Request for Proposal) solicited by anyone below executive management level. Department heads often lack sufficient objectivity to give the outsourcer a fair hearing. Responses to RFPs are expensive for outsourcers to produce. Development of these large documents consumes significant resources. The outsourcer will not provide responses to requests that offer such a low probability of a win.
19. Dewan, Sanjeev, Steven C. Michael, and Chunk-ki Min. "Firm Characteristics and Investments in Information Technology: Scale and Scope Effects," *Information Systems Research*, 9:3 (September 1998) 219–32.
20. D'Aveni, Richard and David J. Ravenscraft. "Economies of Integration versus Bureaucracy Costs: Does Vertical Integration Improve Performance?" *Academy of Management Journal*, 37:5 (October 1994) 1167–207.
21. *New York Times* Business Section, March 29, 1997.
22. Leibenstein, Harvey. "Allocative Efficiency vs. 'X-Efficiency'," *American Economic Review*, 56:3 (June 1966) 392–415.
23. Ibid.
24. Meyer, Marshall W. *Rethinking Performance Measurement*, New York: Cambridge University Press (2002).
25. Well, okay. Sometimes this does occur. If so, it should be a red flag to management. The most qualified people leave, when out-packages get offered in a downsize exercise. They know they have other options outside the organization. This scenario is *not* beneficial to the organization overall. It is almost always the dregs that want to stay behind when attractive out-packages get offered.
26. Quinn, James Brian and Frederick G. Hilmer. "Strategic Outsourcing," *Sloan Management Review*, 35:4 (Summer 1994) 19–31.
27. Jorgenson, Dale W., Mun S. Ho, and Kevin J. Stiroh. "Will the U.S. Productivity Resurgence Continue?" *Current Issues in Economics and Finance*, Federal Reserve Bank of New York 10:13 (December 2004) 1–7.

28. Keynes, John Maynard. *The General Theory of Employment, Interest, and Money*, Orlando: Harcourt Brace (1936).

29. Vedder, Richard K. and Lowell E. Gallaway. *Out of Work*, New York: New York University Press (1997).

30. Lewis, William. *The Power of Productivity: Wealth, Poverty, and the Threat to Global Stability*, Chicago: University of Chicago Press (2004) 50–79.

31. Fama, Eugene F. "Agency Problems and the Theory of the Firm," *Journal of Political Economy*, 88:2 (1980) 288–307.

Chapter 5   External Governance

1. Lee, J.A.N. *Computer Pioneers*, Los Alamitos, CA: IEEE Computer Society Press (1995).

2. Bayers, Chip. "The Ultimate Management Team," *Wired Magazine*, 10.01 (January 2002) 77–8.

3. Levin, Doron P. *Irreconcilable Differences: Ross Perot versus General Motors*, New York: Penguin (1989).

4. The company that Herman Hollerith formed (Tabulating Machine Company) later merged with three other companies in 1911. In 1924, it became known as IBM. Austrian, Geoffrey D. *Herman Hollerith: Forgotten Giant of Information Processing*, New York: Columbia University Press (1982).

5. Loh, Lawrence and N. Venkatraman. "Diffusion of Information Technology Outsourcing: Influence Sources and the Kodak Effect," *Information Systems Research*, 3:4 (December 1992) 334–58.

6. Strassmann, Paul. *The Squandered Computer*, New Canaan, Connecticut: The Information Economics Press (1997).

7. Palvia, Prashant C. "A Dialectic View of Information Systems Outsourcing: Pros and Cons," *Information and Management*, 29 (1995) 265–75.

8. Siems, Thomas F. "Beyond the Outsourcing Angst: Making America More Productive," *Economic Letter*, Federal Reserve Bank of Dallas, 1:2 (February 2006) 1–8.

9. Klein, Benjamin, Robert G. Crawford, and Armen A. Alchian. "Vertical Integration, Appropriable Rents, and the Competitive Contracting Process," *Journal of Law and Economics*, 21 (October 1978) 297–326.

10. Grossman, Sanford J. and Oliver D. Hart. "The Costs and Benefits of Ownership: A Theory of Vertical and Lateral Integration," *Journal of Political Economy*, 94:4 (1986) 619–719.

11. New technologies change things all the time. Satellite, DSL, and terrestrial wireless create intermodal competition that blur the traditional boundaries between the entertainment, information, and communication delivery vehicles. These new options make the cable industry look less like a natural monopoly every day. (See http://www.state.ak.us/itg/telecommstudy.pdf, p. 30.) Accessed in November 2002.

12. Zupan, Mark A. "The Efficacy of Franchise Bidding Schemes in the Case of Cable Television: Some Systematic Evidence," *Journal of Law and Economics*, 32 (October 1989) 401–56.

13. Bendor-Samuel, Peter. *Turning Lead Into Gold*, Provo, UT: Executive Excellence Publishing (2000).

14. DiRomualdo, Anthony and Vijay Gurbaxani. "Strategic Intent for IT Outsourcing," *Sloan Management Review*, 39:4 (Summer 1998) 67–80.

15. Moore, Randy A. *The Science of High-Performance Supplier Management: A Systematic Approach to Improving Procurement Costs, Quality, and Relationships*, New York: Amacom (2002).

16. Davenport, Thomas H. "The Coming Commoditization of Processes," *Harvard Business Review*, 85:6 (June 2005)101–8.

17. Banker, Rajiv, Gordon B. Davis, and Sandra A. Slaughter. "Software Development Practices, Software Complexity, and Software Maintenance Performance: A Field Study," *Management Science*, 44:4 (April 1998) 433–50.

18. As a footnote to the story, some of the related software development by the outsourcer was to take place in a northern U.S. state in the winter months. The outsourcer asked the communications company if it would receive relief from the terms of the agreement in the event the programmers were unable to travel to the development site due to snow or inclement weather. Since the communications company would lose revenue on a late implementation with or without snow, management told the outsourcer that it would not receive any relief (the communications company retorted that the outsourcer might consider relocation of the development effort to a warmer climate).

19. EDS 10K Filing for the fiscal year ended December 31, 2004.

20. Cringley, Robert X. "A Lose-Lose Situation: Sometimes IT Integration Just Isn't Worth the Trouble," in *Cringley PBS Column*, March 18, 2004 at http://www.pbs.org/cringely/.

21. Klein, Benjamin, Robert G. Crawford, and Armen A. Alchian. "Vertical Integration, Appropriable Rents, and the Competitive Contracting Process," *Journal of Law and Economics*, 21 (October 1978) 297–326.

22. Davenport, Thomas H. "The Coming Commoditization of Processes," *Harvard Business Review*, 85:6 (June 2005) 101–8.

23. Jones, S.R.H. "Transaction Costs and the Theory of the Firm: The Scope and Limitations of the New Industrial Approach," *Business History*, 39:4 (October 1997) 9–26.

24. Hagel, John. *Out of the Box: Strategies for Achieving Profits Today and Growth Tomorrow through Web Services*, Boston: Harvard Business School Press (2002).

25. Porter, Michael E. "Attitudes, Values, Beliefs and Microeconomics of Prosperity," *Culture Matters: How Values Shape Human Progress*, Lawrence Harrison and Samuel Huntington, eds., New York: Basic Books (2000) 14–28.

Chapter 6   The Global Perspective

1. Lewis, William. *The Power of Productivity: Wealth, Poverty, and the Threat to Global Stability*, Chicago: University of Chicago Press (2004).

2. "Things Have Changed." Written and performed for the movie *Wonder Boys* by Bob Dylan. Dylan won the 2000 Academy Award for Best Original Song.

3. It should be noted that while insurance companies implement techniques such as remote diagnosis, in-country market forces remain underutilized as a force, to better manage costs. Methods employed in domestic markets rely too much on blunt tools such as heavy-handed regulation or coalitions of insurance providers. The picture starts to look very different once healthcare providers start operating outside these constraints. Look at the costs for elective procedures, which may not be covered by health insurance. Cosmetic surgery (e.g. breast augmentation, liposuction) presents a good example. Costs continue to come down all the time because consumers must pay for these surgical treatments out of their own pocket. They tend to shop for the best price-value provider in the healthcare marketplace. Providers are spurred to find ways to become more efficient.

4. Feenstra, Robert C. and Gordon H. Hanson. "Globalization, Outsourcing and Wage Inequality," *American Economic Review*, 86 (May 1996) 240–45.

5. Fairbanks, Michael and Stace Lindsay. *Plowing the Sea: Nurturing the Hidden Sources of Growth in the Developing World*, Cambridge, MA: Harvard Business School Press (1997).

6. Greider, William. *One World, Ready or Not: The Manic Logic of Global Capitalism*, New York: Simon and Schuster (1997).

7. Ricardo, David. *The Principles of Political Economy and Taxation*, London: Guernsey Press (1973).

8. Cheung, Steven N.S. "The Transaction Costs Paradigm: 1998 Presidential Address, Western Economic Association," *Economic Inquiry*, 36 (October 1998) 514–21; see also Deavers, Kenneth L. "Outsourcing: A Corporate Competitiveness Strategy, Not a Search for Low Wages," *Journal of Labor Research*, 18:4 (Fall 1997) 503–19.

9. Schumpeter, Joseph. *Capitalism, Socialism and Democracy*, New York: Harper and Brothers (1942).

10. Cox, W. Michael and Richard Alm. "The Churn: The Paradox of Progress," *Annual Report*, Federal Reserve Bank of Dallas (1992) 4–9.

11. Chast, Roz. "All-But-Completely Unskilled Labor," *Harvard Business Review*, 76:1 (January-February 1998) 109.

12. Useem, Jerry. "Churn, Baby, Churn," *Inc. Magazine: The State of Small Business* (May 1997) 25–32.

13. Rajan, Raghuram and Luigi Zingales. *Saving Capitalism from the Capitalists*, New York: Crown Business (2003).

14. Casson, Mark. "The Nature of the Firm Reconsidered: Information Synthesis and Entrepreneurial Organisation," *Management International Review*, 36 nSPEISS (1996) 55–95.
15. Casson, Mark. "Institutional Economics and Business History: A Way Forward," *Business History*, 39:4 (1997) 151–72.

Chapter 7   Management Style

1. Evans, Philip B. and Thomas S. Wurster. "Strategy and the New Economics of Information," *Harvard Business Review*, 75:5 (September–October 1997) 71–82.
2. Caves, Richard E. and Ralph M. Bradburd. "The Empirical Determinants of Vertical Integration," *Journal of Economic Behavior and Organization*, 9 (1988) 265–79.
3. Dyer, Jeffrey H. "Effective Interfirm Collaboration: How Firms Minimize Transaction Costs and Maximize Transaction Value," *Strategic Management Journal*, 18:7 (1997) 535–56.
4. Levy, David T. "The Transactions Cost Approach to Vertical Integration: An Empirical Examination," *Review of Economics and Statistics* (1985) 438–45.
5. Frank, Robert H. and Philip J. Cook. *The Winner-Take-All Society: Why the Few at the Top Get So Much More Than the Rest of Us*, New York: Free Press (1995).
6. Barker III, Vincent L. "Traps in Diagnosing Organizational Failure," *Journal of Business Strategy*, 26:2 (2005) 44–50.
7. Weber, Max. *Selections in Translation*, Runcinman, W.G. ed., New York: Cambridge University Press (1978).
8. Rein, Irving, Philip Kotler, and Martin Stoller. *High Visibility*, New York: Dodd, Mead and Company (1987).
9. Pfeffer, Jeffrey and Robert I. Sutton. *Hard Facts, Dangerous Half-Truths and Total Nonsense*, Boston: Harvard Business School Press (2006).
10. Pulley, Brett. "The Boss, Out of Control," *Forbes*, 178:6 (October 2, 2006) 42.
11. Peter, Lawrence J. and Raymond Hull. *The Peter Principle*, New York: William Morrow and Co. (1969).
12. Sterngold, James. *Burning Down the House: How Greed, Deceit, and Bitter Revenge Destroyed E.F. Hutton*, New York: Simon and Schuster (1990).
13. Finkelstein, Sydney. "When Bad Things Happen to Good Companies: Strategy Failure and Flawed Executives," *Journal of Business Strategy*, 26:2 (2005) 19–29.
14. Levin, Doron P. *Irreconcilable Differences: Ross Perot versus General Motors*, New York: Penguin (1989).
15. Tuck School of Business at Dartmouth. "Learning from Mattel," Case Study No. 1–0072 (2002).

16. Burrough, Bryan and John Helyar. *Barbarians at the Gate: The Fall of RJR Nabisco*, New York: Harper-Collins (1991).

Chapter 8   New Rules for Governance

1. Skinner, C. Wickham. *The Impact of New Technology: People and Organizations in the Service Industry*, St. Louis: Elsevier Science (1982).
2. Eldredge, Nigel and Stephen Gould. "Punctuated Equilibria: An Alternative to Phyletic Gradualism," in *Models of Paleobiology*, T.J.M. Schopf, ed. San Francisco, CA: Freeman, Cooper and Co. (1972) 82–115.
3. Claburn, Thomas. "More Than Fun and Games," *Information Week* (April 17, 2006) 51–54. Also McGee, Marianne Kolbasuk. "No E-Learning Gap Here," *Information Week* (April 17, 2005) 51–54.
4. Barber, Felix and Rainer Strack. "The Surprising Economics of a 'People Business,'" *Harvard Business Review*, 83:6 (June 2005) 80–90.
5. Meyer, Marshall W. *Rethinking Performance Measurement*, Cambridge: Cambridge University Press (2002).
6. Reichheld, Frederick F. and W. Earl Sasser, Jr. "Zero Defections: Quality Come to Services," *Harvard Business Review*, 68:5 (September–October 1990) 105–11.
7. Brimson, James A. *Activity Accounting: An Activity-Based Costing Approach*, New York: John Wiley and Sons (1991).
8. Palepu, Krishna G. "Predicting Takeover Targets: A Methodological and Empirical Analysis," *Journal of Accounting and Economics*, 8 (1986) 3–35.
9. Edward, Ben. "A World of Work: A Survey of Outsourcing," *The Economist*, 373:8401 (November 13, 2004) 1–20 (special insert).
10. Tunstall, Thomas. *Firm Governance Mechanisms: An Empirical Analysis of the Determinants of Information Technology Outsourcing*, unpublished doctoral dissertation, University of Texas at Dallas (2000).
11. Cox, W. Michael, John V. Duca, and Richard Alm. "Productivity Gains Showing Up in Services," *Southwest Economy*, Federal Reserve Bank of Dallas, 6 (November–December 2004) 1, 5–8.
12. Brynjolfsson, Erik. "Information Assets, Technology and Organization," *Management Science*, 40:12 (December 1994) 1645–62.
13. Lee, Chi-Hyon and N. Venkatraman. "New Organizational Arrangements for Information Technology Resource Leverage: Empirical Test of Value Capture," *Working Paper*, Boston University (1999).
14. Hornstein, Andreas. "Growth Accounting with Technological Revolutions," *Economic Quarterly*, Federal Reserve Bank of Cleveland, 85:3 (Summer 1999) 1–22.
15. Srivastava, Rajendra K., Tasadduq A. Servani, and Liam Fahey. "Market-Based Assets and Shareholder Value: A Framework for Analysis," *Journal of Marketing*, 62 (January 1998) 1–14.

16. Coyne, Kevin P. and Renee Dye. "The Competitive Dynamics of Network-Based Businesses," *Harvard Business Review*, 76:1 (January 1998) 99–109.

17. Newman, Richard J. "Can America Keep Up?," *U.S. News and World Report*, 140:11 (March 27, 2006) 48–56.

18. Wolfram, Stephen. *A New Kind of Science*, Champaign, IL: Wolfram Media (2002).

19. Dembo, Ron and Andrew Freeman. *Seeing Tomorrow: Rewriting the Rules of Risk*, New York: John Wiley and Sons (1998).

20. Schelling, Thomas C. *Micromotives and Macrobehavior*, New York: W.W. Norton and Co. (1978).

21. Bandler, James and Charles Forelle. "Embattled CEO to Step Down at UnitedHealth," *Wall Street Journal* (October 16, 2006) p. 1.

22. Mufson, Steven. "Gold-Plated Exit for Exxon CEO," *Washington Post*, (April 13, 2006) D3.

23. Pfeffer, Jeffrey and Robert I. Sutton. *Hard Facts, Dangerous Half-Truths and Total Nonsense*, Boston: Harvard Business School Press (2006).

24. Weidenbaum, Murray L. *Business and Government in the Global Marketplace*, Upper Saddle River, NJ: Pearson Prentice Hall (2004) 349.

25. Simon, Herbert. *Administrative Behavior*, 3rd edition, New York: The Free Press, Macmillan (1976).

26. Granovetter, Mark. "Problems of Explanation in Economic Sociology," in *Networks and Organizations*, Nohria Nitin and Robert G. Eccles, eds., Boston: Harvard Business School Press (1992) 25–56.

27. Rousseau, Denise M. "Is There Such a Thing as 'Evidence-Based Management'?," *Academy of Management Review*, 31:2 (April 2006) 256–69.

INDEX

Printed in the United States
122885LV00003B/7/A

9 781403 979674